BECOMING
ANABAPTIST

BECOMING ANABAPTIST

*The Origin and Significance
of Sixteenth-Century Anabaptism*

Second Edition

J. Denny Weaver
Foreword by William H. Willimon

HERALD PRESS

Harrisonburg, Virginia

Herald Press
PO Box 866, Harrisonburg, Virginia 22803
www.HeraldPress.com

Library of Congress Cataloging-in-Publication Data

Weaver, J. Denny, 1941-
　　　Becoming Anabaptist.

　　　　Bibliography: p.
　　　　Includes index.
　　　　Anabaptists.　I.　Title.
BX4931.2.W38　　1987　　　　　　284'.3　　　　　　86-33650
ISBSN 0-8361-3434-6

BECOMING ANABAPTIST
© 1987, 2005 by Herald Press, Harrisonburg, Va. 22801. 800-245-7894.
Second Edition 2005.
All rights reserved
Library of Congress Catalog Card Number: 86-33650
International Standard Book Number: 978-0-8361-3434-6
Printed in the United States of America
Cover design by Gwen Stamm

21 20 19 18　　14 13 12 11 10

To the memory of Gideon G. Yoder,
the teacher from whom I first began to learn
the ongoing Anabaptist story,
and for whom the story meant to "get involved"

Contents

Foreword

Here is a book that is against just about everything we believe in. I say that as a Methodist bishop who ought to know what we believe in. Methodists are those Christians who believe in trying to follow Jesus and attempting to be the church without letting any of that get in the way of our being successful. In other words, we Methodists are just about everything that every Anabaptist lives in fear of becoming.

Denny Weaver knows, about as well as anybody, what Anabaptists believe in. In this masterful treatment of his beloved Anabaptist vision, he writes in measured, scholarly, orderly fashion. But I warn you: Do not be deceived by his Mennonite reserve. This book is a clinch-fisted protest against what the rest of us have made of the church, a defiant act of resistance against the predominant American way of being Christian, a song of love (disconcerting thought—Mennonites making love) to a Jesus that the rest of us are reluctant to follow and a people who, in every generation, Jesus has loved into being out of nothing. To subvert the present ecclesiastical order, Weaver on nearly every page of this book lures us into a respectful discussion of how Anabaptists got here and what they believe. Typical of the Mennonites I have known, he politely reassures us that he is a pacifist Christian who bears us no harm, then hands us a ticking bomb.

I say thank God that the Anabaptists were run out of Europe so that they took up residence in Indiana and elsewhere.

God has sent them into the wilderness that is contemporary American culture in order to keep the rest of us honest about Jesus, or at least to make us feel guilty. Here, as elsewhere, they have exercised an influence upon the extended body of Christ far out of proportion to their numbers. They have been salt, light, yeast, an unassimilatable lump in an otherwise comfortable and accommodated Christendom. God bless them for their witness, though most of the rest of us despise them for it.

I met Anabaptism in my undergraduate thesis, "The Anabaptist Vision of the Church," a sophomoric rehash of Harold S. Bender's analysis of the church. That paper was provoked by my encounter with a real live Mennonite after a peace demonstration in Washington. We had made our heroic stand against the Vietnam War the afternoon before, had made a great party out of it that night, and were now sleeping it off on that Sunday morning. I awoke and, through bleary eyes, saw a homely little woman bending over my sleeping bag, large trash bag in her hands, asking, "Dear, you don't mind if I clean up this mess you have made, do you?"

In conversation with that woman, I found out that she was a Mennonite—a rare bird in my native South Carolina—that she and her husband had been at this peace thing long before the 1960s, and that Jesus had made her into the sort of person who quietly cleaned up and kept at it when the rest of us had lost interest because peace was no longer popular. Shortly thereafter I had my mind blown by John Howard Yoder, and I was rendered permanently uneasy with the mainline Protestant political settlement. When in a lecture in a church history class at Yale, I was told that, "In every reform movement, there are always those irresponsible people who will take things too far, and in the Protestant Reformation, those people are called Anabaptists," I remembered that woman and knew that my professor was lying.

Denny Weaver continues that good woman's work in this book, cleaning up after the rest of us have made a mess of the church. One of the few things that all Catholics, Lutherans, and

Calvinists could agree on in church history was that Anabaptists were a threat and ought to be killed. Thousands died for their conviction that the church is called to more pressing business than to be socially significant, and thousands still die. We're all state churches now who don't appreciate anybody walking around loose who is under the impression that there is a king other than Caesar. Anabaptists continue to have the distinction of being among the few American Christians who can look at the United States of America and the body of Christ and tell the difference. We Americans thought that we were open-minded, basically peaceful, well-meaning people until we met the Mennonites. They have always managed to bring out the worst in us and to demonstrate the limits of our bogus "religious freedom." They have always served as a rebuke to the Niebuhrian claim that Jesus is a sweet-spirited idealist who is utterly irrelevant to responsible ethics.

As Weaver shows, only the Anabaptists both went backward to Scripture for their marching orders and forward out of the medieval synthesis of church and state. By their very being, they were an argument, not so much over baptism, but over the church. Is the church the called-out, visible embodiment of Jesus in our world or not? Does the church have the politics to be able to demonstrate, by its existence, what the world, left to its own devices, is not?

Despite our innate, mainline Protestant, establishmentarian annoyance with the Anabaptists, it is a great tribute to the Anabaptist vision of the church that you Anabaptists have—in a book like this or in your life together—continued not only to annoy us but also to inspire us. You awaken that sense, buried deep within our otherwise compromised souls, that discipleship is a practice and not just an idea, that the faith is meant to be performed and not simply believed, and that the followers of Jesus always produce disorder and resistance whenever we are faithful. There you Anabaptists are, refusing assimilation or accommodation, reminding us that church is called to be more than the cement of social conformity. Church is the invigorating adventure of walking behind Jesus.

With Denny Weaver as your guide, I am sure that you will find it a great joy to walk through the adventure called Anabaptism.

—*William H. Willimon*
Bishop, The North Alabama Conference
of the United Methodist Church
Birmingham, Alabama

Author's Preface

A second, revised, and expanded edition of *Becoming Anabaptist* is evidence that the first edition has garnered a certain amount of respect. A second, revised edition also indicates that the useful life of the first edition has ended. Conversations with colleagues who have used the book, whether in classroom teaching or in congregational settings, revealed significant interest in a new edition. I am grateful that Herald Press staff agreed with that assessment, and it has been a pleasure to work with Levi Miller in producing this edition.

The two editions of this book stand as bookends to my career. The first edition was my first book and came relatively early in my professional career. The second edition comes quite near the end of my teaching career. Much has happened in between. On the side of Anabaptist scholarship, there were a number of revisions and additions to the "polygenesis" school of thought, which shaped the first edition. The current edition has incorporated much from those efforts to go "beyond" polygenesis. The effort to move beyond polygenesis has also provoked a new debate about the significance and meaning of Anabaptism. I have not pursued that debate in the five chapters of the book, but interested readers may engage it in the interpretive essay in the appendix.

On the personal side, my professional interests have followed a number of other paths that at first glance appear unrelated to sixteenth-century Anabaptism. I worked extensively in nineteenth-century Amish and Mennonite theology and also pursued a major project to develop a nonviolent approach to the doctrine of atonement. In the course of this work, I also became significantly engaged in the discussion of what is variously called postmodernity or the crisis in modernity. Through these varied discussions, I developed a deeper and stronger sense that every belief or doctrine or statement of belief has a history behind it. It was thus a natural progression to move from developing a nonviolent atonement theology to work again on the history of Anabaptism, which is one of the important historical points of origin for the modern peace church. Dealing with the interactions of historical narrative and contemporary theologizing appear particularly in chapter 5, which is rewritten and almost entirely new for this edition.

In the time between these two editions, one of my important learnings concerns the number of contemporary Anabaptists who are members of churches other than Mennonites, Amish, Brethren in Christ, and Brethren churches, which comprise the denominations that trace their historical roots to sixteenth-century Anabaptists. This book is written to be equally accessible and useful to Anabaptists who are Anglicans and Presbyterians and Methodists and Pentecostals as well as to Mennonites and their larger faith community. But the volume is also addressed to all Christians of any dimension. For these Christians, it will serve as an introduction to an Anabaptist perspective on the world; and it may even serve as a call to embrace this perspective whose foundational idea is the acceptance of the life and teaching of Jesus as authoritative for ethics.

This revised edition is still a synthesis of current literature, although on occasion there are references to sixteenth-century primary sources. The primary intent in chapters 2 through 4 is to tell a coherent story—a synthesis. It is not an encyclopedic account, attempting to know and mention everything. One colleague, upon learning that I was working on a revision, wrote me that the first edition "reads nicely without being simplistic." His primary admonishment was not to clutter up the flowing text with a lot of new details. I did add material to expand the story into additional areas, but readers will have to judge whether I succeeded in maintaining the first edition's "flowing text."

I am grateful to many people who contributed in one way or another to this second edition of *Becoming Anabaptist*. That list includes the professors who assigned it and all the students who read the book over the years. It includes many face-to-face conversations, whether I was supported or challenged. The impact of such conversations on one's thinking remains, even when a particular conversation is forgotten. I owe much to Gerald Biesecker-Mast, with whom I have processed this manuscript, as well as many others on an almost daily basis. In addition to Gerald, I owe many thanks to a number of other colleagues who shared their time in reading and discussing portions of the manuscript with me. These include Trevor Bechtel, Neal Blough, Laura Brenneman, Ray Gingerich, Ted Grimsrud, Randy Keeler, Hannah Kehr, Mark Thiessen Nation, Mary S. Sprunger, and Earl Zimmerman. Hannah Kehr also provided invaluable assistance in preparing the final version of the computer files of the manuscript as well as performing superb work on the index. Other colleagues who contributed comments or material help of various kinds include Lynn Miller, John Roth, and Zachary Walton. I am grateful for all these interactions, even when I chose not to accept all the advice offered. I remain eternally grateful to my wife, Mary, whose acceptance and support of my desire to write remains constant.

I first heard about the Anabaptist story as an undergraduate student in a class at Hesston College taught by Gideon G. Yoder. Even when I was embarking on a career as a math major at that point and had no inkling that Anabaptist studies would ever become an integral part of my career, I caught Uncle Gid's enthusiasm for this story and his belief that it meant to "get involved." This book is dedicated to his memory.

—*J. Denny Weaver*
Bluffton University
Spring 2005

1

Introduction

Martin Luther posted his 95 theses on October 31, 1517. The first rebaptisms occurred in Zurich on January 21, 1525. If one takes the posting of the theses as the symbolic beginning of the great drama known as the sixteenth-century Reformation and the baptisms as the formal beginning of the Anabaptist Reformation, action was already far along in the first act when Anabaptism appeared on the crowded stage. This book presents the story of these newcomers to the Reformation drama.

All of Europe knew about Martin Luther, who several years before these baptisms had published the core of his new theology. Many commoners picked up at least a part of that message and pushed reforming ideas across western and central Europe. Luther's Wittenberg University led in attracting students who wanted to study in the new perspective. Other important cities like Strasbourg and Zurich had also committed themselves to the reforming way, guided by men also well known if not so renowned as Luther. The idea of furthering reformation was established to the point that, in Zurich, a number of those who ended up in the party called Anabaptist had already worked diligently for reform as colleagues of Ulrich Zwingli. Yet other future leaders were still years from entering the reform drama. Young John Calvin, whose name would become synonymous with reform in Geneva, was about to transfer from Paris to the University of Orleans to begin study in civil law. In Pingjum,

Menno Simons, the newly ordained Catholic priest whose name is borne by many of the heirs of the Anabaptist story, had barely begun his first parish assignment.

Many, even most, of the principal Reformation actors already present protested the appearance of the Anabaptist arrivals and tried to prevent their participation in the drama. Some of the new players forced their way into the drama, while others found themselves dragged in unwillingly or even unwittingly. Some of the new actors developed roles that became a permanent part of the Reformation play even into the twenty-first century. Other players disappeared after a few months or years on stage, leaving marks but no living legacy.

The original cast of Anabaptist players included a wide variety of characters—priests, monks, laymen, laywomen, scholars, tradesmen, artisans, peasants, noblemen, and noblewomen—who reflected a variety of religious backgrounds and came from regions across western and central Europe. These backgrounds helped to shape the roles that the newcomers would fashion in the drama and contributed to the complex context in which the drama played. Because of the variety of backgrounds, sixteenth-century Anabaptism could not, and did not, develop as an entirely homogeneous movement. It had no single theological leader, and its several manifestations cannot all be traced to a single source. Anabaptists differed among themselves just as Martin Luther and Ulrich Zwingli failed to attain unity on crucial questions. The other non-Anabaptist participants in the drama never really figured out what truly characterized the new arrivals and whether they belonged to the main drama or to an alternative cast of characters. While the Anabaptists clearly were no longer Roman Catholic, neither did they fit comfortably within the multifaceted Protestant camp. As outcasts from both these great traditions, the Anabaptists encountered many more enemies than friends in high places. Several thousand surrendered their lives rather than their wills to the established churches and political authorities.

On the basis of their most famous churchly practice, their opponents often identified them by the pejorative names of *Anabaptist,* or *Wiedertäufer*—categories already condemned in the law books of the time. Meaning "rebaptizer," these terms came to designate almost anyone not included in the Roman Catholic, Lutheran, or Reformed (Calvinist) traditions. Since not all individuals so designated actually advocated or practiced rebaptism, and since it lumped together individuals who differed markedly on other key issues, the nomenclature was not and is still not an entirely successful name for the movement. The Anabaptists themselves rejected this designation since they did not consider their practice a rebaptism. They preferred the name of *Brüder* (brethren) in German-speaking areas, and *Doopsgezinde* (baptism-minded) in the Low Countries. But as has happened with other nicknames given to groups by outsiders (with the designation *Lutheran* a prime example), those called Anabaptists eventually accepted the nomenclature, and it still serves to identify sixteenth-century as well as contemporary adherents to this Christian tradition.

Anabaptist, or rebaptizer, is a functionally definable name. It serves well to designate the majority of individuals central to the story: though state churches had baptized them as babies, they joined an Anabaptist community and accepted baptism again as adults confessing the faith. Anabaptist is probably the most commonly used designation for the sixteenth-century movement in question. This book tells the story of the movement that came to be designated by this practice, and the narrator tries to include all significant characters from the early years of the movement. No character is excluded from the story because of deviation from some standard norm, whether the norm be Christendom's theological orthodoxy or twentieth-century Mennonite definitions of nonresistance.

A caution is also in order concerning the use of the term *Anabaptist*. Describing this practice which names the group does not truly define the orientation and the character of the movement. Much more is involved in depicting Anabaptism than in listing a baptismal practice. The narrative chapters of this book indicate additional aspects of an Anabaptist outlook in terms of historical development, while chapter 5 presents a multifaceted statement about the orientation and character of Anabaptism as a distinct Christian perspective on the world.

Anabaptism developed an ecclesiology—an understanding of the church—new to the sixteenth century. This ecclesiology emerged when people decided that the story of Jesus and of the early church was the norm for Christian faith and Christian behavior. Although not all early Anabaptists were pacifists, the idea of measuring Christian practice by Jesus and the New Testament made rejection of the sword an issue central to Anabaptism. The new ecclesiology was an understanding of the church independent of political authorities, which meant that it rejected the state church. More important, this ecclesiology also rejected the idea that the church encompassed the entire social order. Stated another way, the Anabaptist view of the church was a rejection of the idea of a "Christian society" and of the idea that the civil government, backed by the sword, should enforce churchly practices for the entire society. Chapter 5 develops a number of implications of Anabaptist ecclesiology in face of contemporary efforts to assert or promote North American society as "Christian society." Chapter 5 also demonstrates that the ecclesiology of Anabaptism is a comprehensive perspective with potential implications for every aspect of Christian life and thought.

If Anabaptism developed into a new ecclesiology, it also emerged from the existing milieu of Catholic tradition and several reforming initiatives. Some elements of Anabaptism developed in opposition to either Catholicism or the reforming initiatives, while other elements of Anabaptism show continuity with Catholicism and the reforming trends. Since at least the third quarter of the twentieth century, one of the debated issues about Anabaptism has concerned its relationship to these other movements and initiatives.

A closely related debate concerns the character of Anabaptism. Varying answers have appeared. One recent effort has stressed commonalities between Anabaptism and both Catholicism and the majority Reformation traditions; it thus defines the core of Anabaptist theology in terms of the majority Christian tradition. The book in hand tells a different story and draws different implications. Readers interested in the arguments for understanding the essence of Anabaptism in terms of difference from, rather than commonality with, Catholicism and the other reforming traditions should consult the "Essay on Interpretation" in the Appendix. As already indicated, the following narrative emphasizes Anabaptism as a new and distinct movement in the sixteenth century. Both Roman Catholicism and the majority Reformation options assumed a church governed by or in cooperation with civil authorities as well as the idea of a "Christian society" or a church that encompasses the entire social order. Anabaptism rejected these options, and the narrative reveals that the new ecclesiology developed because of other differences from the existing alternatives, and it also set the stage for the development of additional foundational differences. Chapters 2, 3, and 4 make visible those aspects that produce the new Anabaptist ecclesiology, and chapter 5 points to a number of implications of this ecclesiology.

The Anabaptist story has several separate centers or theaters of activity. Each of these theaters has its own story, which are told in chapters 2, 3, and 4. The history of Anabaptism has gone through several major revisions since the second quarter of the twentieth century. Chapter 5 has a brief recitation of some of these historiographical developments. When the first edition of this book was written nearly twenty years ago, the "polygenesis" of sixteenth-century Anabaptism prevailed. In the view called polygenesis, the several theaters of Anabaptist activity had independent points of origin, which produced great diversity. Anabaptism was thus a pluralistic rather than a homogeneous movement.

Recent scholarship has moved beyond polygenesis. These scholars do not deny the existence of distinct Anabaptist centers nor the diversity thereby reflected, but they also show more regional links than previously recognized. The revised edition of *Becoming Anabaptist* incorporates this new material into the narrative. The links among Anabaptist centers are incorporated in the narratives of chapters 2, 3, and 4, which discuss Anabaptism in Switzerland, South Germany, and Moravia, and in the Netherlands. The links involve both people and ideas. Some particular links involve people who were part of both the Swiss and the South German and Moravian Anabaptist stories. Thus, the idea of community of goods is documented in a congregational order written and briefly implemented in Switzerland and used extensively in Moravia. And there is the possible common acceptance of Erasmus's reading of Matthew 28:19 by the earliest Anabaptists in Zurich and by Menno Simons. Further, by the 1550s, Dutch and South German Anabaptists were in conversation as fellow Anabaptists, even if the conversations produced disagreements that ended in excommunication.

Anabaptists and *Anabaptism* designated a sixteenth-century movement. No contemporary denomination is officially named Anabaptist, but the name still has currency and serves a contemporary function. Adherents of any current denomination who have come to embrace the Christian outlook and insight of this movement can and do identify themselves as Anabaptists. The story in the pages to follow belongs to all these contemporary Anabaptists, who come in several guises.

One obvious category of contemporary Anabaptists consists of those movements and denominations whose present historical roots can be traced to sixteenth-century Anabaptists. These include all denominations of Mennonites, Amish, and Hutterites, as well as the Brethren in Christ, who originated as a revival movement among Mennonites in the nineteenth century. This category also includes the several Brethren denominations, who trace their origins to Alexander Mack Jr.

Mack espoused Anabaptism combined with Pietism, and Swiss or German Mennonites were influential for the "brethren" around Mack when he organized the Church of the Brethren in Schwarzenau/Eder, Germany, in 1708. When he formed the Brethren, Mack chose not to join Mennonites because he thought they had strayed from the doctrine and life of historic Anabaptism. The Brethren denominations thus claim historical roots in sixteenth-century Anabaptism.[1]

Modern congregations of these historic Anabaptist denominations frequently contain members with family roots in other denominations as well as the to-be-expected members with ancestral Mennonite or Brethren roots. What unites them is their common commitment to peace and justice issues. Such congregations frequently appear in university towns. When I have spoken in these congregations, I have been impressed that whether members were recent adherents or had long family roots in Anabaptism, in the new congregation in the city they all stood on equal footing. The city and the university offer many options, and these modern Anabaptists were there because they *chose* to belong to an Anabaptist peace church, as sixteenth-century adherents *chose* to join the Anabaptist movement. The Anabaptist story clearly has relevance for these congregations and denominations that trace historical lineage to the sixteenth century.

A second category of people for whom the Anabaptist story is relevant has a quite different historical lineage. It consists of individuals and groups who still find their church homes with denominations that belong historically to the established churches of Christendom. Note, for example, the people who participate in the Anabaptist Network, organized in the United Kingdom by London Mennonite Center. People who identify themselves as Anabaptist from across Great Britain retain membership and participate in their local parishes or congregations of Anglicans, Methodists, Baptists, Seventh-Day Adventists or others, but they also meet regularly as Anabaptists in seminars to discuss issues such as peace and nonviolence that are integral to an Anabaptist Christian perspective. When I spoke to this group, I had many conversations that went something like this: "I belong to ____, but I am really an Anabaptist." In an informal way, this phenomenon is represented in the many people I meet at conferences and speaking engagements who tell me that within their denomination they represent an "Anabaptist perspective." On another occasion I spent two days lecturing to a class of doctor of ministry students at an Episcopalian seminary. A number of students told me they were pacifists. When I drew a diagram to show how the Anabaptists of the sixteenth-century had rejected the established churches of Christendom, these Episcopalians were quick to tell me that in the past their church had become too identified with the social order, but now they sensed themselves a minority that had affinity with many elements of a contemporary Anabaptist outlook.

In Latin America the base community movement perhaps consists of another example.[2] From within the Catholic Church and with a number of parallels to sixteenth-century Anabaptists, these communities that originate in the majority peasant societies assume responsibility for their own biblical interpretation. Their reading of the Bible expresses a strong critique of the economic and social policies by which a wealthy elite, with collaboration of established church, predominantly Catholic authorities, exploits the majority peasant class. These Latin American base communities represent groups around the world involved in struggles for justice. Individuals involved in these struggles are not the church per se any more than the Peasants' War participants of the sixteenth-century story were the church. However, as was the case in the sixteenth-century, a contemporary Anabaptist orientation can draw on those who struggle for justice, and Anabaptism has the theological perspective to challenge injustice.

The story of Anabaptist origins as a church movement that challenges the status quo belongs to the base communities and to these Episcopalian and other "mainstream" Christians as much as it belongs to the Mennonites, Brethren in Christ, and the Brethren denominations. It is my prayer that this book serves all these constituencies, whether a reader is coming to the story for the first time or as an adherent of long standing who is renewing appreciation for the significance of Anabaptism.

Another set of such developments also points to the potential relevance of the Anabaptist story for people whose historical roots are in the established churches. In the decade of the 1980s, a number of denominations descended from the churches of Christendom took steps that made them more supportive of peace and nonviolence. *Gaudium et spes* (1965), a publication of Vatican II, contained what was apparently the Roman Catholic Church's first acknowledgment of pacifism as an official Catholic position.[3] The 1983 *Pastoral Letter on War and Peace* issued by the National Conference of Catholic Bishops situated the Catholic Church within its tradition of justifiable war, but called attention to the significance of Vatican II's support for a pacifist option for both the church and the wider society.[4] In 1980 and again in 1983, Presbyterians affirmed a commitment to peace across a spectrum of issues, and a forum document *Peacemaking: The Believers' Calling*[5] was adopted by nearly all synods and presbyteries and more than half of the individual congregations of the denomination. A similar impetus developed within the United Church of Christ, which voted in 1981 to become a peace church. A Peace Theology Team produced a report received by the General Synod in 1985, with a reaffirmation of the UCC as a "peace church."[6] United Methodists issued a number of statements on peace in the 1980s, and they affirmed support for conscientious objectors to war as well as support for those who oppose payment of war taxes.[7] Drawing on earlier statements, Lutherans followed suit in 1995 with adoption of the statement *For Peace in God's World*. They affirmed their historic, justifiable-war tradition, but also declared that any decision for war must be a "mournful one." Lutherans also affirmed support for selective conscientious objection and affirmed the stance of those who are opposed to any participation in war.[8] These peace initiatives were no doubt slowed by the patriotism generated by the attacks of September 11, 2001, as well as two wars with Iraq. Nonetheless, they demonstrate potential interest in the Anabaptist story and possibilities for fruitful conversations around an Anabaptist focus on peace and nonviolence. An invitation to such dialogue is the book *A Declaration on Peace*. Sponsored by the Fellowship of Reconciliation and representatives of the Historic Peace Churches (Mennonites, Brethren, Quakers), this book issues an ecumenical invitation to "Christians everywhere" to engage in conversation on "peace, war, militarism, and justice."[9]

Clearly indicative of potential conversation about peace is the action of the World Council of Churches to declare the years 2001–2010 as the "Decade to Overcome Violence." In connection with that initiative, representatives of the Historic Peace Churches held a consultation on peace theology at Bienenberg, Switzerland, in June 2001. WCC General Secretary, Dr. Konrad Raiser, addressed the conference and expressed clear interest in dialogue with the peace churches. Presentations from this conference were then copublished by the World Council.[10]

Anabaptists became known as a peace tradition. This developing interest in peace theology (just described for a number of denominations) broadens the constituency for this book even more. In addition to telling the Anabaptist story for several constituencies of contemporary Anabaptists, the book becomes an avenue to discussion of peace concerns across a wide spectrum of Christian denominations. In developing the meaning of the Anabaptist story in chapter 5, it becomes clear that the outlook of Anabaptism that attempts to live as a witness to the reign of God made present in Jesus is the story of a Christian tradition that challenges every person who claims a relationship to Jesus Christ.

2

Anabaptism in Switzerland

The Cradle

On December 27, 1518, Ulrich Zwingli moved permanently to Zurich, Switzerland, to take up duties as people's priest. Initially, the position included the saying of mass and preaching. The religious authorities responsible for the staff of the Grossmünster, known as the chapter, had not hired him as a Reformer, and Zwingli did not move to Zurich with the intent of leading the city in a break with the Roman tradition. In not too many years, however, the Reformation in Zurich would become synonymous with his name, and Zwingli would be the leading Reformer among the several independent, reformed Swiss city-states.

A complex mixture of social, economic, and religious factors combined to form the cradle for Swiss Anabaptism. For one, it emerged from the region administered by Zurich with radicalized followers of Zwingli as one of its sources.

A second impulse was the hostility to the Roman clergy—anticlericalism—of the sixteenth century. While anticlerical impulses contributed to Luther's early popularity and his doctrine of the priesthood of all believers, and also sparked some of Zwingli's earliest impulses to reform, anticlericalism found its clearest outlet in the early Anabaptist movement. It would also bring the radicals to accuse Luther and Zwingli of the kind of abuses perpetrated by the old order.

The widespread peasant protests and uprisings that culminated in 1525—frequently called the Peasants' War—comprised a third, important element in the origin of Swiss Anabaptism, and even more so for Anabaptism in South Germany, the story told in chapter 3. The peasant concerns, which related to greater local autonomy, ran parallel to and were provoked by anticlericalism. For a time peasants swelled the ranks of the anticlerical and Zwinglian radicals.

Zwingli brought twelve years of experience as a priest with him to Zurich—ten at Glarus from 1506 to 1516, and then two at the pilgrimage town of Einsiedeln. He opposed the mercenary system by which young Swiss men hired themselves as soldiers to the military powers of Europe, sometimes to fight against each other. It was a source of income for the various cantons, and at first Zwingli opposed only the French connection but not service to the papal or imperial forces. Zwingli also carried a reputation for good preaching. The reports of his sermons that pilgrims to Einsiedeln carried back to Zurich had initially made Zwingli a candidate for the vacant preaching appointment at the Grossmünster. Zwingli came as an admirer and student of the renowned humanist scholar Erasmus. As a general principle humanists rejected the church's claim that under the guidance of the Holy Spirit what was implicit in the teaching of the apostles was clarified and made explicit over time, which meant that modern teachers were deemed best and most authoritative. In contrast, Christian humanists believed that the sources closest to Christ were most reliable, beginning with the apostles and with the Bible—rather than modern clarifications—as the purest source of Christian truth. As a humanist scholar, Zwingli was widely read in the church fathers—the theologians from the first centuries of Christian history—and a master of Greek and Hebrew. Already in Einsiedeln his preaching demonstrated his humanist orientation, as his sermons utilized passages directly from the Bible.

In Zurich he continued the practice of preaching directly from the Bible, beginning each sermon at the place in the Scriptures where he had finished the day before. Eventually, a particular biblical interpretation from the humanist Erasmus would also prove to be a significant factor in the break between Zwingli and his young disciples in Zurich.

Exactly when Zwingli became evangelical is not clear. It is reasonably certain that he was an "orthodox Catholic priest" at least until the end of 1518. However, by 1522 that label no longer applied. While Zwingli at this time had no direct contact with the early writings of Martin Luther, the critical approach fostered by the humanist scholars was becoming a part of the fabric of the age. The period during which Zwingli's religious outlook changed corresponds closely to his learning of Greek. By 1519 he had acquired sufficient mastery to read the New Testament in the original Greek and to compare it with the Latin Vulgate. For reading in Greek, Zwingli would have used Erasmus's Greek New Testament, along with his series of annotations published in 1516, 1519, and 1522. Quite possibly, writings of Andreas Karlstadt played a part in pushing Zwingli beyond humanism into the role of a Reformer. In a further contributing factor, Zwingli nearly died of the plague in September 1519. He emerged from this grave illness with "an intense sense of purpose, [and] complete self-confidence, arising from the assurance that God would use him and direct his steps and thoughts to His chosen ends."[1]

Those men who would play influential or visible roles in the emergence of Swiss Anabaptism came from two loosely defined, and at times overlapping, groups. One group consisted of radical, urban followers of Zwingli who were willing to go further and faster than he in rooting out the old order. Most of these came from the ranks of the common people rather than the authorities and ruling class. The leader was Andreas Castelberger, a bookseller from the canton of Grisons, who supplied Zwingli with pro-reform literature.[2] By early

1522 Castelberger had organized a "school of heretics" or circle of like-minded persons who met regularly to study the Bible. As was the case for Zwingli, this circle used Erasmus's Greek New Testament and *Annotations* as their primary source.[3] These associates of Castelberger were other artisans from Zurich, including weaver Lorenz Hochrütiner; carpenter Wolfgang Ininger; tailor Hans Ockenfuss; shoemaker Klaus Hottinger; bakers Heinrich Aberli and Barthlime Pur; Felix Manz, son of a canon of the Grossmünster; and a Zurich patrician's son, Conrad Grebel, who had spent twenty months in Paris and environs, carousing and wasting scholarship money. When Grebel associated himself with this group following his religious awakening and espousal of the Zwinglian direction sometime in 1522, his superior education eventually enabled him to play a leading role among them. Priests from small, rural towns within the jurisdiction of Zurich made up the second category. Leading individuals were Simon Stumpf at Hönng, Wilhelm Reublin at Witikon and also at Zollikon, and Johannes Brötli, who arrived at a Zollikon that already reflected the influence of Reublin. Parallel with the reform impulses in Zurich, these men sought to establish populist reformations in their villages, a goal that precipitated a direct confrontation with Zwingli and the authorities in Zurich.

These future Swiss Anabaptists were immersed in the ideas and outlook of Andreas Karlstadt, absorbing much more of his outlook than did Zwingli. Much of the influence came through literary sources, culminating with personal contact in 1524. Karlstadt was the first proponent of the theological outlook given structure in the Anabaptist movement. While he did not found Swiss Anabaptism, the radicals in Zurich attempted to implement much of the reform program that emerged from his experiences in Wittenberg and then at Orlamünde.[4] The Zurich radicals also owe a particular debt to Erasmus for their interpretation of baptism.

Karlstadt had been Martin Luther's senior colleague at the University of Wittenberg and the initiator there of discussions on reform. Karlstadt had published *151 Theses* in April 1517, but it was Luther's *95 Theses* of October 31, 1517, that caught the attention of Europe and sparked the Reformation. Karlstadt defended Luther's theses and participated with Luther in the public debate with Johann Eck at Leipzig in 1519. Eck added Karlstadt's name to *Exsurge Domine*, the papal bull threatening Luther's excommunication.

Following his appearance and condemnation before the imperial diet at Worms in April 1521, Luther for his own safety was removed to the Wartburg castle at Eisenach. In his absence, Karlstadt pushed reform in Wittenberg. He performed the first reformed communion service on Christmas 1521—in German, wearing lay clothing. He became the first Reformer to repudiate his monastic vows, including celibacy, and married sixteen-year-old Anna von Mochau in January 1522. The town council enacted a new welfare system advocated by Luther and Karlstadt, and Karlstadt pushed for removal of images from churches. Unwilling to wait for official permission, an unruly mob acted on its own to destroy a number of images.

The rapid pace of reform upset both the Elector Frederick as well as Luther. In March 1522 Luther returned to Wittenberg from the Wartburg and preached what came to be known as the eight "Invocavit sermons." Luther sided with the conservatives and attacked Karlstadt. A writing of Karlstadt was censored and his preaching was curtailed. Disgraced and with a number of his reforms undone, Karlstadt continued his university lectures on an abbreviated scale.

Karlstadt felt betrayed by his colleagues. Gradually he withdrew to Orlamünde, the source of the churchly stipend that paid his salary. There Karlstadt became increasingly disillusioned with academia. He rejected academic titles as contrary to Christ's words to call no man "master" and adopted a life quite close to the peasants' style. Called "Brother Andreas" in Orlamünde, he encouraged interruptions and discussion during sermons, which he delivered while sitting in the midst of the congregation. He translated psalms into German and collaborated with the town council in removing the organ and the images from the church building. He abolished the baptism of infants.

Karlstadt's activities at Orlamünde continued to draw the attention and opposition of Luther. In August 1524 Luther visited the region, preached against Karlstadt, and implicated him in the revolutionary schemes of Thomas Müntzer, whose story is told in the following chapter. At a face-to-face meeting at the Black Bear Inn in Jena, Luther challenged Karlstadt to refute him in print. Although Karlstadt's polemical works did not eliminate Luther, they proved powerful enough to splinter the Reformation movement on the question of the sacraments and other issues.

Due in part to complaints from Luther, the town council in Orlamünde was overridden by regional authorities. Karlstadt was expelled from Orlamünde toward the end of September 1524. His ensuing travels included Strasbourg, Zurich, and Basel. In the latter city, in the company of Andreas Castelberger, Felix Manz, and his brother-in-law Gerhard Westerberg, Karlstadt attempted to publish a number of his books. Following a period of secret refuge in Rothenburg on the Tauber, Karlstadt worked out a compromise with Luther in 1525 for the sake of his family. He published an ambiguous recantation and promised to remain silent. In return, Luther lodged Karlstadt in his own house until he could settle in the vicinity of Wittenberg. For the next four years, Karlstadt eked out a wretched living. He was kept under surveillance, and his letters to Caspar Schwenckfeld and the Anabaptists at Nikolsburg were routinely intercepted.

Meanwhile, the earlier writings of Karlstadt expressed ideas that would prove formative in the minds of the Zurich radicals. By the end of 1521, he had developed a view of the sole sufficiency of Scripture. His understandings of liturgy, the church, baptism, and the Lord's Supper were based upon what he considered the teaching of the Bible alone. He rejected the Lutheran doctrine of predestination. He rejected infant baptism as a sacrament, refused to baptize infants, and advocated adult baptism as a sign of faith. His view of church rejected all hierarchy and emphasized the equality of members. The pastoral calling was not to a higher status, but to an office performed only for the sake of order. While he was not present in Zurich at the beginning of tension between Zwingli and the radical party, the radicals to a significant extent reflected the influence of Karlstadt's early writings.

Karlstadt had begun reform with the idea that the restored or reformed church would be established by the legal authorities. He withdrew from Wittenberg only after his reforms were crushed. The city council in Orlamünde enacted his reforms. Only when expelled from Orlamünde did he develop a view of the church as a persecuted remnant, a church independent of magistrates. Thus, the development of a disestablished or separated church was originally a matter of circumstances more than an act of principle.

Karlstadt reflected the anticlerical attitude of the time. He insisted that the pastor communicate with the laity, and he disregarded clerical vestments and titles. Laity were endowed with clerical rights such as reading and proclamation from Scripture and celebration of the Lord's Supper in private homes. For the sake of order, in public assembly the chosen pastor simply exercised such functions for all.

Karlstadt rejected the revolutionary violence of Thomas Müntzer, but allowed magistrates to wield the sword of law. He opposed the sword and other means of coercion in matters of religion. Karlstadt was nonresistant at a personal level, but his rhetoric did incite followers to iconoclasm, which contributed to Luther's misguided charges of revolution on Karlstadt's part.

The Beginning of Reform

The first direct attack on the old order in Zurich came with the breaking of the Lenten fast in March 1522. In the home of printer Christopher Froschauer, a small company included sausage in the evening meal. Zwingli was among those present.

While he ate no meat himself, he also did nothing to stop those who did so. Other participants included Zwingli's future co-worker Leo Jud, as well as Simon Stumpf, Heinrich Aberli, and Barthlime Pur.[5] (The latter two would later sign Grebel's September 1524 letter to Thomas Müntzer.) When the matter of the sausage came to public attention, it would have been easy to explain the incident as an accident or mistake, or to seek absolution for it. Instead, Zwingli defended it in sermon and in print. Since the Bible did not require abstinence from meat, choosing what to eat was a matter of freedom in Christ.

Zwingli, aided and abetted by various of his zealous followers, expressed himself publicly on other issues in 1522. They included the desire of the clergy to marry and the validity of monastic vows, indulgences, and the use of images. Grebel, Aberli, and Pur, for example, interrupted sermons of monks in order to expose their unbiblical content. Stumpf and Zwingli were among ten priests who published a petition to the bishop of Constance asking for permission to marry. The writings of Luther—and more so of Karlstadt and Erasmus—were instrumental in the development of Zwingli's early ideas on most of these issues.

Toward the end of 1522, the city council allowed Zwingli to resign his position as priest in order to preach under the direct authority of the council. He further persuaded the council to call a disputation for the purpose of a public validation of his reform program. This First Zurich Disputation, which occurred in January 1523, was called by city council in order to assert its supremacy in matters of religion, and it had a largely predetermined outcome. The council affirmed the principle that all preaching and reform must conform solely to the Bible. Not wanting to validate the right of the council to act independent of his authority, the bishop of Constance had sent no representatives authorized to enter into the debate. Consequently, no real opposition to Zwingli had been expressed during the disputation. The council's hiring of Zwingli and the affirmation of his position through the disputation marked Zurich's official declaration of independence from the Roman hierarchy.

Since the beginning of 1523, several of those who had participated in breaking the Lenten fast and in interrupting monastic sermons had given themselves to systematic study of the Bible. Castelberger led the circle whose members also included Hottinger, Ockenfuss, Aberli, Hochrütiner, Pur, and Grebel. This group of Zwingli loyalists of early 1523 furnished one component of the opposition to Zwingli that emerged later in that year. Many members of this group were immersed in the writings of Karlstadt, and their later reform program resembled much of Karlstadt's reform, while their particular formulation on baptism—the issue for which they would become most known—likely came from Erasmus's paraphrases and *Annotations* of the New Testament.

More than any other single issue, it was the question of the tithe that came to the fore in 1523 and precipitated the break between Zwingli and his radical supporters. Primarily, it was the inhabitants of rural areas who confronted the tithe, and its discussion extended far beyond Switzerland. It consisted of a tax of 10 percent on the produce of the land, collected by the religious establishment for the support of churches. Much more than a question of money, opposition to the tithe was a matter of authority and the assertion of local autonomy by the rural communes. This striving for independence also showed itself in the attempts of the rural churches to select their own priests.

Already in 1522 Simon Stumpf at Hönng had raised questions concerning payment of the tithe. In an independent act at Christmas 1522, Witikon made Reublin its priest. The following March, Zurich and Witikon arrived at a kind of compromise. The council would accept Reublin as priest in Witikon at least to the end of the year, provided they continued to pay for his support. In other words, the commune had permission to reform its own religious life as long as it continued to finance the traditional order.

The impetus to oppose the tithe came from the rural priests rather than from the radical Zwinglian conventicle in Zurich. Perhaps the priests took some of their theoretical arguments from Zwingli's earlier expression of doubt about the tithe. Quite possibly a collection of Karlstadt's theses, with references against tithes and published in Basel early in 1522, provided the impetus that made the tithe a full-fledged controversy in the summer of 1522.

In June, six communities, including Witikon and Zollikon under Reublin's influence, protested to the Zurich city council about the collection of the tithe by the chapter of the Grossmünster, claiming that the tithe was not in accord with the Scriptures and was used for unnecessary purposes. The council supported the continuation of the tithe but stated that they would work with the chapter to avoid abuses. Earlier, Zwingli had expressed doubts about the tithe from a humanist and anticlerical perspective. Now, however, he supported the council. Two days after their action, he preached a sermon—"On Divine and Human Righteousness"—stating that as long as the council required payment of the tithe, it was the Christian's civic duty to pay it.

Zwingli's statement enraged his radical supporter Conrad Grebel. Already in the previous year, Grebel had claimed that the devil sat on the bench with the council, and that in the tithes affairs, they acted like tyrants and Turks. Now Grebel's invective turned on Zwingli as well, calling him an "archscribe" (*Erzschriftgelehrten*). Grebel had now identified himself with the local communities striving for autonomy. Although it did not yet seem irreparable, Grebel's break with Zwingli dates from this point. At this same time, Stumpf encouraged his church in Hönng not to pay the tithe, and Zwingli reported a statement from Stumpf that declared reforming activity worthless if the established clergy were not rooted out and killed.

About this time Grebel, Manz, and Stumpf came to Zwingli to argue for the creation of a new church, independent of the traditional religious institutions. In effect, they asked for the creation of a new political party, which would elect a new, reform-minded city council. Zwingli rejected this solution as politically divisive. While Zwingli's reform resulted in a break with the Roman tradition, he had no intention of creating a new institution outside of or apart from the city polity.

Questions of Authority

The responses and reactions of the radicals and Zwingli show that originally they agreed on the principle of Scripture as the norm for reform, and on the aspects of the old order that needed change. It was thus questions of authority and church order—not of theology—that caused the break between Zwingli and the radicals. Both the radicals and Zwingli expected to win the approval of the city government and assumed that the city council would carry out the reform of the old order. Where they differed was on the point at which resistance to reform by council became intolerable.

Another difference was also developing beneath or alongside the differences of strategy and speed of reform. Although the agreement of the radicals and Zwingli on the principle of Scripture as the norm for reform masked it for a time, the radicals and Zwingli were developing different approaches—different hermeneutics—to the interpretation of Scripture. Zwingli's humanist approach reserved the interpretation of Scripture for himself and his learned associates. This approach left control of the meaning of the Scripture with the authorities of the established church.

In contrast, the radicals came to understand the gathered congregation as the interpretative or hermeneutical community. For them, the ultimate authority rested with the congregation rather than with the literate, educated elite. Putting the Bible into the hands of the laypeople in the congregation is apparent in the list of Scripture texts published by Hans Krüsi, which he had likely received from Conrad Grebel. Of the fifty-three references, sixteen deal with baptism. Other Anabaptist writings reflect a similar approach. Circulating lists of texts in this way enabled the peasant, who had little formal education, to learn the essentials of the scriptural message. This method was a "genuine outgrowth of taking seriously the priesthood of all believers, of making biblical knowledge attainable for the laity, and closing the gap between ordinary lay people and literate leaders."[6] This difference in approach to interpretation between Zwingli and the radicals was not immediately apparent to either side in their growing disagreements. Baptism was the issue that eventually produced clear polarization on the interpretation of the Bible.

Zwingli envisioned the furthering of reform on a different scale than did the radicals, which precipitated the break on the question of authority and church order. He assumed the necessity of a centralized authority, responsible for the entire territory administered by Zurich, and a reform that encompassed this territory. Although Zwingli had initial doubts about the tithe, he saw its role in maintaining the authority of Zurich in the territory under its jurisdiction. He thus came to support and even intensify the tithe system. It was a means of implementing and strengthening the centralized Reformation.

When examined from his perspective of desiring to eliminate the old order throughout the entire territory under Zurich's jurisdiction, Zwingli's policy was obvious. The radical priests from the rural communities, on the other hand, represented localities that had chafed under the control exerted from the urban religious establishment. When the radicals lost patience with the pace of Zwingli's reform, they began to assert the right of local control of reform—a kind of reform from "the bottom up" rather than from the "top down."

For these rural communities, Reformation developed an additional connotation not present in Zurich: the assertion of local control as expressed in opposition to the tithe. This approach to Reformation has been called "reformed congregationalism"[7] and more recently the "communal reformation."[8]

From the perspective of this approach to Reformation, Zwingli was a continuation of the abuses of the old order. From the perspective of radical congregationalism, Zwingli's support of the system of tithes and the opposition to local autonomy was a betrayal of the Reformation. The radicals thus turned on Zwingli the anticlerical impulse that had first motivated their zealous support of Zwingli against the old order.

The assertion of independence by a local parish was not at that point, however, given an ecclesiological rationale. They were not attempting to separate individual believers into a gathered, free church. The radicals all assumed the continuation of one church encompassing all the inhabitants of the town. At this juncture, the organization of a gathered church consisting of believers only and standing as an explicit alternative to the mass church was still some months and years away. It was stated first at Schleitheim in February 1527.

The formation of radical, reformed communities continued with the arrival of Johannes Brötli in Zollikon, which was already influenced by Reublin. He presented himself as one following the example of the apostle Paul, supporting himself through a trade rather than living from a churchly benefice. Brötli still wanted official acknowledgment of his position, however, and issued a request that the council confirm his service in Zollikon.

The first direct action in the reform of worship came in the fall of 1523 with an instance of iconoclasm. At Hönng near the end of September, Stumpf preached against the use of images. The congregation removed them the same day. In order to assert and maintain its authority and to provide an orderly basis for the coming changes in the religious order, the council in Zurich called the Second Zurich Disputation for October.

The disputation involved principally persons committed to reform. The results of the debate were clear statements rejecting both the mass as a sacrifice and the use of images in the churches. It was ruled that neither practice had any foundation in the Bible. The disputation also brought into the open the dissonance between Zwingli and his radical supporters. On the basis of the consensus that the mass was not a sacrifice, Grebel requested that the gathered priests should receive immediate instructions on how to reform the mass. Grebel's question provoked the following oft-quoted exchange:

Zwingli: Milords [the Council] will decide how to proceed henceforth with the Mass.

> Stumpf: Master Huldrych! You have no authority to place the decision in Milords' hands, for the decision is already made: the Spirit of God decides. If therefore Milords were to discern and decide anything that is contrary to God's decision, I will ask Christ for his Spirit and will teach and act against it.

> Zwingli: That is right. I shall also preach and act against it if they decide otherwise. I do not give the decision in their hands. They shall also certainly not decide about God's Word—not only they but [also] the whole world should not. This convocation is not being held so that they might decide about that, but to ascertain and learn from the Scripture whether or not the mass is a sacrifice. Then they will counsel together as to the most appropriate way for this to be done without an uproar, etc.[9]

In this exchange, Zwingli clearly locates the authority for reform with the city council. Stumpf, on the other hand, as shortly becomes clearer, gives the initiative to the local authorities.

The Second Zurich Disputation marked the linking of the radicals in Zurich with the radicals outside the city. Participating in the disputation were several individuals who for various reasons supported local initiatives. These included Sebastian Hofmeister from Schaffhausen and Balthasar Hubmaier from the Austrian-ruled Waldshut. Particularly Hubmaier was prepared to support the side of local initiative in reformation. Two months after the disputation, in defiance of the ruling Austrians and on the basis of local authority, he instituted reform in Waldshut.

Implementation of the decisions of the October 1523 disputation came slowly—too slowly for the radicals. While he had proposed a reformed Lord's Supper for Christmas 1523, Zwingli deferred to the caution of the council, and introduction of the new order was delayed until April 1525. Expressing his now several-months'-old disillusionment with Zwingli, Grebel wrote caustically: "Whoever thinks, believes, or declares that Zwingli acts according to the duty of a shepherd, thinks, believes, and declares wickedly."[10] The comment displays the way in which the radicals from the city had identified with the cause of the rural communities who opposed Zwingli's assertion of Zurich's control over them. As yet, however, the rural leaders had more importance than Grebel, who lacked their congregational base from which to confront Zwingli.

Soon after the October disputation, the authorities launched an investigation of Stumpf's role in the iconoclasm that had challenged the council's authority and elicited the debate. In spite of a petition from the congregation at Hönng, the council removed Stumpf from office. He moved to the nearby town of Weiningen in Baden, where Catholic authorities still ruled. Here he also precipitated a local reformation and persuaded the local priest to marry. When the Vogt (warden) of Baden tried to arrest Stumpf and his colleague, an armed force that included men from nearby Hönng defended the two leaders. Stumpf escaped. However, deprived of activity in his sphere of influence, he gradually returned to the old church. This first leader of a radical, reformed congregation no longer played a part in the movement when it finally reached the occasion of the first baptisms.

Baptism was the first issue that precipitated significant theological differences as well as differences of authority between the radicals and Zwingli. The radicals' public attack on infant baptism began in 1524. Already in 1523 the radical

Bible circle in Zurich had come to a theoretical opposition to baptism of infants.

It appears that the future Anabaptists' insistence that teaching must precede baptism, which in turn necessitated baptism of adults, was based on the interpretation of Matthew 28:19 from Erasmus's paraphrases and his *Annotations* that accompanied his Greek text of the New Testament. Until Erasmus, the text of the so-called great commission was used to show that valid baptism had to be in the name of Father, Son, and Holy Spirit, a view that first developed in the Arian controversy of the fourth century. Using a historical methodology, Erasmus gave the text a quite different emphasis. He assumed that the apostles were the best interpreters of Jesus's words about teaching and baptizing. Thus, Erasmus looked to apostolic practice in the book of Acts to see how they carried out the injunction of Matthew 28:19. A significant dimension of Erasmus's interpretation was his conclusion that the specific order of teaching followed by baptism in Matthew 28:19 characterized apostolic practice in Acts. Only Anabaptists followed Erasmus in this interpretation. And the soon-to-be Anabaptists in Zurich were reading Erasmus's Greek New Testament in the circle led by Castelberger and then Grebel, which also means that they were reading Erasmus's paraphrase and *Annotations* where he emphasized the order of teaching followed by baptism.[11]

Erasmus himself never received a second baptism, and in spite of his severe critique of the Catholic Church, he never left it to join the Reformation. How could the view of one who did not leave the Catholic Church become so important for those who did? The answer lies in Erasmus's larger framework and the place of the paraphrases and *Annotations* in his worldview. Erasmus held to a Platonic framework, in which ideas or the ideals are what is real, with their particular expressions in the world existing only as pale shadows of the ideals. The earthly church, for example, is at best only a pale shadow of the ideal form. Thus, Erasmus could issue sharp critiques of Catholic practices while remaining in that church, since any particular church would be nothing more than a shadow of the ideal. At the same time, Erasmus believed that the teachings of Jesus were a statement of the ideal. Hence, he sought to present this ideal—by publishing the New Testament in Greek along with his *Annotations* and paraphrases, in which he tried to clarify these ideal teachings. As presentations of the ideal of Jesus's teaching, the *Annotations* and paraphrases were bare of the Platonic worldview of ideals and shadows. Since the future Anabaptists studied these writings of Erasmus, they received a view of Jesus's teachings as the correct form for the church. And whatever the source of their biblicism, Erasmus's view that the order of teaching and then baptism in Matthew 28:19 was specifically taught by Jesus and put into practice by the apostles became a central feature of the radicals' own understanding and practice of baptism.

It remained for the inhabitants of Witikon and Zollikon, in the spring of 1524 under the influence of Reublin, to take the initiative in actually refusing to baptize infants. In August, Reublin was imprisoned briefly because of his preaching against infant baptism. On the point of infant baptism, perhaps even more than with the tithe, Zwingli was vulnerable to the radicals' attack. He had earlier expressed the opinion that adult baptism should perhaps be part of the future reformed order, which he could have learned from Erasmus since he had read Erasmus before arriving in Zurich. Rejecting this view would give real significance to the Anabaptists' later claims that Zwingli reversed himself on baptism. Hofmeister in Schaffhausen and Hubmaier in Waldshut had made similar statements about adult baptism, although neither was prepared in 1524 to advocate opposition to infant baptism.

The radicals' common front against Zwingli masked a tension between the radical circle in Zurich and the rural priests. Lacking the communal base of Stumpf, Reublin, and Brötli, the Bible circle members came earlier than their rural colleagues to recognize the powerlessness of the radical movement and their inability to influence the course of Zwingli's Reformation. Already in 1524 the circle to which Grebel and Manz and Castelberger belonged was showing evidence of the idea of a separatist critique, which would reach fruition in the Schleitheim Confession of February 1527. These urban radicals also displayed a consistent pacifism, which contrasted with the communal-based radicals, a number of whom accepted or encouraged local armed defense of their Reformation.

Sensing themselves unable to advance their program for Zurich, the radicals sought support outside of Zurich. Early in September they wrote to Thomas Müntzer. Both Grebel and Castelberger had written to Karlstadt earlier in the summer. Only Grebel's letter to Müntzer has survived.[12] It shows both the developing idea of a separatist critique of church and social order as well as the points of tension between the city radicals and the radical rural communities. Their sense of separation appears in such statements as the claim that there are only a few, "not even twenty who believe the Word of God," and their expectation of coming persecution. The letter lays out Grebel's reform program for a much simplified worship service, bare of music and images, and calls for refusal to participate in the unreformed churches. The letter also expresses opposition to baptism of infants and states clearly that the Reformation should not be defended with the sword. Several times the letter scores the "false forbearance [*faltsch schonen*]" of Zwingli and Luther, who were delaying the institution of reform. In most of these points, Grebel was a close follower of Karlstadt.

Grebel had read enough of Müntzer's writings to deepen his sense of alienation from the established Reformers. However, if he had been better informed about Thomas Müntzer's violent revolutionary direction, Grebel would not have praised Müntzer as he did.

The now-lost letters from the Zurich radicals to Karlstadt must have reached him at the time when his expulsion from

Orlamünde seemed imminent. In early October Karlstadt's brother-in-law, Gerhard Westerberg, who had heard Luther's challenge to Karlstadt at the Black Bear Inn in Jena, was sent to Zurich, where he could anticipate a favorable reception. Westerberg spent six days reading several of Karlstadt's manuscripts to Castelberger, Grebel, Manz, and others in the radical conventicle. The radicals responded to Westerberg by raising much of the money necessary for the publication of these materials.

Westerberg, Castelberger, and Manz rode on horseback to Basel, where they persuaded Johannes Bebel and Thomas Wolf to print seven of the treatises. Karlstadt secretly joined them in Basel but left the city before the printing process was actually accomplished. He later visited the radicals in Zurich. Another manuscript, the baptismal treatise *Von dem Tauff*, was returned to Manz as too radical and likely to produce scandal. Manz and Castelberger left Basel with well over five thousand copies of Karlstadt's booklets. This effort displays the radicals' immersion in Karlstadt's thought. The radicals spread these copies widely throughout Switzerland and to nearby Waldshut, where they eventually contributed to the thought of the future Anabaptist Balthasar Hubmaier.

Anabaptism

In the course of 1524, the baptism of adults became attached to the Radical Reformation. Toward the end of the year, Zwingli and the radical opponents of infant baptism engaged in discussions on the theme. Within a month of the trip to Basel and the meeting with Karlstadt, Felix Manz wrote a personal defense of adult baptism, his *Protestation* to the city council of Zurich. Large sections of this statement were copied from Karlstadt's *Von dem Tauff*.

On January 17, 1525, the first formal baptismal disputation took place. Like the earlier disputations, this one also had the purpose of strengthening the position of the authorities. Consequently, infant baptism was ruled biblical, and the city council issued a mandate that required the baptism of all infants within eight days. It forbade further meetings of the circle of Grebel, Manz, and Castelberger, and expelled from Zurich the opponents of infant baptism who were not Zurich residents, which included Brötli and Reublin.

Apparently having given up on the Zwinglian Reformation, the radicals carried out the first rebaptism of adults as a direct response to the council's ruling on infant baptism. This time, in contrast to the action on tithes and images and even the refusal to baptize infants, it was the radical circle in Zurich that took the initiative. Soon after the council's decision, likely the evening of January 21, 1525, the date of the mandate, the group met in the home of Manz's mother, Anna, in the Neustadtgasse, to consider what to do. After some discussion, George Blaurock requested baptism from Grebel. Blaurock then baptized the remainder of those present. The radical movement already had an identity prior to these rebaptisms, and the reform of baptism had not constituted their most central concern, but the events of January 21, 1525, nonetheless have become recognized as the formal beginning of Anabaptism.

The cessation of infant baptism in the rural communities of Witikon and Zollikon and the first adult baptisms in the radical circle in Zurich did not constitute the establishment of gathered and separated congregations of adult believers. The initial acts of rebaptism did not carry the connotation of separation, which later accrued to adult baptism. The initial refusal of the baptism of infants, like opposition to the tithe and local hiring of priests, was an act that affirmed independence from Zurich, and it was initiated when the council's actions of January 1525 dashed any remaining hope of an official baptismal reform. The baptismal acts represented a desire to align baptism with their understanding of the New Testament, to purify another aspect of the order of worship for the mass church when Zurich hesitated. In a measure, the rebaptisms completed the purification of worship, and the participants acted with the expectation that other reforming communities would follow their example. While an act of defiance, it was also born of the desperate feeling that Zwingli had betrayed the Reformation. The action generated opposition, which would mark the movement for centuries.

The first adult baptisms took place two months after the radicals' personal contacts with Karlstadt. The leaders had immersed themselves in Karlstadt's thought and had worked to disseminate it. Yet Karlstadt's person and impact were soon forgotten, for several reasons. Karlstadt himself had spurned the personality cult of early Lutheranism. Complementary to this outlook, the radicals and Karlstadt considered themselves to be restoring the New Testament church on the basis of Scripture alone, rather than starting a new church based on the ideas of a contemporary leader. They had likely learned from Erasmus the distinct component of their understanding of baptism, that Jesus specifically commanded the order of teaching followed by baptism. And finally, the radicals would soon learn of Karlstadt's compromise with Martin Luther, which enabled him to live again in the vicinity of Wittenberg.

Radicals like Felix Manz, who would be the first to die in Zurich for the Anabaptist cause, must have been disappointed at Karlstadt's shrinking from martyrdom and pulling back from what they considered as known truth. They may have thought him another example of the dangers of being learned. In fact, after another interlude of work for more radical reform with Melchior Hoffmann in 1529, Karlstadt reconciled himself to Zwingli and moved to Zurich in 1530. Eventually he obtained the chair of Hebrew Bible at the University of Basel and preached at the University Church of Saint Peter. Similar disaffection perhaps followed Erasmus's failure to leave the church he so strongly critiqued.

In the days following January 21, 1525, with major assistance from Grebel, the majority of the inhabitants of Zollikon received rebaptism in institutional form. Even though the experiment resisted the authority of Zurich for only a few months, this rebaptized church constituted the first Anabaptist congregation. Grebel, Manz, George Blaurock, and others spent the months after January 1525 in the regions outside of Zurich, preaching and baptizing.

After their expulsion from Witikon and Zollikon, Reublin and Brötli established a base of operations in Hallau, through which that city underwent an Anabaptist Reformation, and from which Reublin exerted considerable influence in the surrounding area. From Hallau, Reublin went to Waldshut to baptize Hubmaier before Easter 1525. The radicals developed considerable followings in Grüningen, Schaffhausen, Waldshut, Appenzell, the region of Bern, St. Gallen, and other areas. In a number of these instances, such as at Hallau, Tablat near St. Gallen, and Waldshut, these were churches that encompassed the entire community, and they were prepared to defend themselves in an armed way.

Hubmaier possessed the only doctor's degree among all the first-generation Anabaptists. He had wide acquaintances among humanist and Reformation figures. These included contacts with Zwingli and active participation in the October 1523 disputation in Zurich. As a priest schooled in nominalist theology, he came to Waldshut in 1520, not far from Zurich but just across the border in Austrian territory. By early 1523, Hubmaier was known as an evangelical preacher, and at the October disputation in Zurich, he demanded replacement of the mass with a plain ceremony in line with Zwingli's ideas. While the higher ecclesiastical authorities and the Austrian rulers were demanding Hubmaier's extradition, the city council of Waldshut supported his reforming work. At an April 1524 disputation in Waldshut, Hubmaier defended the Reformation and attacked the old church as superfluous. The Catholic priests left town. When Archduke Ferdinand of Austria threatened to use force against the city, Hubmaier spent a kind of voluntary exile in Schaffhausen, looking for political support.

Upon his return in October 1524, Waldshut received

Hubmaier enthusiastically. Mass was celebrated in German, and images were removed from the church. When the political situation worsened, volunteers from Zurich, including members of the Grebel circle, came to defend the town. Waldshut also received defensive support from the peasants of South Germany, whom Hubmaier actively supported in their demands.

Hubmaier had read the writings of Karlstadt and Müntzer against infant baptism (and likely had met Thomas Müntzer near Waldshut in 1524). He also knew of the Grebel circle's doubts about infant baptism. His writing *Old and New Teachers on Believers Baptism* of 1526 quotes Erasmus's 1523 paraphrase of Matthew, which says that "baptism was instituted by Christ for those instructed in faith and not for young children."[13] But Hubmaier had still not committed himself to adult baptism when Reublin and Brötli arrived in Hallau following banishment from Witikon and Zollikon in January 1525. From this town placed strategically between Waldshut and Schaffhausen, Reublin worked for the conversion of both towns to the Anabaptist cause. Brötli, who tended to work in Hallau, succeeded in converting most of the city to the Anabaptist Reformation. From Hallau, Reublin traveled the countryside to create a territorial base for a radical Anabaptist variety of reformed Christendom, to challenge the more conservative model of Zwingli in Zurich. In Schaffhausen, Reublin met with Conrad Grebel and the town's priest, Sebastian Hofmeister, in a concerted effort to convert the town to the Anabaptist cause.

Later, Manz would make a similar journey to Schaffhausen. Hofmeister wanted to move in the radical direction. He had the support of peasants and some guilds, but he had to exercise caution in moving a reluctant city government toward reform.

The conversion of Hallau occurred primarily through the support of the peasants against the town's authorities, and it included an assertion of independence from Schaffhausen. Hallau wanted freedom from the bishop of Constance, but not as part of a reformed territorial church emanating from Schaffhausen. This striving for local autonomy united the peasants' movement and the Anabaptist movement in a common cause.

Reublin paid several visits to Waldshut. Although Reublin may have baptized the first Waldshuters as early as February 1525, Hubmaier himself delayed until Easter, when he and sixty others received baptism from Reublin. In the following days Hubmaier then baptized three hundred other residents of Waldshut.

Hubmaier still hoped for some kind of accommodation with Zwingli, but his literary efforts on baptism in 1525 erupted into a sharp battle with Zwingli. Hubmaier's *On Christian Baptism of Believers* of July 1525 was one of the best arguments for believers baptism of that time. In that year he also produced a *Summary of the Christian Life* and a second book on baptism. His publication work would continue in Nikolsburg, where he wrote on the Christian life and ethics, orders of worship for baptism, the Lord's Supper, church discipline, free will and predestination, and the sword. He also developed a catechism. Before his death less than two years after departing Waldshut, Hubmaier produced what was by far the greatest literary legacy of any first-generation Anabaptist.

Communal Reformation and the Peasants' War

This story of efforts to convert towns was played out against the backdrop of what has been called the "Communal Reformation" and the "reformation of the common man," which came to a rather abrupt end in the Peasants' War of 1525.[14] Contemporaries understood the "common man" as those strata of society who did not generally share in the exercise of political power, the counterparts to clergy and nobility. The "common man" carried the Reformation until 1525, when it was taken over by established authority to become the Magisterial Reformation, or the reformation of the princes. Seeing the emergence of Anabaptism out of and as a response to these events will serve to focus the distinct character of Anabaptism.

In the late medieval period, the hierarchical world of feudalism was collapsing and giving way to social structures with more horizontal relationships. In place of serfs tied to the land of a feudal lord, ownership was passing to towns of equal owners, who controlled their own affairs. In villages and towns, the commune became the primary organizing structure, and people began to assume responsibility for their own lives. This process was particularly developed in those areas of the Communal Reformation—around Zurich, in South Germany, and in the Tyrol—that are also important to the story of Anabaptist origins. In these locales of increasing local, communal control, peasants appropriated a part of Luther's new gospel in a way that supported communal control of the church. The peasants demanded preaching of the "pure gospel," by which they understood a church guided by the Reformation principle of *sola scriptura*.

In addition to secure preaching based on Scripture alone and without abuses and accretions from the Roman hierarchy, the commune demanded the right to hire its own resident pastor. Reform began with local hiring of a pastor, and it became the issue that signified local control. In other words, the communal was demanding the right to exercise authority traditionally exercised by the nobility and the ecclesiastical hierarchy. Local control of hiring concerned pastoral care, which suffered greatly in a system that allowed for many absentee priests. Intertwined with the desire to hire a pastor was the question of the tithe. Local hiring required that the commune also pay the pastor—either from money withheld from the tithe or by redirecting the money to the salary of a resident pastor. In brief, such were the central demands of the peasants and the driving force of the Peasants' Reformation. At heart, it was a challenge to the existing authorities, both political and ecclesiastical, and a drive to reorder society.

In a parallel movement, burghers—city dwellers—also demanded reform. Since burghers had long had more local control through elections than the rural peasants, the burghers did not focus on hiring a pastor. In cites, the issues concerned abolition of the mass and the removal of icons, and abolishing clerical privilege, which meant the integration of the clergy into burgher society by requiring such things as payment of taxes and standing guard duty.

Common to both the rural and urban reformations was the communal focus, putting the church under local control. The goal was to cut ties to the pope and bishops and to a regional prince or lord, and to assert local control.

In this seeking of reform via the commune, influence could pass in either direction. In some cases, peasant demonstrations pushed forward reform in the cities, while in other cases the city reforms were carried into the countryside. Together these peasant and urban drives for reform constituted the Communal Reformation. These reforms were not always achieved, but the push from them constituted the Communal Reformation, which was the dominant phase of the Reformation until 1525.

What came to be called the Peasants' War grew out of this communal reformation. It began as a series of protests by peasants and commoners that spread from the edge of Switzerland across South Germany as far as Thuringia and Saxony from 1524 to mid-July 1525. These peasant protests included issues related to use of land and forests, and to hunting and fishing rights, as well as to church reform. There were preliminary manifestations already in June of 1524 in the Black Forest region, and an additional phase that continued into 1526 in the Tyrol, which impacted Anabaptism in Moravia. Although the protesters were armed, approximately the first third of the uprising consisted of nonviolent protests, more like a general strike than a war. Crowds reached as high as thirty thousand participants. Their objective was to seek redress of grievances against landlords and rulers. Grievances touched a number of social, political, and economic issues that varied from one region to another. Whether paid to secular rulers or religious landholders, the tithe brought all economic, political, and religious dissatisfaction to bear on a single issue.

Common to the whole of this uprising was the Reformation. Although Martin Luther came to harshly denounce this uprising of common people, the movement used the new Reformation language as justification, and in many ways it was the form that the Reformation took among the common people until 1525. The introduction to Twelve Articles, a well-known manifesto of peasant grievances that originated in Swabia in March 1525 and was the model for many local statements, makes clear its identification with the Reformation. It denounced opponents of the Reformation and presented a Christian justification for the uprising, stating that the "basis of all the [twelve] articles of the peasantry is to hear the Gospel and to live accordingly."[15] The movement turned violent when negotiations did not yield results. The rulers recognized that their authority was threatened by the demands for local control and that the peasant program sought a reordering of society. Thus, for the most part the rulers confronted the peasant movement harshly. Following several military confrontations, the peasant revolt and the Communal Reformation were effectively ended with the massacre of six thousand peasants at Frankenhausen on May 15, 1525. Chapter 3 tells the story of several men from the Peasants' War and the defeat at Frankenhausen, men who are important to Anabaptism in South Germany and Moravia.

Early in his reforming career, Martin Luther had written in support of the local community hiring pastors. However, as the peasant movement progressed, Luther turned against it and condemned their appeal to the gospel as the basis of reform. Luther considered authority sacrosanct, ordained by God to preserve order in the wicked world. The peasants challenged that order. Hence, Luther called on the rulers to "stab, strike, slay" the "robbing and murdering hordes of the peasants."[16] Luther called on the rulers for reform, and his reformation became a reformation of the princes. In contrast, Ulrich Zwingli agreed with the peasants' assertion that the gospel should shape the political order (the position vehemently rejected by Luther). Zwingli's Zurich enacted a good deal of the program of the Communal Reformation, and these reforms enjoyed generally widespread support in both the city of Zurich and the surrounding countryside. Zwingli's opposition to the rural radicals came at the point of preserving the authority of Zurich's political authorities, which Zwingli defended on a regional basis.

To grasp the distinct character of the Anabaptist Reformation, it is important to recognize a way in which the Communal Reformation of peasants and burghers, Zwingli's Reformation, and Luther's Reformation, which vigorously opposed these reformations, all share a common presupposition. Although in different ways, all assume that the church or the Christian faith—however defined—encompasses the entire social order, and each sought political support for the reform program being advanced. The peasants who asserted local control assumed that they were hiring a pastor for the entire community, and they sought validation from local political authorities for their action. These demands were made to the city authorities of Zurich, who refused to grant such authority to the villages of the area. The reformation of the burghers sought approval of the city authorities for abolishing the mass and removing images and restructuring the role of the local clergy. It was true of Zwingli's reform, as he sought and waited for the support of city council for local initiatives, but procured council's support for his added qualifiers against Anabaptist resistance. And it is most certainly true of Martin Luther, who called on the German princes to carry out churchly reform that supported the political status quo. These actions all presuppose that the church encompasses the social order, whether those seeking reform thought in terms of commune, their region, or the empire.

The single most significant element in the emergence of Anabaptism as a distinct movement is its rejection of the idea that the church encompasses the entire social order. It was not an idea that the first Anabaptists articulated as an operative principle—but it was implicit in the first rebaptism in the house of Felix Manz's mother, when George Blaurock, Conrad Grebel, Felix Manz, and others on their own initiative carried out a reformation of the practice of baptism. Through a series of efforts at reform, with successes and failures in the next two years, this idea took shape and was first given articulation in February 1527 at Schleitheim, as following paragraphs recount.

The intertwined relationships among Anabaptism, Reformation, the peasants' movement, and the striving for civic independence are visible in the story of how the radicals in Zurich made common cause with those in the countryside, and in the careers of Hubmaier in Waldshut, and of Reublin and Brötli in Hallau. The tithe precipitated the break between Zwingli and the Zurich radicals. Reublin was prominent in that dispute, and Grebel's letter to Müntzer mentioned the burden on the poor imposed by ecclesiastical taxes. Zollikon, where Brötli was priest, had been prominent in the early resistance to tithes. In their work from Hallau, where Reublin and Brötli moved after their expulsion from Zurich, they forged links between a Reformation that involved baptism of adults and the peasants' campaign of disobedience to the ruling lords.

Hubmaier was the most prominent Anabaptist to participate in the Peasants' War as an Anabaptist (in contrast to those who joined the Anabaptists after having participated in the peasants' uprising). Hubmaier's Anabaptist town of Waldshut sent an armed contingent to join a peasant army in siege at Radolfzell, and also supplied armed assistance to Hallau in one of its quarrels with its overlords. Hubmaier did not author the Twelve Articles, but he was instrumental in drafting local statements of peasant programs.

The Peasants' War was much broader than Anabaptism. With a few exceptions such as Hubmaier, in regions impacted by the uprising, former rebels joined Anabaptists after an interval of months or years. For some erstwhile rebels, Anabaptism became the religious expression that continued critique and resistance to the established church and civil authorities. Grebel, Manz, and Blaurock were not Peasants' War participants, but they recruited Anabaptists in Grüningen after the uprising there, and Grebel continued to move around scenes of peasant uprising. Michael Sattler was a peasant sympathizer. Connections between the peasant uprising in the areas of Swiss Anabaptists are looser, however, than in South German Anabaptism, where as we shall see, the connections are many and direct.

For the most part the populist or mass-church form of Anabaptism was short-lived. It collapsed with the defeat of the peasant forces defending the cities. By August 1525 the Catholic authorities had regained control in Schaffhausen, where Sebastian Hofmeister had supported much of the radical program but had not yet put baptism of adults into practice. Catholic Schaffhausen then reasserted its control of Hallau. Reublin and Brötli became refugees once again.

After spending time in Strasbourg, and then in the Neckar Valley, where he worked with Michael Sattler, and again in Strasbourg as a colleague of Pilgram Marpeck, Reublin surfaced in Moravia[17] and played a role in that Anabaptist story as well (which is told in chapter 3). Although exiled from Schaffhausen, Hofmeister eventually returned to the good graces of Zwingli and ended up exercising the office of a Reformed minister in Zurich and then in Bern.

In December 1525 the Austrians drove Hubmaier from Waldshut and reestablished the Catholic order. After a stop in Zurich, where he was tortured and forced to recant, Hubmaier established himself in Nikolsburg in Moravia, where he once more led a populist or mass Anabaptist Reformation of the city on a model like that of Waldshut. (Chapter 3 picks up Hubmaier's story in Nikolsburg.) One could relate a similar story about St. Gallen, where the radicals developed a large following and tried to lead the city in a mass rejection of the

Zwinglian reform. Along with other individuals, Joachim von Watt, known as Vadian, brother-in-law of Conrad Grebel, enabled the Zwinglians to retain the upper hand.

The existence of these attempts at a mass or territorial version of Anabaptism, defended with peasant arms, shows that by no means were all of early Anabaptists either separatist or nonresistant. The extent to which the Anabaptist leaders actually supported revolution, or merely profited from the peasant cause, is not clear in every case. Connections obviously existed between Anabaptism and the peasants' revolution, and there was an attempt to establish Anabaptism on a mass scale.

In Zurich in February and March of 1525, informal and private discussions took place between Zwingli and the radicals. However, they were not successful in narrowing their differences. After spending periods of time in Schaffhausen, St. Gallen, and Waldshut, Grebel worked in Grüningen from June until his arrest on October 8, 1525. He was incarcerated, along with Manz and Blaurock, in the Grüningen castle, in which he had spent part of his boyhood while his father served as magistrate from 1499 to 1512. The prisoners participated in the formal baptismal disputation in Zurich on November 6-8, 1525. On November 18, Grebel, Manz, Blaurock, and others were tried in Zurich and given prison sentences of indeterminate length. Those radicals not citizens of Zurich were banished from the city. On March 5 and 6, 1526, Grebel, Manz, and Blaurock received a second trial. This time they received life sentences. However, the life sentence lasted only two weeks. The prisoners escaped on March 21.

Neither Grebel nor Manz had long to live. Little is known of Grebel's whereabouts following the escape. He died of the plague at Maienfeld sometime that fall. Manz was rearrested several times. In January 1527 he was once again tried in Zurich for rebaptizing, and received a death sentence. Manz became the first member of the radicals to die in Zurich for the movement. With his mother looking on and encouraging her son to remain steadfast, Felix Manz was drowned in the Limmat, off the Fischmarkt bridge, on January 5, 1527. George Blaurock reappears in the next chapter as one of the key people in introducing Anabaptism to South Tyrol.

It was these experiences of repression and the failure of efforts at local, Communal Reformation, rather than a preconceived and well-thought-out notion of a gathered congregation of believers, that fostered development of the free church or believers church idea among the radical Anabaptists. The radicals had sought support from political authorities. The emergence of a church independent of civil authorities was brought about more by social pressures than by principled acts to separate church and government. It was a pattern first experienced by Karlstadt at Wittenberg and Orlamünde. In a sense this formation of churches controlled by the members continued the Communal Reformation impulse in which local communities sought to control their own affairs. However, Anabaptist congregations also differed in important ways from the Communal Reformation. Anabaptist congregations were based on adult confessions of faith rather than encompassing the entire community. The idea of following Jesus as discovered in the New Testament or of Jesus as authority became the basis for defining the life of the congregation, and accepting Jesus as authority brought the issue of the sword to the fore as a central element of Anabaptist identity.

The remnants of the several failed mass churches in Switzerland founded a new form of church, some of whose people and ideas could be traced to the members of the radical Bible circle in Zurich. These Anabaptist radicals abandoned attempts to reform all of society, and instead they established congregations composed of the few believing persons who would separate from the established territorial church with its worship practices still resembling the old order, and its ethics consisting of the common denominator of society. For this new form of church, baptism of adults became the most important symbol of leaving the old and joining the new church that was distinguished by its rejection of specific practices of the established church.

The presumed authority of the radicals to interpret the Bible apart from the learned scholars of the established church produced frequent claims that the reformed, Anabaptist church would have everything in common, based on the model of Acts 2 and 4. In other words, working to institute community of goods was an effort to apply and live out of the New Testament, alongside efforts to practice baptism and Lord's Supper in the manner of the apostles. Community of goods attained written expression in the Swiss Congregational Order (treated below). In Switzerland, the practice of community of goods meant primarily a common treasury or a sharing between individual families to help needy members in a congregation, and also a refusal to take money from interest or rent. Community of goods meant something different for Hutterites in Moravia, where it eventually came to involve a congregation living together as a household.

The practice of community of goods was short-lived among Swiss Anabaptists. When they came under increasing suspicion and pressure from civil authorities, they made clarifications that they had not advocated confiscating property from wealthy people but only wished to implement apostolic practice in the church. Community of goods became a rule against exploitation and about sharing in the congregation. However, it was also a contribution to Anabaptism that attained much greater visibility in the Anabaptist movement of Moravia.

Anabaptists did separate from the established churches, and they did see their religious faith as an outlook that impacted all of life and made their church a witness to both the mass church and the social order. However, separation from the established church does not mean withdrawal from society. Separation is the stance from which Anabaptists witnessed to and engaged the social order.[18] Their engagement appears even in the *Schleitheim Brotherly Union*, which is frequently viewed as an exclusively separatist statement.

Schleitheim

An Anabaptist ecclesiology, based on the idea that the church controls its own affairs independent of political authorities, first received a systematic statement in the seven articles edited by Michael Sattler, an associate of the Zurich radicals, and adopted at Schleitheim in February 1527. Sattler had a position of leadership—perhaps even that of prior—at the Benedictine monastery of Saint Peter's in the Black Forest.[19] It is likely that he abandoned St. Peter's in May 1525, in conjunction with the siege of it by a peasant troop from the Black Forest, which included volunteers from Anabaptist Waldshut and Hallau.

Now sympathetic with peasant concerns, Sattler settled in the area of Waldshut and Schaffhausen, north of Zurich. His activities are not known until he arrived in Zurich for the November 1525 disputation on baptism and displayed some sympathy with the Anabaptists. Still less than committed to their cause, however, he was expelled from the city rather than jailed with Grebel, Manz, and Blaurock. By late June 1526 he had committed himself to the Anabaptist movement.

Toward the end of 1526, Sattler spent a period of time in Strasbourg, where he argued his case with the city's Reformers, Martin Bucer and Wolfgang Capito. He pleaded with them for mercy for imprisoned Anabaptist brothers. Sattler outlined his differences with the Reformers in a letter of farewell. These views appeared two months later in the Schleitheim Articles, written February 24, 1527.

At the turn of the year to 1527, Sattler abandoned Strasbourg and then did some missionizing in the area of Lahr. From there, he went to Schleitheim for the conference that produced the well-known seven articles. Most likely while at Schleitheim, Wilhelm Reublin persuaded Sattler to take charge of the Anabaptist congregation at Horb on the Neckar River. Within a few days of his arrival there, Sattler, his wife, Margaretha, and a number of other individuals were arrested by Austrian authorities and imprisoned in Rottenberg.

The trial occurred on May 17 and 18, 1527. The execution on May 20, 1527, displayed particular cruelty. Sattler's tongue was cut out and his flesh torn numerous times with hot tongs. He was then burned at the stake. Two days later Margaretha demonstrated similar faith and steadfastness when she was drowned in the Neckar River at Rottenberg.

The seven articles of the Schleitheim Confession[20] are the first true articulation of the "free church"—the idea of a church of believers independent of the established church and civil authorities. The content of the articles reflects the issues debated between the radicals and the official Reformers, and among the peasants and the various Anabaptist groups. Parallels with the monastic tradition appear in the articles' emphasis on discipline, holy living, separation, and imitation of the way of Jesus.[21] In contrast to the earlier efforts to work through the established church and the political authorities and to create Anabaptist mass churches, the accord at Schleitheim expressed a sense of separation or self-declared independence from other institutions. This separation applied to the official church, to the mass-church Anabaptists, and to the revolutionary peasants.

The articles opposed the oath, which became the primary symbol of rejection of political authority. They also made baptism of adults the norm and established a Lord's Supper devoid of any sacramentalism. In contrast to the tendency to use the sword exhibited by Anabaptists at Waldshut or St. Gallen and the peasant revolutionaries, Schleitheim rejected the sword and made pacifism the normative position. The confession also rejected the idea that a Christian could serve in any political office. Following the radicals' initial opposition to the tithe, Schleitheim now counseled payment of it, since refusal did not fit the pattern of nonresistance and suffering.

The articles made the church visible through the admonitions against expensive clothing and food and preserved the visible church through systematic discipline. Schleitheim now advocated not only the establishment of separated congregations, but also opposed any attendance at worship services of the official church. Further, since the Anabaptists had surrendered any attempt to work within the established churches, the confession prescribed pastors hired to shepherd the separated Anabaptist congregations. Designation of such practices indicates that the Anabaptists at Schleitheim were rejecting "certain practices" more than making a "principled withdrawal from the whole world."[22]

The earliest Anabaptist leaders had been expelled or executed. In these articles, Sattler formulated anew the basis of the radical faith as it had gradually come into practice. Schleitheim made the first formal articulation of those elements within the Swiss Brethren that would later constitute the essence of the whole Anabaptist movement. What was once a program for the mass church of all the citizenry, as in the Communal Reformation of the peasants, had become the form for a remnant group sharply separated from the mass church. Whereas Thomas Müntzer had envisioned a new society built by the elect on the remnants of the old through a violent revolution, Sattler and those gathered at Schleitheim saw a withdrawal from the institutions of the social order in order to establish a new society of the elect on a pacifist model, following literally the example of Jesus. This new religious society enfranchised all its members together to read the Bible, to choose its pastors, and to exercise discipline. As such, it rejected control of the church by civil authorities, the hierarchical authority of Catholicism, as well as the Magisterial Reformation's relocation of that authority in academically educated teachers and ministers.

At the same time, the separation in Schleitheim's form of Anabaptism did not envision a complete withdrawal from the social order nor a cessation of interaction with it. Continuing interaction appears in article 6 on the sword. In this article, the brethren acknowledge that the sword appears to play an ordering function in the world that does not confess the rule of God. Thus, the sword functions "outside the perfection of

Christ." Those who follow Jesus under the reign of God cannot bear the sword nor serve in offices of the social order that controls the sword. For them, the ban, established in article 2, is the best form of discipline. But this statement about the sword also does clearly engage the social order. It calls on civil authorities, within their own framework, to respect the limits on the sword's ordering function. By holding up the teaching of Christ to those in the established church who also claim to be Christians, this document is a political engagement and churchly witness—rather than an absolute withdrawal from the social order. However, this political engagement and witness happens on the church's terms rather than on the terms of the civil authorities. "The *Brotherly Union* thus stands as a statement of protest against the religious and cultural and political establishment associated with the status quo in Switzerland and South Germany. It represents the outcome of failed discussions, disputations, and exchanges between Anabaptist leaders and the political and ecclesiastical authorities of Christendom. It is the product of engagement, not withdrawal."[23]

Alongside the Schleitheim Articles is the document that Werner Packull has called "the Swiss Congregational Order."[24] Because of overlapping content with the Schleitheim Articles, some scholars have argued that they come from the same source. Differences between them, however, point toward different origins, and in fact the Swiss Order may well predate Schleitheim. One of the most significant differences is the Swiss Order's fifth article, which calls for community of goods, expressed primarily as a common treasury. "Of all the brothers and sisters of this congregation, none shall have anything of his own, but rather, as the Christians in the time of the apostles held all in common, and especially stored up a common fund, from which aid can be given to the poor, according as each will have need." Whatever its origin, the practice could have endured only temporarily in Swiss locations. Other particulars of the Swiss Order, such as specifying the number of weekly worship meetings and specifying the kind of meal to share when they ate together, indicate that it was likely implemented for a time in a congregation. Possible candidates include Zollikon, Tablat near St. Gallen, or Teuffen in the territory of Appenzell. The more important point, however, is that the Swiss Order and community of goods emerged from a particular context and was the first specific embodiment of the congregation as a hermeneutical community. The influence of this Swiss Order reached well beyond its brief practice in Switzerland. It reappears in revised formats in Moravian Anabaptism, the story that unfolds in the following chapter.

This chapter has related the story of the origins of the idea of a church separated from or independent of the established church and the civil authorities. It consisted of believers, whose intent was to govern the church on the basis of Scripture alone, although as this narrative has made clear, they obviously read contemporary literature as well as the Bible. Baptism was not the defining issue at the beginning of the radical movement, but it became the most important symbol of separation and assertion of churchly independence for the young Anabaptist movement. For this movement, discipleship or the following of Jesus became the normative way to discuss the nature of the Christian life, which made rejection of the sword a central focus in Anabaptist identity.

3

South German and Moravian Anabaptism

Anabaptism in South Germany had different origins and acquired a quite different character from that of the Swiss Brethren and their Schleitheim Articles. An undercurrent of medieval mysticism[1] runs through much of South German Anabaptism. It blended with anticlerical attitudes and apocalyptic expectations to form the basis for a vision of a transformed social order. The events of the Peasants' War provided the wider backdrop as well as producing a number of individuals important for the story. The idea of community of goods that surfaced in the Swiss story became an important part of the South German story, particularly in Moravia, which means that in spite of their differences, South German and Moravian Anabaptism is not entirely separate from the Swiss story of the previous chapter.

South German Anabaptism did not initially focus on developing the structures of ongoing congregational life. More often this version of Anabaptism sought a regeneration of the elect in preparation for the expected and near return of Christ for the last judgment and the establishment of God's reign on the earth. With the disappearance of the first generation of leaders and the failure of the end to come, some elements of the movement died away. Others integrated into the Swiss Anabaptist story or into what became the Hutterite tradition, the most visible institutional legacy of South German and Moravian Anabaptism. It is a complex story, which requires placing a number of characters onto the scene and showing the multiple interactions of their individual stories within a larger narrative.

Thomas Müntzer

Although he never rebaptized anyone and was not a founder of Anabaptism, one cannot separate the story of Thomas Müntzer, Peasants' War leader, from the development of Anabaptism in South Germany. Through the influence of Hans Hut, a transformed version of Müntzer's vision for reform permeated much of this Anabaptist movement.

Very early, Müntzer appeared as a friend of the Reformation, and by 1519 a Catholic polemic denounced him as a "Lutheran." Upon the recommendation of Martin Luther, he received a temporary position at St. Mary's church in Zwickau, and in 1520 he soon found a permanent assignment at St. Catherine's in that city. In just a few months, however, circumstances led him into a more radical social stance, and the "Lutheran" Müntzer turned his mystical-based, anticlerical reform program against Martin Luther.

While Müntzer found support among all the population groups of Zwickau, he identified most with the disenfranchised groups that pressed for a role in government and with those members of the city council who wanted to free Zwickau from outside ecclesiastical control of its affairs. These involvements of Müntzer reflected the widespread anticlericalism that often appeared in combination with economic discontent and social protest,[2] and the impulses of the Communal Reformation depicted in the previous chapter. Müntzer emphasized an inner faith inspired by the Spirit and personally appropriated, and he pursued Reformation with a good deal of social protest. He had several quarrels with the Franciscans and with Pastor Johannes Sylvius Egranus from St. Mary's church, who took a reserved, humanist, intellectual approach to reform. Müntzer was thus forced to leave the city in April 1521.

From Zwickau, Müntzer went to Prague, where he issued a manifesto containing the seeds of the social outlook that his later writings would develop more fully and make him a vocal proponent of the social demands eventually represented by the Peasants' War. Evident were his mysticism and his anticlerical orientation. For Müntzer, each individual's immediate, mystical experience of God undercut the claim of the clergy to be the guardians of God's grace or of divine revelation. Müntzer believed that those who directly experienced the suffering submission to God's work within would become part of a restored divine order. Eventually these restored, elect individuals would inherit the rule of this world. Müntzer envisioned a great separation of the elect from the godless, with the godless annihilated by the elect before they assumed the government. Müntzer came to identify the common people as the elect, and the clergy as the reprobate, who on false authority tried to place themselves between God and humankind. Political authorities soon joined the clergy in Müntzer's godless category.

After only brief stays in Prague and several other towns, Müntzer obtained a pastoral position in the Saxon town of Allstedt. He quickly carried out a wide-ranging local Reformation with support from the majority of inhabitants, including for a time the local political authority. Crowds from the surrounding area came to the services in Allstedt to hear his liturgy, psalms, and hymns translated into German. With his reformed liturgy and preaching, Müntzer wanted to bring people to the experience of inner faith and make them bearers of the new, external, restored order.

This reform quickly provoked the opposition of the Catholic authorities. It also confirmed Luther's growing distrust of Müntzer. At Allstedt, Müntzer began open opposition to Luther, whom Müntzer now included in the category of the clerical enemy. According to Müntzer, Luther advocated a false faith, dependent not on the process of faith within but on an external Scripture, which stood between God and the people. As learned "scribes," the Wittenberg Reformers also placed themselves between the people and God. Müntzer advocated administering baptism in conjunction with the beginning of the new, awakened faith. But in contrast to the radicals in Zurich, he did not initiate a rebaptism of persons previously baptized as infants.

Müntzer's reform in Allstedt created evident disorder. When at Mallerbach his supporters destroyed the chapel dedicated to the Virgin Mary, the court at Weimar decided to investigate. Duke John and his son John Frederick requested that Müntzer present a trial sermon at the castle. He preached from Daniel 2. Attempting to pose himself as an alternative to Luther's Reformation, Müntzer invited the princes to join "the commoners as agents of apocalyptic overthrow of worldly authorities," to establish the reign of God on earth. If the princes refused, Müntzer threatened, God would take the government from them and turn it over to the common people.

The Dukes rejected Müntzer's invitation and forced him to leave Allstedt in August 1524. From this time on, he led a rather unsettled existence. In cooperation with Heinrich Pfeiffer, he tried to initiate a Radical Reformation in Mühlhausen and was twice exiled in the process. During these exiles he contacted Hans Hut in Bibra, whom Müntzer likely already knew through Hut's travels as a book peddler. On one of these visits, Müntzer gave Hut his *Explicit Exposure of the False Faith*, which Hut brought to press in Nuremberg. This document relegated the secular rulers to the same category as the clerical enemy: both were to be resisted whenever their deeds or authority came between God and the people. In November 1524 Müntzer probably met with Balthasar Hubmaier near Waldshut.

After being readmitted to Mühlhausen, Müntzer participated in and helped to organize peasant marches through Thuringia and Eichsfeld in early phases of the Peasants' War. He interpreted the looming confrontation of peasants and the worldly authorities as the last judgment, at which time God's elect—the peasants—would annihilate the godless oppressors. Müntzer eagerly joined himself to the peasant army that met the princely advance near Frankenhausen on May 15, 1525, in the last and most famous encounter of the Peasants' War. The princes slaughtered six thousand peasants while suffering only six casualties themselves. Müntzer escaped the slaughter but later was discovered hiding in an attic in the town. After interrogation under torture, he was executed on May 27, 1525.

An antimaterialism element ran through the heart of Müntzer's social critique. It is disputed whether he actually taught that all things should be held in common. However, his antimaterialistic piety produced a social program stressing equality among Christians, with an economic component. Müntzer believed that attachments to the material opposed the lordship of God over God's creatures. "The order of property was radically opposed to God's lordship." Faith from the Holy Spirit would then destroy creaturely attachments to the material within the transformed believer. James Stayer has called his antimaterialistic piety "the most important thing South German-Austrian Anabaptists inherited from Thomas Müntzer."[3]

A number of Anabaptists had connections to Thomas Müntzer and the Peasants' War. One was Melchior Rinck, who after 1527 became the major Anabaptist leader in the border area of Hesse and Thuringa. It is probable that Rinck's expulsion from Hesse in 1524 provoked his sympathies with the peasants, and he ended up fighting alongside Müntzer at Frankenhausen. An important fruit of his ministry was the congregation with earlier Peasants' War experience that he helped to administer at Sorga after his return to Hesse in 1528. Rinck espoused a community of goods based on sharing within the congregation. When this congregation was expelled from Hesse in September 1533, they made their way to Auspitz in Moravia, carrying the belief in community of goods with them.

Hans Hut

Peasant War participant and Müntzer-follower Hans Hut[4] became one of the most important Anabaptists of South

Germany. His Anabaptist career carried forward a modified version of Müntzer's vision of a restored society beginning with the inner transformation of individuals. It is important to follow Hut's career as an Anabaptist missioner, as well as to trace the elements of his influence that flow into the Hutterite story and that provide one of several links between the Swiss Brethren and Anabaptists in Moravia.

As a book peddler, Hut's travels between Wittenberg and Nuremberg gave him a variety of contacts. He likely visited Müntzer in both Allstedt and Mühlhausen, and Hans Denck in Nuremberg, where Denck had become rector of St. Sebald's school in 1523. At Mühlhausen, Hut was enrolled in Müntzer's covenant of true believers who were involved in the Peasants' War. Hut was with Müntzer at Frankenhausen and was also captured, but was one of the lucky people to be released. Hut had fully accepted Müntzer's interpretation that the peasants' confrontation of worldly authorities constituted the final confrontation of good and evil before Christ came to establish his kingdom. Following Frankenhausen, Hut returned to his home territory of Bibra and preached what amounted to a continuation of the Peasants' War, advocating that the peasants should slay all the rulers and take power into their own hands.

Soon, however, Hut began to modify Müntzer's reform program in light of the new circumstances in which Hut found himself. With the demise of peasant hopes, Hut abandoned the idea of a transformation of all of society, but he continued to expect a great, future confrontation of good and evil, at which time the wicked would be destroyed and the godly would inherit the worldly kingdom. Hut modified Müntzer's end-time calendar. Revising Müntzer's calculation that pointed toward the time of the battle at Frankenhausen, Hut set Pentecost 1528 as the date when the judgment of the ungodly and wicked would begin. Hut also included the Turks in the scheme. They, with the support of the godly, would serve as God's instrument to destroy the godless. The faithful remnant would reemerge later.

Meanwhile, in the interim until Pentecost 1528, Hut called for a cessation of violence. The revolutionary sword should remain sheathed until the time of vengeance in the last days. This sheathed sword enabled some interpreters of later generations to transform Hut into a nonresistant Anabaptist.

Hut also modified Müntzer's definition of the elect. In the case of Frankenhausen, Hut decided, the peasants as identified by Müntzer had suffered destruction because they were not pure. Hut concluded that the Anabaptists comprised the godly. Hut had begun to question pedobaptism as early as 1524, and he accepted baptism as an adult in Augsburg from the hands of Hans Denck at Pentecost in 1526.

Following his baptism, Hut once again returned to his home area in Franconia, to carry out a mission of assembling the elect community that would inherit the reign of God after the wicked were destroyed. It is likely that first of all he sought out folks like himself who had survived the Peasants' War. A likely attraction for them was the idea of vengeance on the perpetrators of the Peasants' War disaster. Meanwhile, they would remain quiet until called forth to carry out God's judgment on the ungodly rulers. Hut's renowned zeal as a baptizer was directly related to this identification of baptism with the sealing of the elect in preparation for coming judgment and apocalyptic vengeance.

Baptism of adults thus carried a significantly different meaning for Hut than it did for the Swiss Brethren. Whereas for the Brethren it had occurred first as a purification of the sacrament and then came to signal the separation of a church of believers independent of secular authorities, baptism for Hut was an eschatological sign sealing the 144 thousand elect or faithful remnant who would escape the approaching judgment of the wicked (cf. Rev 14:3). Hut saw himself as the man of Daniel 12:5 and Ezekiel 9:2-5, whose duty it was to mark as many as possible of the 144 thousand on the forehead with the sign of the cross, his preferred mode of baptism.

Hut preached what he called the "gospel of all creatures."

This gospel stated that in order to attain their ordained purpose, all creatures must suffer. Animals and trees, for example, suffer at the hands of humankind before attaining their intended end of becoming food or houses. Similarly, men and women must suffer—both internally and externally—in order to come to their intended end of serving God. The mystical inner suffering produced individuals purified within and prepared for the coming millennium. This message gave meaning to the suffering experienced by the peasants to whom Hut preached. It also separated the coming violent confrontation of good and evil from the patient endurance of suffering required by the daily lives of the peasants, through which they waited with sheathed swords for the coming day of vengeance. While Hut's message did not require the peasants to observe particular religious norms, he did admonish them to begin to practice the brotherliness that was to distinguish the restored world after the judgment.

Another distinct feature of Hut's Anabaptism was preaching for community of goods, or a common treasury, to help the poor and those too ill to work. Jörg Volck, the most important Anabaptist leader in Franconia after Hut, also preached community of goods in order to care for the poor. Both the gospel of all creatures and community of goods mark the influence of Hut and will reveal his influence in following elements of the story.

In the spring of 1527 Hut spread Anabaptism in the area of northern Franconia, in the villages around Coburg and Bamberg, in the valley of the Regnitz near Erlangen, and south through Nuremberg and Augsburg to Salzburg, Wels, and Steyr. The message about expectations of the coming judgment in 1528 sounded to the authorities like a new peasant rebellion. Although their small numbers posed no real threat to the established order, the presence of these Anabaptist followers of Hut precipitated a general persecution by the Protestant authorities.

Arrests and execution of their converts drove Hut and his traveling companions to Nikolsburg in Moravia, where they had no doubt heard that the town was a haven for persecuted Anabaptists, and where Hubmaier had established another Anabaptist Reformation after his own earlier flight from Waldshut. If Hut expected to be received as a fellow Anabaptist, his hopes were dashed. In Hut and Hubmaier, the two forms of Anabaptism quickly clashed. The "Nikolsburg Articles," Hubmaier's slanted statement of Hut's supposed errors, grounded a public disputation between the two men, in Nikolsburg.[5] Eschatology was the most significant point of difference, with Hubmaier summarily rejecting Hut's apocalyptic speculation. We return to this disputation in more detail below. Following the Nikolsburg Disputation, Hut was imprisoned. He managed to escape and fled to avoid a threatened extradition.

Hut traveled through Austria, establishing small groups in Vienna, Steyr, Linz, Freistadt, Salzburg, and Passau. Evidently, evangelicals frustrated by stalled reforms from the established authorities responded favorably to Hut's message. His converts in these territories included most of the Anabaptist leadership in this region, including Jacob Wiedemann and Philip Jäger. The authorities quickly eliminated most of these by fire and sword, although Wiedemann survived into 1535 or 1536 as leader of the refugee community at Austerlitz. August of 1527 found Hut once again in Augsburg, where he participated in the series of encounters sometimes called the Martyrs' Synod, since many of those present soon after fell at the hands of executioners. Here again tension surfaced between two forms of Anabaptism. Hut rejected the Swiss Brethren's ethic of the Sermon on the Mount, which lay at the heart of the Schleitheim Articles. He did agree, however, to withhold comment on his eschatological speculations except when specifically requested. Hans Denck, who was present at some of these gatherings, perhaps contributed to Hut's agreement.

A few weeks later, Hut was arrested in Augsburg. His trial lasted several months, well into November. Torture as well as information relayed from outside Augsburg brought to light Hut's ties to Müntzer and the peasants, as well as his expectation of an approaching judgment on the present order. The guilty verdict and his execution were never in doubt. Before enactment of the verdict, however, Hut suffered smoke inhalation in a jail fire, which led to a lung infection. He died shortly thereafter, and his body was burned in early December 1527.

The Anabaptism founded by Hut did not develop into an ongoing tradition. With the expectation of the near end, Hut had established no structures for carrying on the movement nor any provisions for permanency. Since he had kept much of his eschatological speculation relatively secret, some of his followers were able to affiliate themselves with other groups within the larger Anabaptist movement. When Hut's deadline for the judgment had passed, others rejected Anabaptism in disappointment. There was an enduring influence of Hut, however, in the idea of a common treasury or community of goods. As the following story recounts, community of goods with an impetus from Hut was practiced among Anabaptists in Moravia and attained ongoing, institutional status in what came to be called the Hutterite tradition. Hut's influence also manifested itself to some extent in the circle of Pilgram Marpeck.

Hans Denck

After Hut, Hans Denck was the most prominent figure of early South German Anabaptism, and his short life crossed that of Hut at several junctures.[6] With roots in humanism and mysticism, Denck's career is another example of the differences between the South German and Swiss Brethren Anabaptist movements.

Denck was born in Upper Bavaria around 1500. After acquiring a literary education at the University of Ingolstadt from 1517 to 1520, he arrived in Basel in 1522. He worked as a proofreader and associated himself with the reform efforts of Johannes Oecolampadius.

On Oecolampadius's recommendation, Denck obtained the position of rector at St. Sebald's school in Nuremberg. He became associated with the radicals who were impatient at the slow reform in Nuremberg, and he likely made the acquaintance of book peddler Hans Hut. His circle in Nuremberg found the ideas of Karlstadt and Müntzer congenial, both of whom had broken with Martin Luther. Denck's associations implicated him in the trial of the "godless painters" who had scandalized the town with attacks on the privileged position of clergy and other irreverencies.

The attack of Denck and other radicals focused particularly on Luther's close association of word of God with Scripture. Denck's theology reflected a mystical outlook. It took as its starting point the empowering word that dwelled within every individual. This word within gave each individual direct access to God. For Denck, Luther's high regard for the written Word and a literate clergy who expounded it seemed like an attempt to pose an external authority between the individual and God. In Denck's view, Luther undercut his earlier statements on the priesthood of all believers, and he seemed to take on the same role as the old Catholic clerical enemy. Denck's view of Scripture also made him suspect to the more literal-minded Swiss Anabaptists such as Michael Sattler, whom he later met in Strasbourg.

In Nuremberg, Denck's outlook brought a direct confrontation with the Lutheran clergy. When his written replies to their questions did not meet their standards, Denck was exiled from the city in January 1525, about the time of the first rebaptisms in Zurich. It is not known precisely how Denck spent all the time until his premature death in the fall of 1527. Müntzer invited him to Mühlhausen, and he may have been working as schoolmaster in this imperial city while it was allied with the cause of the peasants. If so, he escaped when the city was occupied on May 19, 1525. Denck then surfaced in Schwyz and was imprisoned for his opposition to baptism of infants. Following his release from prison, he contacted the Anabaptists in St. Gallen. These Anabaptists had expressed determination to defend themselves and their leader Hans Krüsi with the sword. Denck's associations in these locations indicate his sympathy for the cause of the Peasants' War. It is not known whether Denck's later pacifism had already crystallized by the time he arrived in St. Gallen. The Reformers there, however, took offense at Denck's teaching on universalism.

Perhaps by the time he arrived in Augsburg in September 1525, Denck had become a practicing Anabaptist. We do not know who baptized him and other circumstances of his baptism. In Augsburg, Denck met Balthasar Hubmaier. In the spring of 1526, Denck baptized Hans Hut. Denck's radical activity and teaching provoked a confrontation in Augsburg with Urbanus Rhegius and other Lutheran clergy. He fled the city before a proposed public debate could take place.

Hans Denck's story repeated itself once more in Strasbourg, where he arrived late in 1526. Here Denck encountered opposition from both the city's official clergy, such as Martin Bucer, as well as from Anabaptist Michael Sattler, who was in the city trying to convert Bucer to the Swiss Brethren's version of Anabaptism. Following a debate with Bucer, Denck was expelled from the city. The differing orientations of Denck and Sattler appear in Bucer's defense of Sattler's theological orthodoxy and the simultaneous accusation that Denck denied the atonement.[7]

A similar series of events repeated itself in Worms. Here in cooperation with Ludwig Hätzer, Denck produced a translation of the Old Testament prophets, apparently with collaboration from Jewish scholars. Denck's contacts with Jews and with the radical faction in the city provoked the suppression of the radical movement in Worms. Once again, Denck moved on.

He was present in Augsburg in August 1527 for some meetings of the Martyrs' Synod. While he played only a small role in the discussions that centered on Hut's apocalyptic teaching, he may have had a moderating influence on Hut. Two months later, Denck contacted Oecolampadius and requested permission to live again in Basel. Soon after that, he died of the plague while in the process of reexamining his beliefs.

Oecolampadius published the written product of this reexamination posthumously under the inaccurate title *Recantation*. In it Denck expressed anguish at conflict among believing persons. He actually maintained his mystical, spiritual orientation and his critique of the social order and institutional Christianity, and he moved away only from his Anabaptist practices of baptism and opposition to the oath.

In Denck, one observes the evolution of an Anabaptism with a mystical beginning point—not toward a revolution as in Hut, but toward an eventual "quietistic, socially pacific sect."[8] The story also illustrates, however, that the Peasants' War impacted or produced many South German Anabaptists.

Hubmaier, Hut, and Nikolsburg

After fleeing from Waldshut in December 1525, Balthasar Hubmaier and his wife, Elsbeth Hügline, spent a very difficult four months in Zurich. Following mild confinement, he agreed to recant his Anabaptist outlook. When he reneged on the promise and instead made a speech in favor of adult baptism, he was severely tortured and finally forced into a public recantation. In April, Hubmaier fled the city, and with his wife settled in Nikolsburg[9] in Moravia. Reformation in a Zwinglian sense was already advanced in Nikolsburg. Before long, Hubmaier was able to establish Anabaptism in the city on a model quite similar to that in Waldshut. The lords von Liechtenstein who ruled Nikolsburg supported Hubmaier's reform, and Prince Leonhart von Liechtenstein himself accepted baptism. The city became the center of this territorial Anabaptism.

The tolerant policies of the Liechtensteins toward Anabaptists attracted many hard-pressed refugees from Switzerland and the Tyrol. Some of the Swiss refugees may have brought to Nikolsburg the pacifist stance of the Grebel-circle radicals. In any case, in the early months of 1527 there was the beginning of a schism among the Nikolsburg Anabaptists. Under the leadership of Jacob Wiedemann and Philip Jäger, likely brought to Anabaptism by Hans Hut,[10] a group met separately, outside the walls of Nikolsburg in the town of Bergen. They dissented from Hubmaier on, among other things, the role of the magistrate and the use of the sword, and they had a more developed idea of sharing and community of goods. In recognition of their pacifist stance, the dissenting group acquired the name of *Stäbler* (staff-bearers) in contrast to the main party of Hubmaier and the Liechtenstein lords, who were known as the *Schwertler* (sword-bearers).

The visit of Hans Hut to Nikolsburg in the spring of 1527 polarized this situation, and Hut became a temporary spokesman and leader of the dissenting group. Hut rapidly developed a following among the common people, while he and Hubmaier conflicted on many issues. After private conversations between the two men, Hubmaier invited Hut to a public disputation in the church. Apparently Hubmaier wanted to use the occasion to rout his opposition. The "Nikolsburg Articles," a list of fifty-two errors he attributed to Hut, provided the basis for interrogation. Hubmaier packed the church with his supporters and turned it into what looked like a mock trial. Hut and three others were accused of holding to all the errors. When they wanted to debate the points one by one, Hubmaier cut them off and wanted only a guilty plea. Issues discussed included Christology, the work of Christ, eschatology, the nature and interpretation of Scripture, the sword, the role of the magistrate, angels, and special revelation.

Hubmaier rejected Hut's eschatological speculations outright, with their critique of the established order. Hubmaier feared that such ideas would arouse the authorities and endanger his own effort in Nikolsburg to reform the entire community in cooperation with the local authorities, the lords of Liechtenstein. Hut's mystical assumptions and eschatological speculation underlay their differences. His inner Christ, with whom all believers must suffer, sounded to Hubmaier like a new attempt at denying the work of Christ and affirming salvation by one's own works. Hut's eschatology enabled Hubmaier to accuse Hut of spreading sedition, rejecting the need for secular authorities, and declaring the final judgment within two years.

After the disputation, the prince's guard escorted Hut up the hill to the Liechtenstein castle. Here again, in the presence of Prince Leonhart von Liechtenstein, Hubmaier repeated the accusations against Hut. Hut was warned that there were plans to turn him over to Ferdinand of Austria. That same night, Hut escaped from the castle, apparently aided by sympathizers. The remainder of his life was described earlier.

Within a few months, Hubmaier himself was in the hands of the Austrian archduke, Ferdinand, who had also become ruler of Moravia the previous October. In July 1527, Ferdinand demanded Hubmaier's arrest, at least in part to seek vengeance for Hubmaier's leadership in the revolt of Waldshut against Austrian authority. The circumstances of the arrest are not known. Leonhart von Liechtenstein either could not, or would not, defend his pastor. Hubmaier's loyal and brave wife accompanied him as he was taken to Vienna, where he spent the last months of 1527 until March 1528 in the Kreuzenstein castle outside the city.

Following a lengthy series of trials, torture, and conversations on theology with Johannes Faber, a Catholic theologian and old university colleague, Hubmaier was condemned for treason and heresy and burned at the stake in Vienna on March 10, 1528.

Hubmaier's wife, Elsbeth, who had followed him through all, encouraged him to remain steadfast to the end. A few days later, she displayed her own faith and courage. For refusing to recant her Anabaptist position, she was thrown into the Danube with a stone around her neck.

With Hubmaier and Hut both gone from the scene in Nikolsburg, tension continued between the two parties, with Hans Spittelmaier as leader of Hubmaier's reform direction that worked under the authority of the ruling lords of Liechtenstein, and Jacob Wiedemann as head of the *Stäbler* faction. Wiedemann and the refugees introduced a policy of a self-administered common treasury or mutual aid fund, and they refused to attend the local church. Nonresistance coupled with mutual aid points to a Swiss influence and a synthesis of Hut's teachings.

Leonhart von Liechtenstein desired a uniform religion in the estates under his control, and he did not approve of the pacifist stance of the *Stäbler*. After many efforts to mediate the dispute, early in the spring of 1528 he reluctantly decided to ask the dissidents to leave. In March, under the leadership of Jacob Wiedemann and Philip Jäger, about two hundred adults plus children departed from Nikolsburg. As they left, a conscience-stricken Prince von Liechtenstein reversed his decision and stated a desire that they remain. The dissidents refused to return, however, expressing disapproval of the prince's use of force to resist the Anabaptist hunters of Ferdinand. The Hutterite *Chronicle* describes the scene outside Nikolsburg. They spread a cloak on the ground, on which they pooled their meager resources as a matter of survival. "Thus was born the first historically identifiable Anabaptist congregation known to have practiced full community of goods in Moravia."[11] From that rather inauspicious beginning stems the visible and ongoing Hutterite practice of community of goods that has now endured for more than 475 years. That narrative continues below, following the introduction of another major character.

Pilgram Marpeck

Engineer Pilgram Marpeck was an important leader of South German Anabaptism, whose story also touches community of goods and developments in Moravia.[12] However, Marpeck came to Anabaptism from the side of the establishment and resistance to the commoners' movement. He thus posed a marked contrast to most South German Anabaptists, who came to Anabaptism from the side of the peasant movement, which had resisted the establishment. At the same time, Marpeck's thought reflected the cross mysticism that impacted Hans Hut and Hans Denck.

From his birth around 1495 until early in 1528, Marpeck lived in or around Rattenberg in the Tyrol. At age eighteen the Rattenberg city council made him an assistant administrator of the local hospital. In following years he became a member of the city council, served a term as mayor in 1522, and attained the position of inspector of mines. He was still exercising this important judicial position when Schleitheim was deciding that Christians ought not participate in institutions of governance of the social order. Marpeck also obtained considerable wealth in the city. By the time he identified himself with the Anabaptist movement, many of its original founders had already fallen to executioners or to the plague.

Although raised a devout Catholic, Lutheran influences drew Marpeck to the cause of reform, which prepared the way for increasing interest in the vision of radicals such as Michael Gaismair, Leonhard Schiemer, and Hans Schlaffer, who were active in the area. An Anabaptist community developed in Rattenberg and included members of the miners' guild.

Marpeck's Anabaptist thought came to reflect the influence of the mysticism expressed by the anonymous writer of the *Theologia Deutsch* and by itinerant Anabaptists Schiemer and Schlaffer. From these sources came the cross mysticism that could bring together his concerns for personal repentance and for social responsibility. These concerns shaped his Anabaptist ecclesiology and also supplied an understanding of suffering as salvific, similar to Hut's "gospel of all creatures."

As a city employee Marpeck was expected to assist in the arrest of Anabaptists. He refused these orders, and when Schiemer and Schlaffer were executed, he resigned his position as inspector of mines. That act resulted in expulsion from the city, and much of his considerable wealth was confiscated.

With his wife, Anna, Marpeck became a refugee. They moved for a time to Krumau, a city sought by previous refugees from Rattenberg. Refugees from Krumau had also transferred to Austerlitz in 1528, providing an avenue for Marpeck to be oriented toward Moravia and Austerlitz. Two other individuals important for the story to trace also left Rattenberg at about this time. Melchior Schlosser probably functioned as a contact between Marpeck and the Anabaptist community at Austerlitz. Sigmund Schützinger became an itinerant Anabaptist leader in Upper Austria and North Tyrol, and sided with Jacob Hutter and the group—including Krumau refugees—that broke from Austerlitz and went to Auspitz in 1531. This story of schism is continued in a following section of this chapter.

These contacts with ties to Austerlitz mean that when Marpeck arrived in Strasbourg on September 19, 1528, with a commission to baptize, he was likely a representative of the Anabaptist community at Austerlitz. This connection made Marpeck an advocate of—or at least rather sympathetic to—community of goods. If he did not arrive as an advocate of community of goods, perhaps a visit to Strasbourg in 1530 or 1531 by Jacob Wiedemann made visible the community of goods practiced by the Austerlitz community and led to Marpeck's espousal of that view.

Upon arrival in Strasbourg, Marpeck purchased citizenship and went to work as a city engineer concerned with fuel and drainage problems. Quickly he became a revered leader of the already-existing Anabaptist congregations within the city, and he worked with Wilhelm Reublin, who was in Strasbourg for the second time. For a brief moment in the late 1520s and early 1530s, Strasbourg was a city of relative religious tolerance, and there were significant conversations among various dissenting groups as well as with Martin Bucer and Wolfgang Capito, the leading reform-minded ministers in the city. Marpeck participated in these dialogues. The lines hardened, however, and in January 1532 Marpeck was expelled from the city because he dissented from the established church position on infant baptism. He wrote a confession of faith that was presented to the city council as a part of the proceedings that led to his expulsion.

Although Marpeck was expelled from Strasbourg for

opposing the view of the official church on baptism, a debate among the radical groups, occupying much of Marpeck's writing, is also apparent in his years in Strasbourg. Two writings, published anonymously but attributed to Marpeck, appeared in 1531. *A Clear Refutation* and *A Clear and Useful Instruction* both respond to the spiritualist and spiritualizing element within Anabaptism that was introduced in Strasbourg by Christian Entfelder and Hans Bünderlin. Entfelder came to Strasbourg from Nikolsburg, apparently representing the spiritualizing direction taken by Hans Spittelmaier, the successor to Hubmaier. Entfelder warned that focus on externals—such as differences on baptism, community of goods, and the sword—was creating divisions, as was happening in Moravia. In response to Anabaptist appeals to apostolic authority, Entfelder argued that the authority of the apostles depended on Christ's special command and validation by miracles, but that soon after the time of the apostles, externals had taken over to become more important than inner spiritual regeneration. Since proper externals could not be reinstated without a new divine mandate, it was better to abandon the external forms that caused division and to focus on the inner, cleansing work of the Spirit. Bünderlin made a similar argument, as had Hans Denck.

Marpeck's *Clear Refutation* engaged and refuted such spiritualist arguments in the writings of Entfelder and Bünderlin. Marpeck asserted: (1) The ceremonies had not been hopelessly corrupted, and Christ's ordinances remained in effect until his return. (2) Christ's commission to baptize was not limited to the apostles, as is demonstrated by the practice of deacon Philip, and hence no new divine command was needed to restore apostolic practice. And (3) the apostles had delegated authority to other leaders in the early church, again implying that contemporary leaders could continue apostolic practice. The *Instruction* had similar arguments concerning apostolic authority and practice. Its discussion of Christology implied that the spiritualists had a docetic view of Christ, since they neglected the humanity and the incarnate Christ in favor of a heavenly and divinized Christ. Caspar Schwenckfeld was also in Strasbourg during Marpeck's years there. Although Schwenckfeld's spiritualism was addressed in Marpeck's later works, Schwenckfeld was not the target of Marpeck's writings of 1531 since the lines between Schwenckfeld and Marpeck did not become sharply drawn until the 1540s.

Just before Marpeck's expulsion from Strasbourg, the anonymous tract *Exposé of the Babylonian Whore* was published at Cammerlander's press in Strasbourg.[13] Recent scholarship attributes authorship of this tract to Marpeck,[14] and its content reflects Marpeck's view of the sword while also linking him to the idea of community of goods. The principal focus of *Exposé* was to discredit any religious justification for use of the sword by civil authorities. But the tract tied use of the sword by authorities to the defense of private property. Authorities developed the sword to protect temporal property, *Exposé* said, and in the eyes of the anonymous author, private property was as egregious a sin as participation in civil governance. Linking private property to the sword would fit Marpeck at this time as one who baptized as a representative of the congregation at Austerlitz, which practiced community of goods.

Following expulsion from Strasbourg, the precise whereabouts of Pilgram and Anna Marpeck for the next twelve years are not always clear. For parts of this time they traveled in Switzerland and to Moravia. If he wrote during this epoch, his items primarily surviving were produced late in the period. Following a change in the political climate, Marpeck moved to Augsburg in 1544. Here he was quickly hired as an engineer to manage the city's forests and water supply. He also functioned openly as a leader of the Anabaptist circle in the city, which enjoyed a somewhat tentative status, with intermittent periods of harassment and tolerance. Marpeck managed to survive and work in Augsburg until his death from natural causes in 1556.

A process in Regensburg against Anabaptist Hans Umlauft in late 1539 and 1540 revealed that a congregation in Moravia was distributing Anabaptist literature in the Reich. It is quite likely that Marpeck's 1531 writings against spiritualism were included in this literature. During his years in Augsburg, Marpeck apparently maintained ties with a community in Moravia. These factors help to explain why Marpeck belongs in the story of Moravian Anabaptism.

Marpeck's Anabaptism was grounded in ecclesiology. He sought to build congregations whose goal was to live out of the Sermon on the Mount on a day-to-day basis. This church was an extension of the incarnation of Christ. Marpeck saw the church as an advance party of the reign of God, but in ordinary time rather than with the apocalyptic outlook of someone like Hans Hut. The incarnation showed that God had used the ordinary things of the earth—including the coming of Christ as a natural man—to witness to the presence of God's reign. Since Christ had conquered the devil and restored the potential of creation with his death, the physical world as well as the human body and mind could transcend the fleshy nature and take on a spiritual nature. Through Christ's cross, the Holy Spirit is poured out on believers as the source of restored life. With Christ, then, there is a restoration of right order both among people and within each individual. In Marpeck's church, the physical gathering was indwelled by the Spirit, and inner and outer had become one reality.

Since transformation of the believer comes through spiritual identity with Christ and depends on the restoring power of the Holy Spirit, coercion in matters of faith is both useless and destructive. True community must be voluntary. True faith cannot be coerced, and coerced faith is not true faith. Faith produced by coercion will be destroyed by more coercion. Coercion violates the individual conscience, which was a cardinal principle for Marpeck, along with the physical and spiritual interdependence of the Christian life.

The activity of the Christian believer will inevitably provoke opposition or hostility, Marpeck believed, which means that suffering is to some extent inevitable for Christians.

Suffering challenges the conventional belief in self-sufficiency; it makes clear that the only secure basis of hope is the Spirit. The gospel of all creatures, which said that a creature must suffer in order to attain its intended end, prepares the believer to receive the Spirit, a point on which Marpeck followed Schiemer and Schlaffer. Marpeck situated this suffering in the cosmic context of the struggle between the reign of God and the rule of Satan, a struggle in which the believer does not cling to life but offers it freely to God. In this suffering, believers participate in Christ's cross, suffering, and reconciliation. Marpeck viewed suffering as a contributor to the process of salvation. This cross mysticism also provided a means by which Marpeck could understand his own loss of office and property as well as executions of Anabaptists he had defended.

Challenges to Marpeck's version of Anabaptist ecclesiology came from two sides. From his contacts with the Swiss Brethren, Marpeck concluded that their stress on behavioral conformity constituted coercion in matters of faith and a new form of legalism. In his view, they had reduced the visible church to an external form that lacked a spiritual principle from the incarnation. Similarly, he abandoned his earlier support for community of goods and came to reject the required communitarianism of the Hutterites as a coercive law that both the New Testament and the Holy Spirit considered optional. From the other side, Marpeck's visible ecclesiology was challenged by Schwenckfeld's spiritualist orientation. Schwenckfeld understood the true body of Christ as the inner communion of believers. A visible community was desirable but not necessary for the Christian life. In essence, Schwenckfeld's spiritualism would render Marpeck's visible church unnecessary. In addition to the theological difference, the practical reality was that Marpeck's Anabaptists, with a visible church, were more vulnerable to persecution than Schwenckfeld's spiritualists, for whom the inner communion of believers left the visible church optional.

In 1542, Marpeck did some judicious editing on Bernard Rothmann's *Bekenntnis,* or *Confession of the Two Sacraments,* and published it as his own work with the title *Vermahnung* or *Admonition* (Rothmann's story at Münster is told in chapter 4). It was directed against the spiritualism of Caspar Schwenckfeld and was sent to an Anabaptist in Augsburg, Helena von Freyberg, who likely passed it to Schwenckfeld's circle before Marpeck arrived in the city. The debate with Schwenckfeld and opposition to Schwenckfeld's spiritualism became the orienting features of Marpeck's writing after his arrival in Augsburg. In 1544 he wrote the first part of the *Response* to Schwenckfeld. The second part of *Response* and the *Explanation of the Testaments* were written by Marpeck and his circle in Augsburg. Since the limited toleration of Anabaptists prevented open evangelism, baptisms were rare. The Lord's Supper replaced baptism as the ritual that sustained congregational life and became the central issue in the debate with Schwenckfeld in *Response.*

These debates concerning legalism and spiritualism show the shifting character of concerns in the radical reforming movements. When Marpeck was expelled from Rattenberg in 1528, the challenge faced by Anabaptism was still that of a repressive state allied with an established church, and the radical groups were more complementary than competitive. By the time Marpeck moved to Augsburg in 1544, this order had been reversed, and the radical groups were more concerned with each other than with the state church. Marpeck's debate with Schwenckfeldian spiritualism reflects this reversal.

In the context of these debates, Marpeck had a centrist theology. He rejected Schwenckfeld's spiritualism. He reflected the concerns of Denck and Hut, stressing the idea of a new life as a gift of God's grace, appropriated by faith, while opposing the increasing tendency of the Swiss Anabaptists toward legalism and literalistic biblical interpretation. The Swiss in turn accused Marpeck of stretching the freedom of Christ too far. Marpeck dissented from the community of goods of the

Moravian Anabaptists, with whom he was in contact. He also rejected both Luther's sacramentalism and Zwingli's spiritualistic symbolism.

Marpeck wanted a clear separation of church from political authorities. On the other hand, his work as a civil engineer in several cities shows that he could cooperate with civil authorities, and his valuable work as a city engineer placed him in the role of colleague and friend with potential persecutors. This work may have contributed to his survival as an Anabaptist leader.

The writings of Marpeck, many of them products of the controversies in which he involved himself, are more extensive than those of any other Anabaptist of the sixteenth century. At the same time, many were circulated in manuscript form, which limited their visibility, and publication of his voluminous literary output in recent times may give Marpeck a broader modern theological significance than he had in his own time. To a modern reader, Marpeck's theology stands in a mediating position, but his views were a minority among Anabaptists in the sixteenth century.

The careers of Hut, followed by Denck and Marpeck, display elements of the South German Anabaptist movement that for the most part did not produce a continuing or visible institutional legacy. There is evidence that materials written by members of Marpeck's circle had a significant influence on Swiss Brethren leadership in the 1570s and 1580s. This influence is also visible in the publication of the second edition of the Swiss Brethren's *Ausbund*,[15] which is discussed below. However, Marpeck's circle did not leave a visible or permanent structural legacy as Marpeckites, and remaining parts of the Marpeck tradition apparently merged gradually with the Swiss Brethren. It is significant to recognize, nonetheless, that contributions of the Marpeck circle to the Swiss Brethren constitute the closing of a circle, since Swiss elements also contributed to the development of Anabaptists in Moravia. The presence of some Anabaptists in the region of Alsace and the Palatinate did continue into the seventeenth century, maintained by a trickle of Anabaptist refugees moving down the Rhine River from Switzerland, but was then virtually wiped out by the widespread devastation of the Thirty Years' War (1618-48).

If structural or visible elements of South German Anabaptism disappeared, a perturbation of the Hut legacy, along with other previously noted elements, did carry on in Moravia, and in the face of great persecution achieved a structural legacy. What came to be called the Hutterite tradition, named for Jakob Hutter, who supplied its major ideas, displayed traces of Hut's theology of mystically transformed individuals and was expressed most vividly in the antimaterialistic piety and advocacy of community of goods in Moravian Anabaptism. Although community of goods in some form was common to all Moravian Anabaptists, it was the followers of Jacob Hutter who would give it an enduring institutional legacy. To reach that legacy, the narrative rejoins the group expelled from Nikolsburg.

Community of Goods in Moravia

After three weeks of travel, the Nikolsburg refugees reached Austerlitz, some twenty-five miles from Nikolsburg. The local lords granted them permission to settle, with freedom of conscience and exemption from war. Rapidly, biblical and theological justification was added to the survival rationale for community of goods. With the protection and permission of the local rulers, the group could establish itself, acquire supplies, and undertake the building necessary to become a viable community. The overall leader of the group remained Jacob Wiedemann. As the group prospered at Austerlitz, it soon became a beacon of hope and an attractive destination for persecuted Anabaptists from neighboring territories of Austria and South Tyrol and elsewhere. The community soon numbered six hundred adults. A group of new arrivals from Krumau, Marpeck's initial refuge from Rattenberg, included future Hutterite leader Hans Amon.

The *Chronicle* of the Hutterites refers to a Church Discipline or congregational order in use in 1529. The congregation in

Moravia that used this Discipline is not specified, but it may well have been the one established at Austerlitz by the refugees from Nikolsburg. The precise means by which it attained status in Moravia is not clear. Important, however, is the fact that the Discipline is a rewritten and expanded version of the Swiss Order introduced at the end of the last chapter. Swiss Anabaptist refugees reached Moravia by a number of different paths, and there are several possible ways by which the Swiss Order could have arrived in Moravia. The point is that Swiss Anabaptism did influence Anabaptism in Moravia, including the idea of community of goods.[16]

Exposé of the Babylonian Whore, published anonymously in Strasbourg in 1531, likely contributed to the discussion of community of goods in Moravia. As recounted earlier, the principal focus of *Exposé* was to discredit any religious justification for use of the sword by civil authorities. However, this tract tied the use of the sword by authorities to the defense of private property. *Exposé* becomes particularly significant for the current context when Pilgram Marpeck is accepted as its author. Published just before his expulsion from Strasbourg, the link of the sword to community of goods would reflect Marpeck's early association with Austerlitz.

The community at Austerlitz was not the only Anabaptist presence in Moravia. Other groups were established at Rossitz and Auspitz.[17] A series of schisms and moves interrelated the stories of these three groups, whose geographic locations form a triangle of about ten or twelve miles per side. Many of the actions and quarrels of the leaders prove less than edifying.

Gabriel Ascherham led a group of as many as two thousand people from Silesia, who settled in the neighborhood of Rossitz in 1528, on the estate of Bohunda of Pernstein. How he came to Anabaptists is not known, but there are likely some Swiss Anabaptist influences in his background. The community he established at Rossitz was the largest of the early Anabaptist settlements in Moravia. Gabriel established a common treasury and voluntary community of goods. Within a few years, the community numbered about twelve hundred adults.

Others who joined Gabriel's community were a group from Swabia under leadership of Philipp Plener. Considering Plener better qualified, Ascherham at first allowed him to have leadership of their combined groups. However, some differences and inadequate accommodations at Rossitz soon led to an amicable separation, in which Philipp's group, which came to be called Philippites, established a new community at Auspitz in 1529. Both Gabrielites and Philippites experienced considerable growth from refugees in the next several years. Another of the refugee groups was the congregation from Sorga whom Melchior Rinck had served as leader after the Peasants' War and who were expelled from Hesse in September 1533. By the end of 1534, just before the harsh repression of 1534-35, the Philippites at Auspitz had reached some four hundred adults, meeting in three separate households. Whatever their differences, the Philippites recognized Gabriel Ascherham as their senior bishop.

Social conditions contributed directly to the growth of these three communities and their brief existence as a haven for harassed Anabaptists from elsewhere. For one thing, the local ruling lords of Moravia proved themselves reluctant to apply the policy to exterminate Anabaptists that Austrian Archduke Ferdinand demanded. Ferdinand had inherited the crowns of Bohemia and Hungary only in 1526, and his immediate efforts to impose his will in Moravia ran into a long tradition of religious toleration practiced by the local nobility. An external political factor contributed to the success of the lords's initial resistance to Ferdinand. The threat posed by the Turks to the east periodically distracted Ferdinand and strongly influenced when he could vigorously pursue the policy against Anabaptists. Balthasar Hubmaier was the most prominent Anabaptist victim of a first round of the campaign of suppression. The community at Austerlitz, as well as the Philippites at Rossitz and the Gabrielites at Auspitz, were established at a time when Ferdinand was focused on a threatened Turkish invasion. Ferdinand's application of pressure on the reluctant Moravian lords and his extreme measures against Anabaptists in 1534-35 and again in 1535 to 1537 accompanied a waning of the Turkish threat.

Jacob Hutter, whose name the Hutterite tradition still carries, emerged as the leader of Anabaptists in South Tyrol in the years 1528-29. Two earlier movements prepared the way for Anabaptism in the Puster region of South Tyrol. In this area there had been many supporters of revolutionary Michael Gaismair, a representative of the Communal Reformation, who projected a wide-ranging, revolutionary program that had social, political, and ecclesiastical elements. His economic plan called for reforms in care for the sick and the poor, increased availability of arable land, placing control of mines under elected managers who would operate them for the common good, and more. Politically, this movement called for an independent republic, similar to a Swiss canton. Ecclesiastically, the program included calls for rejecting the sacramental powers of clergy, replacing the mass with a sermon, allowing local congregations to choose their pastors, and establishing the Bible as sole authority for religious beliefs and practices. Gaismair's program contained many more elements as well, but this sketch indicates why future Anabaptists would have affinity with it.[18] The second set of events that prepared the way for Anabaptism consisted of the itinerant preachers who were already carrying reform ideas throughout the countryside in 1524-25. In particular, they preached against the mass, sacramental theology, and the sacramental authority of priests. It was reported that one of these preachers induced Jacob Hutter to buy a New Testament in 1526. Each of these challenges to the established church and its theology contributed to preparing the seedbed for Anabaptism.

Another Swiss connection enters the story here. George Blaurock, who participated in the first adult baptisms in Zurich, introduced Anabaptism and played a significant role in its spread in the territory of South Tyrol in 1527. After being expelled from Zurich, Blaurock made at least two journeys to South Tyrol. The first was between May and September of 1527, in the region of Bozen and Klausen. Blaurock was confrontational, disrupting traditional worship services and denouncing both churchly and secular authorities. These tactics no doubt appealed to the supporters of Michael Gaismair, a number of whom were among Blaurock's first converts. Later in September, Blaurock was back in Switzerland, escaping arrest at St. Gallen, undergoing brief imprisonment at Appenzell, and then participating in the Bern disputation of 1528. In the spring of 1529, Blaurock was once again in South Tyrol and active in a number of towns. He was arrested in July and met death by burning in Klausen on September 6, 1529, a victim of the repressive measures of Archduke Ferdinand.

Certainly not all supporters of Gaismair became Anabaptists, and not all Anabaptists had been Gaismair supporters. There were nonetheless clear affinities between the two programs, but at the same time Anabaptism marked a different reform direction. The communal reformation of Gaismair made the social order the focus of reform. Anabaptism meant rejecting "in principle the entire sacramental, sacerdotal, hierarchical church." Preeminent for Anabaptists was the effort to reinstitute the New Testament church, which focused on "following Christ, on discipleship,"[19] and is identified by the assertion of Scripture as ultimate authority and baptism of adults to indicate those who belonged. The church rather than the social order thus became the primary locus of moral authority and activity, which meant that they abandoned the goal of reforming all of society. This orientation was not a separatist withdrawal from interaction with civil authorities and the social order, but it did inaugurate a new kind of interaction. Anabaptists professed respect for civil authorities but refused to grant them ultimate allegiance or reverence. Their interaction became that of witness to injustices from the perspective of an independent church rather than speaking as supporters of and within the established order.

Jacob Hutter

Jacob Hutter was born about 1500 in Moos in the Puster valley of the Tyrol. As his name indicates, he practiced the hat-making trade for a living. He had contacts with the sacramentalist preachers and had acquired a New Testament by 1526. Likely he had been a Gaismair partisan. It is not known how he came to join Anabaptism or who baptized him, but it appears that he was organizing an Anabaptist congregation at Welsberg in late 1528 or early 1529. Pusterers were known for their toughness. Hutter's emergence as leader happened in the years that Archduke Ferdinand was effectively pursuing his vigorous and cruel policy to suppress Anabaptists. Hutter's stubbornness and persistence reflected the well-known Puster temperament and served him well in organizing Anabaptists in the very difficult task of surviving the hostile policies of Ferdinand.

In 1529 Hutter visited Austerlitz to check out reports that it was a faithful community in which people cared for each other. He liked what he found enough to unite with it, which meant that the community accepted Hutter as its representative, and that he accepted Austerlitz as the model of Anabaptist community, including community of goods and presumably pacifism. In other words, Hutter had become a representative in South Tyrol for the Anabaptist community of Austerlitz in Moravia. He returned to his organizing work in South Tyrol with a glowing report on the community in Moravia. It appears that Hutter introduced a common treasury on the basis of the model at Austerlitz, and he began to organize Anabaptists to move to that haven. The first such group, under the leadership of Jörg Zaunring, arrived at Austerlitz in early summer of 1530.

Throughout that first year, other Anabaptist refugees from the Tyrol and elsewhere joined or visited this group. The community at Austerlitz existed alongside the Anabaptist communities at Rossitz and Auspitz. From this time forward, Jacob Hutter would have a hand in the affairs of Anabaptists in Moravia. Eventually the Tyrolean refugees under Hutter's leadership came to dominate Anabaptism in Moravia.

Yet another Swiss element entered the story with the reappearance of Wilhelm Reublin, who played a major role in the 1531 schism in the Austerlitz community.[20] In late 1530, after being banished from Strasbourg, Reublin traveled to Austerlitz and associated himself with the Anabaptist congregation there, still under the leadership of Jacob Wiedemann. Due to the size of this group, in the winter they met for worship in three different places. A separate leader was appointed for each subgroup, while Wiedemann retained leadership of the community as a whole.

Immigrants from Tyrol, with Zaunring acting as their unofficial leader, had high expectations about the perfection of the ideal community in Austerlitz, and they soon found reason to complain about the leadership of Jacob Wiedemann, who seemed either unable or unwilling to enforce uniformity of practice. In spite of Reublin's impressive credentials as an Anabaptist—founding member of Swiss Anabaptism, baptizer of Balthasar Hubmaier, likely aide to Michael Sattler in writing the Schleitheim Articles, and publicizer of the account of the martyrdom of Sattler—Reublin was not given authority to teach in Austerlitz. He soon became the catalyst and spokesperson for voices unhappy with Wiedemann's leadership. A letter to Marpeck from Reublin listed ten charges against Wiedemann. Complaints that implied spiritual problems included authoritarian leadership and unequal treatment of leaders and laypeople, so that the leaders and their spouses dined sumptuously in separate dining rooms on "roasted meat, fish, poultry, and good wine," while the ordinary folks had only "peas and cabbage," and children were perishing of malnutrition.[21] Reublin took his complaints to a subgroup leader, who refused his request to address the entire community. After being refused authorization to release a statement, Reublin in early January 1531 forced a public hearing by reading loudly from Scripture and using the text to criticize the order in the Austerlitz community. Wiedemann returned and tried to discipline and silence Reublin. However, other secondary leaders rallied to the side of Reublin, which in addition to Zaunring included Hans Amon and several others. With this support, Reublin attempted to convince Wiedemann that he was not teaching according to Scripture.

After further discussion failed, Wiedemann issued a public ban against Reublin. In a meeting of the entire community, Wiedemann explained that Reublin had usurped authority and was advocating views contrary to the teaching of the leadership. Wiedemann asked for those who supported the ban to come and stand with him. A group of about fifty refused, led by Zaunring. When Wiedemann then attempted to discipline Zaunring, more people rallied to Zaunring's side, believing that Zaunring and Reublin were being treated unfairly. Reublin played a biblical role by walking out and shaking dust—perhaps actually snow—from his feet.

Schisms

This polarization developed into schism on January 8, 1531, when in the dead of winter Zaunring and Reublin left Austerlitz for Auspitz with a group that included 150 adults. They traveled with minimal provisions, charging those who stayed with mistreatment and misuse of the common treasury. For a time some children and ailing individuals found shelter with sympathetic neighbors. By January 26, the advance party was established in several locations in and around Auspitz, alongside Philipp Plener's group. The remaining dissidents from Austerlitz joined them later in the spring. The newcomers experienced additional misfortune. A loan from Johanka of Boskowitz, abbess of the convent at Brünn, enabled them to survive the winter.

Both those who left and those who remained in Austerlitz sent out accounts of the schism, appealing to Hutter and others for support. Hutter, representing South Tyrol, and Sigmund Schützinger, from North Tyrol, traveled to Ausptiz in the spring of 1531 to assess the situation. They exonerated neither side but placed the most blame on Wiedeman and the faction that stayed in Austerlitz.

Although the schismatics agreed on the failings at Austerlitz, that agreement did not translate into harmonious community at Auspitz. Physical hardships, new and difficult surroundings, financial problems, and different backgrounds soon brought other tensions to the surface. By autumn of 1531 Reublin was disgraced and gone from Austerlitz. First, unidentified arrivals from Swabia revealed a likewise unidentified difference between Reublin and the community on an article of faith. This difference was compounded when it was revealed that Reublin was hiding a significant personal fund. Hutter and Schützinger arrived from Tyrol soon afterward, examined Reublin, and excluded him from the community. Reublin acknowledged the justice of the judgment.

After his expulsion Wilhelm Reublin spent some time in Moravia. In the mid 1540s, he contacted Heinrich Bullinger, Ulrich Zwingli's successor in Zurich, and served him as a messenger. In 1554 he sought shelter in Basel. He lived to be nearly eighty years old. In his last years, Reublin successfully appealed to Ferdinand, under whose authority so many Anabaptists had died, to recover an inheritance. Thus, the story of Wilhelm Reublin, a well-traveled participant in the both Swiss and Moravian Anabaptism, ends back with the opponents of Anabaptism.

Meanwhile, in Auspitz, Hutter and Schützinger installed Jörg Zaunring as servant of the Word, with Adam Schlegel, Burkhart of Ofen, and David of Schweidnitz as assistants. However, Zaunring soon fell into difficulties of his own. Schlegel was accused of licentious behavior but gained the support of Burkhart of Ofen. Eventually these two left to join the Philippites. Soon Zaunring was at loggerheads with his remaining assistant as well. During this dispute David of Schweidnitz leaked the information that Zaunring had been lax in disciplining his wife for an adulterous relationship, and Zaunring was then accused of a cover-up. For a time, Zaunring and his wife were separated from the congregation.

Hutter and Schützinger returned to Auspitz again for Easter of 1532. Zaunring was reinstated but given an assignment outside the community as itinerant preacher in Franconia and Hesse. Lots were cast to replace Zaunring, and it fell on Schützinger to assume the office of servant of the Word. He served with two assistants, Wilhelm Griesbacher and Leonhard Schmerbacher.

Before he returned to South Tyrol, Hutter and Schützinger negotiated an alliance with the nearby Gabrielites and Philippites. Gabriel Ascherham was designated as the overseer of the three communities. The alliance was put to the test in 1532, when marauding soldiers sent to fight Turks turned on the heretics of Moravia. Schützinger's congregation was hit particularly hard, and among other problems, there was difficulty in making payments on their loan from the abbess of the convent at Brünn.

Apparently Leonhard Schmerbacher sent Hans Amon to Tyrol with a message for Jacob Hutter about financial difficulties and problems with Schützinger's leadership in Auspitz. In response, Hutter decided to move permanently to Auspitz and to leave Amon in charge of Anabaptist affairs in South Tyrol. About this move, Amon wrote Schmerbacher but not Schützinger—which indicates the existence of a pro-Hutter faction that was already unhappy with Schützinger. Amon also warned Schmerbacher to do everything possible to avoid a schism after Hutter's arrival.

On August 11, 1533, Hutter arrived in Moravia for his fourth, last, and longest sojourn, bringing along a small sum of money as a "sweet gift." He came convinced that he had a unique calling of God to lead the federated groups, and the move was intended to be permanent. For a time Hans Amon remained in South Tyrol as the chief servant of the Word, but the next year he followed Hutter to Moravia.

Amon's premonition of schism rapidly proved correct. Hutter arrived in Auspitz on August 11, 1533. Some dissidents wanted Hutter to leave with them to found a new group, but Hutter announced that he would stay to correct the abuses in the house of God. Schützinger took this statement as criticism of his leadership, and within two weeks Schützinger and Hutter were deep in conflict over Hutter's leadership role. Hutter posed his own sense of divine calling over and against Schützinger's argument that God had appointed him by the lot. Both Plener and Ascherham supported Schützinger, with Ascherham still functioning as leader of the three groups. Gabriel declared that Hutter's "proud and arrogant"[22] bearing suited him better to be an itinerant preacher than a residential pastor. A compromise of sorts was suggested, which the congregation heartily affirmed. As the one elected by lot and thus presumably having the divine blessing, Schützinger remained in charge, while Hutter held an undefined, subordinate role. Hutter agreed only very reluctantly.

But two weeks later, with Schützinger seriously ill in bed, Hutter assumed the lead role. Since the congregation could not be left without spiritual leadership, the subordinate leaders invited Hutter to assume the role of servant of the Word. Hutter quickly moved to assert his leadership. In a service of admonition on September 28, he castigated the lax discipline regarding community of goods that Schützinger had tolerated. Some members rebelled at this admonition, but others took it to heart and recommitted themselves to the practice. One wife was disciplined as a "new Sapphira"[23] when she withheld money without her husband's knowledge after he had made a gesture of full commitment.

Hutter then claimed divine intuition that perhaps Schützinger's wife was also a Sapphira. A search party went to her quarters and discovered a large supply of linen, shirts, and a sum of money. When Hutter admonished her husband to confess all "in the name and power of the Lord," a shaken and contrite Schützinger produced the sizable sum of forty gulden. Since Schützinger had preached complete community of goods, the offense was enormous, and it demanded an immediate response.

Ascherham and Plener were quickly sent for but could not come immediately. Hutter called a congregational meeting for Sunday, October 5, to deal with the crisis. In the presence of the entire community he denounced the duplicity of the Schützingers. Although Schützinger expressed contrition and made a public confession of his sin, he was excommunicated.

Hutter now stood alone, completely vindicated. Given Schützinger's duplicity, it was obvious that the Holy Spirit could not have guided his selection as leader the previous month and Gabriel's censorship of Hutter. Hutter then declared it uncertain whether he should serve such a congregation and invited them to pray earnestly for a leader. In response, the congregation spent that Sunday and the following week in loud and earnest prayer for discernment. By the end of the week, a consensus was reached that Jacob Hutter was a "gift from God to be their shepherd."[24] On October 12, 1533, he was formally installed as the community's servant of the Word. The former supporters of Schützinger confessed publicly their "sin of ignorance." Ascherham, who returned belatedly to a fait accompli, put his blessing on Hutter and the congregation. In less than two months, apparent divine intervention, Schützinger's illness, and Hutter's admonitions and premonitions about deceitful practices had led to Schützinger's expulsion and Hutter's installation as head of the community.

The seeming harmony following Hutter's assumption of leadership did not long endure. Hutter moved quickly to separate members he considered unfaithful or unwilling to follow his stricter discipline. Several of these appealed to Ascherham and Plener, and within two weeks these two deemed intervention necessary. Accompanied by assistants, Ascherham and Plener arrived unannounced early on Sunday morning, October 26, to confront Hutter. The discussion soon became heated, with raised voices and mutual recriminations, and expanded to include a number of issues and past events. The assembled congregation was left confused, unable to determine who was right. The next day, Hutter sent messengers to the other two communities to inform them that their leaders were liars. Ascherham and Plener replied with a suggestion to establish a joint study commission from the three congregations without their leaders. That suggestion was nearly accepted but broke down when Hutter commented that he already did not regard Gabriel as a brother. Again Hutter's congregation was left wondering and uncertain. It took five days of discussion and prayer before Hutter had reestablished a consensus in his congregation.

A stroke of good fortune, considered a God-send by Hutter, also aided his cause. Hutter had remained in communication with Hans Amon in South Tyrol, and in the midst of these deliberations, on October 31, a contingent of Hutter supporters arrived from the Tyrol. And on that very same day, the group saw celestial events—three suns and two rainbows—that Hutter interpreted as a divine sign in his favor. The Hutterite *Chronicle* would later interpret the three suns dissolving to one, with two rainbows disappearing, as the eclipse of the other two congregations, with only Hutter's remaining. In any case, on the following Sunday, November 2, 1533, Hutter and his congregation in Auspitz severed all ties with and excommunicated all members of the congregations of Gabriel Ascherham and Philipp Plener.

Within a month, 120 to 130 new arrivals from South Tyrol replaced the losses due to the schism in Hutter's community. Hutter was at peace with himself, believing that he had acted with pure motives and under divine guidance against liars and false prophets. Of course, his opponents bitterly disputed such claims. Ascherham wrote that Hutter was ambitious, arrogant, and vengeful, "an evil person."[25] Recriminations between the two sides continued, but in Hutter's congregation at Auspitz, now dominated by refugees from South Tyrol and comprised primarily of Hutter's supporters, harmony finally reigned.

The impact of the schism lingered, however. Excommunicated members complained to the abbess of the convent in Brünn, on whose land the Auspitz community was located. Relations worsened further when Hutter refused to make the abbess a loan, claiming that the congregation had no money beyond that necessary for its own needs. In response, sometime in the second half of 1534, the abbess imprisoned three leaders, including Hutter and Amon, as well as other community members. During this dispute, Hutter and his associates decided that they could do no work for any church-related institution, since those efforts would contribute to idolatry. Although the confining of Hutter and the others evidently involved ransom, which would have meant paying money to a church institution, the circumstances of their release are not known. But henceforth, the community decided it would seek accommodations only with civil or temporal lords. On May 6, 1535, the community moved to the land of the lord of Lippe at Schackowitz, where they began constructing a large communal dwelling.

Construction was still underway when the lord of Lippe informed Hutter that they would have to leave. Along with Ferdinand's avowed Catholicism was the spectacle of the Anabaptist kingdom at Münster (1534-35), which caused alarm all across Europe, a story told in the following chapter. Determined to rid his lands of the heretics and to prevent any development comparable to Münster, Archduke Ferdinand forced the tolerant Moravian lords to expel Anabaptists. Often sympathetic to Anabaptists, but finding no other alternative, the local authorities reluctantly asked their Anabaptists to leave. In the case of Hutter's congregation, the expulsion happened with great fanfare, for the benefit of Ferdinand and the hostile citizenry, while Lord Lippe was quietly telling Hutter to keep his people together and that they could return as soon as the situation warranted. Seven hundred adults and three hundred children from Hutter's congregation, as well as Gabrielites and Philippites, all camped in the open in a desolate area near Tracht.

In a stern confrontation with investigators, Hutter adamantly refused to leave the area and expressed anger at Ferdinand's policy of extermination. A written grievance from Hutter against the policy of Ferdinand became part of the Hutterite literary legacy. Although Hutter's response showed courage, it also proved unwise. The governor ordered Hutter's immediate arrest. The authorities could not locate Hutter but did arrest two others, Wilhelm Griesbacher and Loy Salztrager. Salztrager recanted under torture, but later regretted his weakness. Griesbacher remained steadfast and was burned at the stake in Brünn.

This outcome made clear that Hutter had little chance of surviving in Moravia. At the urging of his group (at least he claimed that they compelled him), in July 1535 Hutter sought refuge back in South Tyrol. The traveling party consisted of Hutter, his wife of about two months, Katherine Präst (or Prust), and three other companions. Hans Amon, who had a lower profile than Hutter, was given the leadership of the congregation that remained in Moravia. Thus, Hutter's direct guidance of the community lasted only from August 1533 until the late spring of 1535. Nonetheless, he made a lasting impact, and his name became permanently attached to the group.

Few Anabaptists remained in Tyrol after Amon led the exodus to Moravia in 1534. Thus, on his return, Hutter set about developing or restoring an Anabaptist network. However, he was arrested in Klausen on the evening of November 30 and taken to the fortress above the city. Two days later he was moved to Brixen, and on December 9, he was taken, bound and gagged, to Innsbruck and placed in the Kräuterturm. His torture included flogging; immersion in ice water until nearly frozen followed by thawing in a hot room before being beaten; cutting, with the wounds filled with brandy and then burned. The outcome of his trial was a foregone conclusion. His death was by public burning in the market square of Innsbruck, Ferdinand's seat of government. The date is unclear but occurred perhaps in mid-March 1536. Hutter remained defiant to the end, challenging his tormentors to test their faith with him in the fire.

Through all, Hutter retained a high sense of mission for himself and his people, seeing them as the righteous element who would inherit the kingdom of God. For their part, he believed that the righteous can expect suffering, as happened to the prophets who were stoned and the apostles martyred after Christ's resurrection.

Katherine, Hutter's wife, was arrested with him but escaped from prison sometime between May and August of 1536. Katherine came from Tauffers in the Puster region. She learned about Anabaptism while working as a maid in a household that associated with Anabaptists. In this way she met and was baptized by Hutter. She was arrested, released upon recantation, continued as an Anabaptist, and arrested again. At some point she escaped and joined the trek to Auspitz in 1534, where she became a member of the inner core of Hutter's supporters from the Puster region. She was likely in her early 20s, and thus significantly younger than her husband when they married. After escaping in 1536, she remained in Tyrol and was arrested two years later in Schöneck. This time she was executed. In her six years as an Anabaptist, she was imprisoned four times.

Dissolution and Continuation

The Anabaptists who stayed in Moravia had two primary choices for survival: leave the region or disband into small clusters to wait out the oppression. Most opted for the former solution. Hutter's community followed the second course.

Those who chose to leave went in many directions; we mention migrations most relevant for the current narrative. Some evidence suggests that a significant number of Gabrielites made their way to Silesia, the original home of Gabriel Ascherham and many of his congregation. In 1540

Gabriel himself was living at Fraustadt (Wschowa), near the border of Poland and Silesia. His writings indicate that his thought developed further in a spiritualist direction until it became analogous to the view rejected by Marpeck in 1531. Gabrielites practiced a voluntary community of goods, which left room for individual choice and variation. No successor followed Gabriel, and when the last of his followers joined the Hutterites, Gabrielites passed from the historical stage.

Traveling in small groups, Philipp Plener and his associate Blasius Kuhn divided their community into small groups who traveled to areas of the Palatinate and the Rhineland. Significant numbers settled in the Württemberg area. Plener and Kuhn continued to search for places of refuge and planned for a meeting in Strasbourg in 1536 to report on progress. Kuhn reached Strasbourg but Plener, who was carrying a large sum of the community's money, did not. Whether he met foul play or absconded with the money is not known. Some indirect evidence suggests that he may have been in later contact with the community, which would make him a thief. Portions of the Philippite community eventually merged into Swiss Anabaptism, which meant that they abandoned community of goods. The ongoing legacy of Philippite Anabaptism is song. One of the traveling Philippite groups—about fifty members and three leaders from the dispersal of 1535—was arrested and imprisoned at Passau, in the fortress at Oberhaus, across from the city. While in prison, they wrote many of the hymns that were published in 1564 in a collection of fifty-three hymns. Titled *Etliche Geseng*, the collection was claimed to be the work of Swiss Brethren and is the forerunner of the Swiss Anabaptist *Ausbund*, which the Amish still use today in North America. Of note is the fact that the earliest compilation of these hymns contained two that praised community of goods as the "practice of the true church in its purest form."[26] Later editions of the *Ausbund* dropped these two hymns.

In 1536 the community at Austerlitz lost its main leader, Jacob Wiedemann. It appears that he and some other members had traveled to Vienna, where they were arrested and eventually executed. Ulrich Stadler and Leonhard Lochmair, second level leaders, took a group from Austerlitz to the east, seeking a place to settle on the borders of Ruthenia and Volynia. Conditions were difficult there as well, and by 1537-38 Stadler and Lochmair had returned to Moravia with a remnant, which eventually joined the followers of Jacob Hutter. An Austerlitz remnant continued to exist for a time.

At the time, the decision of the Hutterites to stay in the area seemed perhaps more perilous than leaving. In historical perspective, however, it was the right, if also costly, decision. They lost their dominant leader, Jacob Hutter, as well as a number of other leaders. In this period, Hans Amon provided continuity of leadership. Survival of the group owes much to his tireless travel for encouragement and admonishment, as shared hardship molded them into a more uniform and cohesive group. In 1537 Leonhard Sailer [or Lanzenstiel] emerged as Amon's most trusted itinerant preacher. Sailer was given charge over South Tyrol. In effect, Sailer was the last productive leader from the line of Jacob Hutter when Puster ceased being a fertile recruiting ground. When Hans Amon died on February 2, 1542, Sailer was well positioned to follow him as leader.

By the time Sailer succeeded Amon, better times had returned to Moravia. By 1540, a community of five hundred had reunited at Schackowitz. It was said that in total, Hutter's group numbered one thousand adults.

Peter Riedemann joined Sailer as a coleader of the Hutterites.[27] Born in 1506 in Silesia, Riedemann appeared on the scene when he was imprisoned in Gmunden for his Anabaptist faith. It appears that he had been drawn to Anabaptism under the leadership of Wolfgang Brandhuber, in the region of Linz, Steyer, and Gmunden, where Hans Hut had done missionizing. Riedemann was imprisoned in Gmunden in 1529-32, during which time he wrote a first, short confession of faith. Released in 1532, he traveled to Moravia and joined with the group at Auspitz that had left Austerlitz in the schism led by Reublin and Zaunring. He accepted the idea of community of goods, married Katherine from the Anabaptist community, and was appointed a minister of the Word. After less than a year at Auspitz, he was sent as a missioner to Franconia. Soon after his arrival, he and his colleague Six Braitfus were arrested. Braitfus was whipped and expelled, but Riedemann was imprisoned for four years, 1433-37.

Riedemann was released in 1537 after promising that he would not preach in Nuremberg. He returned to Moravia, where the Hutterites under Hans Amon were the major communal group remaining during the persecution. Riedemann joined the Hutterites, but he also met with leaders of the other factions to hear their views on the great schism. In the next years, Riedemann succeeded in convincing many of their members to join the Hutterites.

In 1539, in response to a request for help from Anabaptists in Hesse, the Moravian Anabaptists sent Peter Riedemann. He visited Anabaptists in Swabia and engaged in discussions concerning problems in Hesse, which eventually led to a split in the group.

Riedemann briefly returned to Moravia, but in early 1540 was sent back to Hesse. Shortly after his arrival, he was imprisoned. Philip, the ruler of Hesse, exercised a relatively tolerant policy toward Anabaptists. Rather than killing them, he tried to convert them by argument and persuasion. During his two years of imprisonment, Riedemann wrote his *Confession* or *Account of Our Religion* as a product of his conversation with Philip. Copies of the *Account* were carried to the Hutterite communities in Moravia, who quickly accepted it as a definitive statement of their faith.

Escaping from lax imprisonment in 1542, Riedemann returned to Moravia and was appointed a coleader with Leonhard Sailer. They ruled together until Riedemann's death in 1556. These years were a period of relative prosperity, with some persecution in the years 1547-53. At Sailer's death in 1565, Peter Walpot was appointed leader.

Riedemann's *Account* became a defining element in Hutterite thinking. Written to explain Hutterite beliefs and to build credibility with Philip of Hesse, the *Account* begins as an exposition of the Apostles' Creed. However, the explanations of creedal statements, as well as the bulk of text devoted to explaining Anabaptist questions of discipleship and the nature of the church, make the *Account* into much more than a mere statement of agreement with standard theological orthodoxy. For example, in the *Account*, the idea of community of goods is anchored in trinitarian theology. The model for holding all things in common is that "the Father has nothing for himself, but everything he has, he has with the Son. Likewise, the Son has nothing for himself, but all he has, he has with the Father and with all who have fellowship with him."[28] The *Account* features a "specificity of Hutterian discipleship" so woven into the statements of the creed that "it is no longer possible to separate out core from addition." Rather than being a statement showing Anabaptist agreement with standard orthodoxy, Riedemann's *Account* testifies to new thinking. It "is a new and particular Hutterian statement about the commitments and life of Christian faith."[29]

During the leadership of Peter Walpot came the beginning of what is called "the golden years" of Hutterite life in Moravia.[30] Walpot established the structures and patterns of community life that would enable Hutterites to flourish in the relative tolerance that endured into the next century, when they faced the devastation caused by the Thirty Years' War. Under duress, the legacy of community of goods lapsed, to be reestablished again. After a sojourn in Russia, Hutterites immigrated to North America in the 1870s. They are firmly established in both the United States and Canada.

Jacob Hutter's group, the Hutterites, survived as the sole representative of Anabaptism in Moravia. Already in 1536, their correspondence reflected their belief that, in contrast to the Gabrielites and Philippites and Austerlitzers, they alone were the faithful remnant, which retained the apostolic ideal of community of goods as the essential mark of the true, apostolic church. With some lapses, this legacy from Swiss Anabaptism has endured until the twenty-first century in North America.

The story of Anabaptism in South Germany and Moravia is complex, with many differing individuals and a number of twists and turns. Mysticism, biblicism, and commitments to nonviolence and community of goods wend through the story. Although it is a story in its own right, separate from Swiss Anabaptism, this story also has links to Swiss Anabaptism. These links include a series of individuals such as George Blaurock and Wilhelm Reublin, the concept of community of goods as stated in the *Swiss Order* and given real form and substance in the communities in Moravia, as well as the influence of the Marpeck circle reaching from Moravia back to Switzerland.

4

Anabaptism in the Low Countries

Alongside the Swiss Brethren, and South German Anabaptism and its derivatives, a third major Anabaptist tradition developed in the Low Countries, which correspond approximately to modern Netherlands and Belgium. The origin of Dutch Anabaptism is tied to the activities of one individual, Melchior Hoffmann, who planted the movement in a well-prepared field. Contact with Andreas Karlstadt and the major parties of Anabaptism in Strasbourg precipitated Hoffmann's break with the Reformation and his acceptance of believers baptism, but Hoffmann's movement—the Melchiorites—was not simply a continuation of Swiss or South German Anabaptism. It was, rather, a new movement that reflected Hoffmann's background and eschatological emphases, but with some elements that would perhaps give at least Menno Simons's wing an intellectual root in common with Swiss Anabaptism. Several different branches emerged from Dutch Anabaptism. Among others, these included both the short-lived revolutionary kingdom of Münster and the permanent, pacifist tradition, which developed through the guidance of Menno Simons, Dirk Philips, and others.

Sacramentarianism

Anabaptism in the Low Countries sprouted quickly in the soil well prepared by the sacramentarian movement.[1] The *devotio moderna* had arisen late in the fourteenth century. It emphasized a personal and internal spirituality in contrast to the supposed intellectualism of scholasticism. This impulse found a kind of institutional expression in the monastic renewal movement known as the Brethren of the Common Life, and its classic literary expression in the book *Imitatio Christi*. From another direction, humanism emphasized the Bible and called attention to the abuses in the existing church order. For the most part, the *devotio moderna* had an orthodox Catholic character and a high regard for the sacraments. This expression of Dutch piety appears to have no direct lines to Anabaptism.

However, some atypical sacramental theology that emerged from this movement, in conjunction with Christian humanism, eventually developed into the sacramentarian movement. It came to reject not only transubstantiation[2] and the mass as a sacrifice, as did the entire Protestant Reformation, but also the Catholic idea of access to God mediated through the sacraments. In various ways, mysticism and humanism expressed the idea of direct access to God. When pushed to a logical conclusion, the result was a symbolic view of the material of the sacrament and a direct, spiritual communion with God.

Those who had rejected the Catholic ideas of transubstantiation and the mass as a sacrifice and went on to develop a symbolic or spiritual understanding of the Lord's Supper were called sacramentarians. Ulrich Zwingli's symbolic view of the Lord's Supper received an impetus from the sacramentarian movement, via Cornelis Hoen's *Epistola christiana*, which Hinne Rhode had carried to Wittenberg, Zurich, Strasbourg, and other cities. While Luther rejected Hoen's suggestion that "is" means "signifies" in the eucharistic expression "This is my body," Zwingli accepted that interpretation as his own.

The widespread sacramentarianism eventually touched even

the remote villages in the Low Countries. Menno Simons serves as an example. In 1524 he received ordination as a priest, with his first parish responsibilities in Pingjum, Friesland. The next year he began to question whether the bread and wine of the mass were really "the flesh and blood of the Lord." In all likelihood, Menno's doubts mirror the spreading sacramentarian movement. When Melchior Hoffmann reached Emden in 1530, sacramentarianism was already well established and had prepared many persons in a significant way for the transition to Anabaptism.

Melchior Hoffmann

The founder of Anabaptism in the Low Countries began his career as a furrier in his birthplace of Schwabisch Hall in South Germany. Through circumstances not known, Melchior Hoffmann had developed some affinity for the Lutheran cause by 1522.[3] Perhaps traveling in part because of his furrier's trade, for the next several years Hoffmann embarked on a program of wide-ranging itinerant evangelism. He was first established in Livonia, which consisted of parts of present-day Estonia and Latvia. He preached at Wolmar in 1523, where he likely encountered some of the writings or ideas of Karlstadt via individuals who had spent some time in Wittenberg. Following an imprisonment, he was expelled from the city in 1524 and took up residence at Dorpat.[4] Here the emphasis on eschatological speculation in the self-educated Hoffmann's preaching earned him the distrust of the Lutheran ministers, in spite of his popularity with the lower social orders. After being implicated in an iconoclastic riot in January 1525, Hoffmann was promised that he could continue to live in Dorpat only if he could secure a letter of recommendation from Martin Luther. He visited Wittenberg and concealed his iconoclastic differences with Luther well enough to secure the required letter. It is probable that Hoffmann met Karlstadt for the first time during this trip to Wittenberg. Both probably stayed simultaneously in Luther's house.[5]

The letter satisfied the authorities in Dorpat for a time.

However, Hoffmann's eschatological self-consciousness continued to grow. He came to believe himself called to fulfill the end-time role of the witnesses mentioned in Revelation 11:3—a new Enoch or Elijah. His final ouster from the city followed his humiliation of the daughter of one of the burgomasters. When she appeared in his congregation wearing a gold necklace forged from confiscated communion vessels, Hoffmann sarcastically called for the congregation to kneel and to worship the sacred ornaments carried in procession. Resulting outrage from the girl's father caused Hoffmann to abandon the city. Leaving Dorpat, Hoffmann spent a brief interlude in Reval, and then late in 1525 or early in 1526 Hoffmann became pastor of a German Lutheran church in Stockholm.

While he still adhered generally to the Lutheran understandings of justification and predestination, his eschatological interests continued with the publication of his exposition of Daniel 12, in which he predicted major changes for the world in 1533. Probably under the influence of Karlstadt, Hoffmann had begun to develop a spiritual and symbolic view of the Lord's Supper, and to modify his view of the church, liturgy, and Scripture. However, his concern for apocalypticism clearly distinguished him from Karlstadt.

Uncertain of the outcome of events in Stockholm, Hoffmann left that city after being implicated in another iconoclastic riot. He stopped briefly in Lübeck with his wife and son, and then worked for a time in Schleswig-Holstein. He paid another visit to Wittenberg; this time the Reformers were quite unsympathetic to his symbolic and allegorical interpretation of Scripture. Upon return to Schleswig-Holstein, King Frederick assigned Hoffmann to the Nikolaikirche in Kiel. Like Karlstadt, Hoffmann saw a positive role for a Christian ruler, and his views on baptism and Lord's Supper continued to take on the overtones of Karlstadt.

Hoffmann's final and explicit break with Lutheranism came during his stay in Kiel. In January 1529 Hoffmann invited Karlstadt to join him in Schleswig-Holstein. Karlstadt's position at Wittenberg had become untenable when he refused to write a tract attacking Zwingli. Facing imprisonment, Karlstadt fled Saxony in February and joined Hoffmann in March 1529. For five months they worked together in Schleswig-Holstein and in East Friesland.

Issues causing Hoffmann's rupture with Lutheranism included Hoffmann's views on eschatology, his allegorical interpretation of Scripture, his sharp ethical attacks on Lutheran preachers, his rash actions, and also his view of the Lord's Supper. A publication no longer extant presented his nontraditional, symbolic understanding of the Lord's Supper and thereby created a furor. A public disputation at Flensburg ensued on April 8, 1529. Karlstadt helped Hoffmann prepare his defense. The next day, Hoffmann and three other individuals were requested to leave Holstein. Karlstadt may have been in Kiel at the time, and possibly he and Hoffmann left Holstein together.

Following expulsion from Holstein, Karlstadt and Hoffmann appeared together in East Friesland in late April or early May 1529. At Emden, they visited Hinne Rhode, a former student of Karlstadt. Karlstadt visited Oldersurn and stayed with Chief Ulrich von Dornum, with whom Karlstadt maintained cordial relations. Early in July 1529 Karlstadt wrote to Martin Bucer in Strasbourg, recommending Hoffmann to him. When Hoffmann arrived with his family three weeks later, Bucer welcomed him. Karlstadt followed early in 1530.

In Strasbourg Hoffmann encountered a variety of individuals who represented all stripes of the Radical Reformation—from the spiritualists like Caspar Schwenckfeld, Sebastian Franck, or the followers of Hans Denck to the somewhat separatist and biblicist Swiss Brethren. Hoffmann called on Martin Bucer, who introduced him to his co-workers and also to Schwenckfeld, who was a house guest of Wolfgang Capito. Hoffmann's primary concern in Strasbourg was publication. In 1529 and 1530 a number of writings by Hoffmann appeared—all dealing with parts of his end-time speculations and his interpretation of the prophetic and eschatological parts of the Bible. In one work, Hoffmann identified King Frederick of Denmark, who had protected Hoffmann for two years in his domain, as one of the two kings from Revelation 12, who would protect the spiritual Jerusalem.

In another work Hoffmann wrote an introduction and conclusion to seventy-seven eschatological prophecies by Ursula Jost, through whom Hoffmann believed God spoke as a favored one. Ursula and her husband, Lienhard, came from Esslingen, and their outlook almost certainly betrayed a strong influence from Hans Hut. They did much to confirm and stimulate Hoffmann's own apocalyptic leanings.

While Hoffmann did not arrive in Strasbourg as an Anabaptist, his experience there was more a continuation of directions already adapted from Karlstadt than a radical turning point. The exact circumstances through which Hoffman came to espouse Anabaptism are not known. However, as had been the case with the Zurich radicals and Karlstadt, Hoffmann accepted adult baptism soon after personal contact with Karlstadt.

The contacts in Strasbourg also provided other impulses with which to articulate his rejection of the Magisterial Reformation. He developed his Christology in conversation with Schwenckfeld, who also pushed Hoffmann in a spiritualist direction. Somewhere Hoffmann also picked up the idea of free will and a tendency toward universalism. He may have received these from Denck's followers or from Jacob Kautz, leader of one of the three principal Anabaptist groups. Karlstadt may also have influenced him in these directions.

However, it is also clear that during his career as an evangelist, Hoffmann never fully identified with any of the Reformation groups, including the various Anabaptist movements that were themselves still somewhat in flux. A good deal of friction existed between Hoffmann's followers and the Swiss Brethren, stemming from their differences on apocalypticism, Hoffmann's more positive view of government and the Christian's role in it, and the more congregational expression of the Swiss faith. The other Anabaptist groups were all uncomfortable with the apocalyptic speculations that he brought with him into Anabaptism. His sense of being an end-time messenger whose authority others should accept also kept him from joining one of the existing Anabaptist congregations. Further, Hoffmann's Christology continued for some time as a controversial subject among Anabaptists.

Along with Schwenckfeld, Hoffmann held to the idea of the celestial flesh of Christ. Briefly stated, this view of the incarnation held that while Christ had genuine flesh, it was flesh that had originated in heaven. Thus, Christ became flesh in Mary but not of Mary, and he passed through her as "water through a pipe."[6] As discussed below and in chapter 5, Menno Simons and some of his colleagues in the Low Countries accepted a version of this Christology, but it was uniformly rejected by the Swiss and South German Anabaptists.

Their meeting in Strasbourg in March and April 1530 was the last personal contact between Karlstadt and Hoffmann. The nearly destitute Karlstadt family left Strasbourg for Basel, where his three children begged for bread in the streets. Finally, after working out a compromise with Zwingli, Karlstadt was welcomed in Zurich. In 1534 he attained university preaching and teaching positions in Basel.

Meanwhile, before Hoffmann fled from Strasbourg toward the end of April, he had already denounced Karlstadt's act. To Hoffmann, the compromise with Zwingli was an appeasement, a deliberate falling away from the truth and a return to being a "belly servant" after having known the truth.[7] While Karlstadt's impact on the Zurich radicals exceeded his influence on Hoffmann, for the second time Karlstadt's action for the sake of his family led to the rapid erasure of his memory from a movement on which he had made a real impact.

Hoffmann left behind a Strasbourg group identified as his own followers. Between 1530 and 1533, through the influx of refugees from the north, Melchiorites became the strongest Anabaptist group in Strasbourg. In spite of the conflict between the Melchiorites and the Swiss Brethren led by Marpeck and Reublin, the three Anabaptist groups in Strasbourg apparently cooperated in a project for poor relief.

A public act of Hoffmann on behalf of the city's Anabaptists led to his flight from Strasbourg. Although Anabaptism had been illegal in Strasbourg since July 1527, the city tolerated Anabaptists up to a point—somewhat as objects of missionary endeavor by the established church. Hoffmann made a public petition to the city council, requesting that a church be made available to the Anabaptists for public worship. Never in sympathy with his interpretation of Scripture (the council's charge against Hoffmann included his equating the emperor with the dragon of Revelation), on April 23, 1530, the council decided to try Hoffmann and punish him.

Hoffmann and his family had already disappeared when officials came to search for him. He left the city without credentials or letters of recommendation either from the official Reformers of Strasbourg or from the Anabaptist community. Hoffmann became an apostle to spread his version of Anabaptism in the Low Countries to the north.

Spread to the Low Countries

Anabaptism dominated the Reformation current in the Netherlands from 1530 to about 1560, before being supplanted by the Reformed tradition. Hoffmann's message about the breaking in of a new world found a ready ear among the poor populace of the Low Countries, as well as among some of the rich whose nascent Dutch nationalism was stimulated by its anticlerical implications. Thus, Dutch Anabaptism benefited from the same type of impulses that also played a role in the origins of the Swiss Brethren. The Melchiorite Anabaptist movement was the first Reformation in the Low Countries, and Anabaptism attained a popular following there that it achieved nowhere else. After Menno gathered the scattered followers of the Melchiorite movement, in 1550 perhaps 25 percent of the population of northern Netherlands was identified with Menno's stripe of Anabaptism.

The birth of Anabaptism in the North may have been Hoffmann's baptism of nearly three hundred persons in the *Grosse Kirche* in Emden in June 1530. Hoffmann's *Ordonnantie Godts*,[8] which appeared soon after his arrival in Emden, laid out the Anabaptist message he preached in East Friesland: In the power of the great commission, Christ sends out messengers to unite with Christ those in darkness, through repentance and the symbol of baptism. Hoffmann saw baptism as a covenant binding the individual in a close fellowship with Christ and the church, in which discipleship and discipline are practiced. Since the covenant was "instituted solely for the old, the mature, and the rational, who can receive, assimilate, and understand the teaching and the preaching of the Lord," only adults could receive it.[9]

However, different from Swiss Anabaptist leaders, Hoffmann did not use baptism as the basis for forming permanent congregations. His conventicles kept the covenanted ones pure while awaiting the near return of Christ rather than organizing them for ongoing congregational life. He could declare a suspension of baptism for two years when ten of his Dutch followers were executed in 1531, even as he continued to preach and to denounce infant baptism. His view of baptism thus had a spiritualist component to it, and Hoffmann's expectations for the near end of the world in just a few months clearly constituted the most important part of his message.

Hoffmann considered himself a new Elijah, one of the two witnesses to the apocalypse that he thought Revelation 11:3 predicted. Hoffmann believed that his own time—the era of the Reformation—would be the third revelation of divine glory in history, following the two that had come during the era of the original apostles and at the time of John Hus. A great fall of the church followed each outpouring of the Spirit. In Hoffmann's apocalyptic understanding, the world would be prepared for the return of Christ through a great cleansing.

Hoffmann defined the role for a Christian magistrate during this purge. The free imperial cities, with Strasbourg as the center and leader, would protect the true gospel and the true believers from an unholy trinity of emperor, pope, and false teachers like Martin Luther and Ulrich Zwingli. The Turks would wield the sword to carry out the actual extermination of the godless from the land. Throughout the time of vengeance, the Anabaptists would have no direct military role. They would not carry the sword themselves, but they would support the struggle with prayer and through construction work on the fortifications in cities such as Strasbourg. At the collapse of the wicked enemy, the 144 thousand of Revelation (14:4), led by the two witnesses, of which Hoffmann considered himself one (11:3), would march across the face of the earth, proclaiming the joyous, universal message of divine grace and dispensing the baptism of faith. Following the elimination of the wicked, a new theocracy would be established as in ancient Israel, with a pious king and a Spirit-filled prophet working hand in hand. While Hoffmann envisioned a revolutionary new age beginning on earth, it was still a new age begun by God rather than by human initiative.

Radical followers of Hoffmann, soon to institute the revolutionary kingdom in Münster, switched the origin of the revolution from above to below. They believed that their followers constituted an avenging army of believers who would slay the godless and thus initiate the coming of God's kingdom. Menno Simons's reshaping of the Melchiorite tradition, on the other hand, would begin with the assumption of the essentially peaceful and pacifist role of the believers in Hoffmann's end-time speculation.

His success at Emden in June of 1530 resulted in Hoffmann's forced departure from the city. He left behind Jan Volkertsz Trijpmaker as his deputy. In December 1530 Jan Volkertsz was also driven from the city, along with the recently baptized

Sikke Freerks Snijder. Jan Volkertsz carried Hoffmann's message to Amsterdam. Sikke Freerks fled to Leeuwarden, where he established a small Bible circle around the ideas of Melchior Hoffmann.

When Sikke Freerks was publicly beheaded in Leeuwarden on March 20, 1531, he became the first Anabaptist martyr in the Low Countries. His brief activity in Leeuwarden recruited several other individuals eventually significant to the Melchiorite movement. Although they were not baptized until January 1534, it is likely that Obbe and Dirk Philips belonged to Sikke Freerks's circle. Further, the execution caught the attention of the priest Menno Simons,[10] on the point of moving to his second parish assignment in his hometown of Witmarsum. This first lowland execution for rebaptism caused Menno to question the Catholic Church's position on infant baptism; it thus contributed to his renunciation of the Catholic Church some five years later.

During 1531 Jan Volkertsz preached and baptized in Amsterdam as a representative of Melchior Hoffmann. The first baptized converts included Bartholomeus Boekbinder and Pieter de Houtzager. Hoffmann himself arrived that summer and together with Jan Volkertsz baptized about fifty persons in a public ceremony. Such activity aroused the opposition of the Court of Holland, which demanded that the local magistrate arrest Jan Volkertsz. Instead of taking advantage of the magistrate's offer to flee, Jan Volkertsz sought martyrdom by turning himself in. The court sent him to The Hague, where he reported the names of those baptized in Amsterdam. Since the tolerant magistrate's wife warned many of them, only nine were arrested. The nine were beheaded along with Jan at The Hague on December 5, 1531.

The ten executions shocked Melchior Hoffmann. He recommended a *Stillstand* or suspension of baptism for two years, until the end of 1533, just prior to the end-time events he expected soon thereafter. Without the practice of baptism, the Melchiorites seemed like a radical version of the sacramentarian movement that was tolerated throughout the Low Countries.

For the most part, they escaped execution and grew rapidly during next two years. The Melchiorites thus benefited directly from the conflict between the imperial court and the local magistrates, who asserted local independence by refusing to carry out the mandates of Emperor Charles V against dissenters.

Hoffmann visited Strasbourg briefly in December 1531 and again in the spring of 1533. The latter visit led directly to a trial and imprisonment. According to Obbe Philips, Hoffmann returned to Strasbourg to court imprisonment when an old man predicted that Hoffmann as the new Elijah would undergo only figurative death—that is, six months' imprisonment—just before the spreading of his message and the return of Christ.

While Hoffmann likely did not hurry to Strasbourg and request imprisonment, when arrested he considered it the beginning of the end, and he welcomed the opportunity that the coming trial afforded him to present his case to the authorities in Strasbourg. The trial resulted in a life sentence for Hoffmann. He spent the remaining ten years of his life in prison, ailing and then dying in 1543. He was the object of pity and scorn and finally no longer convinced of his eschatological prophecies.

The entire Melchiorite movement followed Hoffmann in the belief that they were in the end times and that quite soon major changes would occur in the world. There were differing views, however, on the geographic center of the changes and the means by which the new righteous reign of God would be established. Was the center in Strasbourg or elsewhere? Would the changes be precipitated by an act of God or by the return of Christ or by God's human agents wielding swords of vengeance against the godless? It was several years following Hoffmann's imprisonment before these various impulses were sorted out and solidified into separate and distinct movements.

Münster

The most spectacular and infamous events of the Melchiorite movement occurred at Münster, tied in large part to the

Melchiorite career of a baker from Haarlem, Jan Matthijs.[11] Hoffmann had converted and baptized Jan Matthijs in 1531. In the absence of the imprisoned Hoffmann, Jan moved to assume leadership of the Melchiorite Anabaptist movement. Jan claimed to have experienced the special outpouring of the Holy Spirit that Hoffmann had prophesied. Thus, as Hoffmann had done, Jan Matthijs now claimed for himself the role of Enoch, one of the witnesses of Revelation 11:3. As the now self-anointed leader of the Melchiorite movement, Jan lifted Hoffmann's *Stillstand*, arguing that the nearness of the end made it precisely the time to begin baptizing again in order to assemble the end-time faithful. He moved the predicted end of the world from Hoffmann's appointed 1533 to Easter 1534.

In Leiden for several days, Jan Matthijs met with Jan Beukels, often called Jan van Leiden. Jan van Leiden had earlier visited Münster, where he was impressed with Bernhard Rothmannn's preaching against infant baptism. And he had already come to accept Hoffmann's predictions about the nearness of the end of the old order. Jan van Leiden now accepted baptism from Jan Matthijs, on All Saints' Day (Nov. 1) of 1533. Jan Matthijs then sent Jan van Leiden, along with Gerrit Boekbinder, as "apostolic messengers" to Briel, Rotterdam, Amsterdam, and other cities.

Jan Matthijs went directly from Leiden to Amsterdam, the location of the oldest of Hoffmann's followers. As a first act, he rejected his wife and took instead the pretty young Diewer, the future queen of Münster. Through a combination of threats of eternal damnation and acts of love, Jan Matthijs persuaded the Melchiorites in Amsterdam to accept his leadership.

The acceptance of Jan Matthijs's leading role by some of Hoffmann's oldest followers—Pieter Houtzager, Bartholomeus Boekbinder, and Willem de Kuyper—sent a signal to the Melchiorites everywhere. As Jan Matthijs' special messengers, Pieter de Houtzager went to Friesland and baptized many people into the end-time congregation of 144 thousand who would resist the antichrist. Meanwhile, Bartholomeus Boekbinder and Willem de Kuyper went to Leeuwarden and persuaded the unbaptized Melchiorites to accept baptism, with the promise that soon all the tyrants would be removed from the earth. Those baptized in Leeuwarden included the brothers Obbe and Dirk Philips. At this time, Obbe and another individual also received ordination as elders to preach and baptize.

The events in Leeuwarden created a stir that resulted in an edict for six individuals wanted by the authorities. Included on the list were Melchior Hoffmann and Obbe Philips. Near the end of 1534, Obbe fled from Leeuwarden. In Delft, before making his way to Amsterdam, Obbe baptized David Joris, future opponent of Menno Simons.

Meanwhile, under the leadership of Bernhard Rothmann, the city of Münster was proceeding toward Reformation. In a few months, Anabaptists would win out over Catholics and Lutherans in a multifaceted, three-cornered struggle to control the religious direction of the city. A council and the United Guild, which represented the various guilds, ruled the city. The United Guild usually supported the council, but in times of controversy, such as in this religious struggle, it could and did oppose the council. The following describes only the outline of this struggle.

After visiting centers of Reformation such as Marburg, Wittenberg, and Strasbourg, Rothmann in 1532 had introduced a Reformation in Münster, strongly influenced by Melchiorite Anabaptist positions on the Lord's Supper and baptism. By August 1532 reforming preachers controlled all the city's churches except the cathedral. By February 1533 a number of preachers were known for Anabaptist leanings, and tolerant Münster was attracting harassed Melchiorites from Amsterdam. When Rothmann and others questioned infant baptism, the evangelical party was split. Following a public disputation on August 7-8, 1533, it was ruled that all infants had to be baptized. City council dismissed Rothmann from his position in November 1533 and tried to banish him and his supporters from the city.

Rothmann replied with his first Anabaptist treatise, *Bekentnisse von beyden Sacramenten* or *Confession Concerning the Two Sacraments*, published in November 1533. It used sacramentarian arguments from preachers such as Heinrich Roll, who had come to Münster the year before. This *Confession*, a "classic peaceful Anabaptist statement,"[12] advocated believers baptism and a symbolic view of the Lord's Supper. It had wide repercussions and became the theological foundation for the Anabaptist movement in Münster. The Reformed ministers from Strasbourg wrote a refutation of it in March 1534. Pilgram Marpeck used it to rally the divergent South German Anabaptist groups, and he copied from it extensively in his *Vermanung* or *Admonition* of 1542.

Believers baptism itself was introduced in Münster by Jan Matthijs's special emissaries, Bartholomeus Boekbinder and Willem de Kuyper, who arrived from Leeuwarden on January 5, 1534. They immediately baptized Rothmann and a number of other preachers. Within the next week, Rothmann and his assistants baptized fourteen hundred others.

Jan van Leiden and Gerrit Bookbinder entered Münster on January 13, 1534, followed closely by Jan Matthijs. Jan Matthijs persuaded Rothmann that the time had come for a sharp break with the old order. The time was near for the righteous to use the sword against the godless. Rothmann took on the role of providing a theological rationale for the political measures advocated by Jan Matthijs. Rothmann's book *Van der Wrake*, which appeared in December 1534, argued that the people of God were called not only to defend themselves but also to help God to punish the wicked.

On January 23, 1534, Bishop Waldeck issued an edict demanding the imprisonment of Anabaptists. Since Anabaptists drew support from a number of guild members and conservative evangelicals, the edict threatened evangelicals as well as Anabaptists. There was enough popular support that the bishop's order could not be carried out. Rothmann preached openly. Heinrich Redeker, a powerful alderman with the United Guild, organized burghers against the rumored attack on the city by the bishop, and the United Guild became the real power in the city.

Waldeck withdrew from Münster and established a military headquarters at Telgte. He began a siege of the city, which prevented entry of soldiers and foodstuffs, but did not stop communication or traffic in and out of the city.

Events of February 9-11, 1534, solidified the Anabaptists' hold on power in the city, but they were under threat of attack from the bishop as well as by an imported peasant levy and armed supporters of the council. Their prophets were instructing the outnumbered Anabaptists to take up arms, yet they considered themselves as sheep ready for the slaughter. However, accompanied by unusual meteorological phenomena, a compromise was reached that left the pro-Anabaptist members of the ruling group in control. On February 23, Redecker and the United Guild organized the election of an Anabaptist council. Bernhard Knipperdolling, wealthy businessman and supporter of Rothmann, became mayor. Jan Matthijs declared Münster a divinely appointed city of refuge for the end-time tribulations. Letters went out to Melchiorites in Westphalia and the Netherlands, declaring the political events of February 1534 to be a miracle.

Meanwhile, on February 25 Jan Matthijs announced that all the godless—those who refused to accept the covenant of adult baptism—should be killed. Mayor Knipperdolling moderated the demand by convincing him to give the citizens a week to decide whether to accept baptism or abandon the city. From this point until his death at Easter 1534, the date to which Jan moved the end of the world from the late 1533 prediction of Hoffmann, Jan ruled in Münster with absolute authority. This authority was reinforced, for example, by killing on the spot the blacksmith—Hubert Ruescher—who had dared to call him a deceiver.

At this point, several positions on the sword of vengeance existed within the diverse Melchiorite movement. Both

Hoffmann and Jan Matthijs believed that a radical change in the world was on the point of appearing through the mission of the apostolic messengers and the destruction of the godless. These events would immediately precede the appearance of Jesus. Hoffmann expected a new outpouring of the Holy Spirit that would render the faithful invulnerable. The outpouring would also stimulate the cooperation of the governments of the free cities (like Strasbourg) in the fight against the antichrist, whose forces included the false priests of all confessions.

In the ideology of Jan Matthijs, Münster replaced Strasbourg as the new Jerusalem, where God would protect his faithful and persecuted children. He placed the temporal rulers as well as the clergy in the camp of the enemy, to be rooted out. While the cooperation of legal governments was desirable, it was also unexpected. Therefore, the righteous element, with sword in hand, would proceed without them to eliminate the wicked.

Other Melchiorites could advocate use of the sword in self-defense (like Balthasar Hubmaier), or still awaited a command from God before seizing the sword (like Hans Hut), or rejected completely any use of force (like Michael Sattler). Only in the few years after the fall of Münster did distinct groups coalesce around these differences. At the time of Münster's rise, it was not the use of the sword but the rival claims of being the new Jerusalem and the acceptance of polygamy that characterized the dispute between the Melchiorite factions in Strasbourg and Münster.

During the period from February to Easter 1534, Jan Matthijs enjoyed virtually unchallenged charismatic authority, and Münster became the focus of apocalyptic excitement in Westphalia and the Netherlands. The banned Anabaptists had placed their people in the seats of political power in the city. In March, Jan Matthijs sent out another call to all of Holland, urging refugees to come to Münster as the city of God, to escape God's coming judgment on the wicked. They were to bring only money, cloth, and weapons. Anabaptists and sympathizers began to move to the city in large numbers. Social conditions—war, plague, high unemployment—undoubtedly contributed to the climate that produced refugees, although evidence indicates that the representatives of all social classes were among those on the move.

Many of the immigrants did not reach Münster. It seems that apocalyptic speculations provided more motivation than organized revolution. Near Genemuiden, for example, less than a hundred soldiers arrested a company of about three thousand armed persons, who offered no resistance. They were waiting on the heavenly Jeremiah to come and organize their march to the new Jerusalem and would not resist without his approval. A group near Zwolle waited for the Holy Spirit. When the "seventh trumpet" failed to blow and Jeremiah did not appear on the clouds, the group disintegrated.

In Amsterdam, Anabaptists allowed large quantities of weapons and ships to be seized without resistance. As a sign of protest, Willem de Kuyper, Bartholomeus Boekbinder, and Pieter de Houtzager ran through the streets of Amsterdam with uplifted swords, proclaiming "woe" on the city. They allowed themselves to be arrested and were executed three days later.

The supernatural deliverance of the city predicted by Jan Matthijs for Easter 1534 did not happen. For reasons not entirely clear, on April 4, 1534, only six weeks after assuming leadership in Münster, he led a small expedition against the besieging army of Bishop Waldeck—perhaps to precipitate a miracle, perhaps provoked to prove himself by Jan van Leyden. In any case, Jan Matthijs and his companions were killed.

There were other radical attempts at following the Bible. After hearing of Judith and Holofernes[13] in a sermon, the young woman Hille Feikes (or Feyken) wanted to reenact the story by assassinating Bishop Waldeck. When discovered infiltrating the enemy lines, she pretended to have a desire to betray the city in order to gain entry to the besiegers' camp. Before she reached the bishop, however, her true intent was discovered and she was beheaded.

At Jan Matthijs's death, Jan van Leiden immediately seized control of the city. He abolished the city council and instituted a kind of messianic kingship on the order of Old Testament Israel. To resist Jan van Leiden was to resist the divine order. Acting as the voice of the Lord, he chose twelve elders of the twelve tribes of Israel. On the basis of a prophecy received, King Jan made Knipperdolling the city's executioner. Capital punishment was frequently threatened for failure to observe the stated code of behavior that Jan also claimed to receive by divine revelation. Under the new order, which referred to the citizens as "Israelites," capital crimes included blasphemy, seditious language, scolding parents, a servant's disobedience of a master, adultery, gossiping, and complaining.

In addition to their revolutionary use of the sword, the Anabaptists in Münster were also distinguished by the practices of community of goods and of polygamy. Community of goods was instituted by Jan Matthijs and had already been advocated in Rothmann's *Confession*. Drawing on Sebastian Franck's *Chronica*, Rothmann tied community of goods to the Christian solidarity of the Lord's Supper, in which those who partake are one body and one bread. In a later writing Rothmann equated community of goods with the abolition of a money economy. He wrote that Münster had eliminated "buying and selling, working for money, and indebtedness and usury."[14] Although Jan Matthijs abolished private property and declared all goods common to everyone, the practice of community of goods in Münster never attained the egalitarian life pattern that it attained among Hutterites. King Jan modified the practice, and exceptions developed for the wealthy, the powerful, and the privileged minority of the royal court. Its practice became as much a way to deal with refugees and the city's needy, and then with the wartime siege, as it was a matter of egalitarian sharing.

Jan van Leyden forced polygamy upon the community, using biblical arguments. He held up Old Testament examples to follow literally, and argued from the New Testament that

Paul's hierarchy of Christ/man/woman required that every woman be attached to a man for salvation. However, polygamy also had a practical basis. It was a way to regulate sexual relations and the supposed male control of females in a context in which women outnumbered men in the city three to one.

Jan van Leiden did not institute polygamy without resistance. In fact, a group of dissidents led by Heinrich Mollenhecke surprised and imprisoned him on July 29, 1534, with the intent of forcing Jan to abandon the practice. Townspeople loyal to Jan then released him and imprisoned the dissidents. Jan responded by executing Mollenhecke and forty-eight others.

Jan van Leiden rallied the city to repel successfully a direct attack by the bishop's forces on August 31, 1534. On the basis of a vision and some biblical passages, Johann Dusentschuer declared van Leiden "King of the New Zion." At the height of his power, Jan van Leiden was crowned king. He erected a throne in the market square from which to hold court, and he wore royal symbols on a chain around his neck. The new king used terror tactics and on-the-spot executions to subdue those who did not show great enthusiasm for the royal developments, or who in other ways resisted his rule.

The last months of the kingdom of Münster were severe for the city. Within the city, King Jan continued to rule through terror. For example, he beheaded one of his spirited wives in the marketplace and then trampled on the body in front of his entire harem when she dared to criticize his rule. Events in the city—as well as actions by fanatical Melchiorites in other places—had stiffened resistance to Anabaptists throughout the Low Countries, and movement into the city was virtually stopped. Jan sent out more messengers with appeals to come to the new Zion. Many were captured and executed. Both supplies and spirits within the city sagged. Due to lack of supplies, King Jan sent the women, children, and old men out of the city in June 1535. Many of these were cruelly killed by the besieging army.

Treachery brought about the actual fall of the city. A

guard abandoned his post and showed the besieging army how to enter the city. When the bishop's forces finally entered Münster on June 25, 1535, about eight hundred men remained to repel three thousand soldiers. The killing continued for two days. Nearly all the defenders perished, and the bishop reasserted his control of the city.

Likely Bernhard Rothmann died in the attack on the city; his body was never found. Jan van Leiden, Bernhard Knipperdolling, and Bernhard Krechting, a member of King Jan's council, were captured alive. In the next months the three became a public spectacle and were interviewed by a number of people in attempts to establish a direct, conspiratorial link between them and Melchior Hoffmann, who was still imprisoned in Strasbourg.

Their end came finally on January 20, 1536, in Münster. After horrible torture—their flesh was torn and then their tongues ripped out with hot pincers—they were executed by piercing the heart with a hot dagger. The bodies were placed in three cages and hung on the tower of St. Lambert's church as a warning for all to see. Replicas of the cages still hang there today.

Anabaptism lived under the shadow of Münster for a long time. In the public mind throughout Europe, Anabaptism became virtually synonymous with Münster. In spite of the peaceful and pacifist stance that came to be the norm for Anabaptism, religious and political authorities feared and assumed that Anabaptism's rejection of the established ecclesiastical authority would inevitably lead to another Münster. Repression of Anabaptists was the result. For instance, as earlier reported, fear of another Münster caused the Moravian lords to expel the Hutterites from their lands.

Historiography has reflected the presumed identity of Münster and Anabaptism. In a virtually unbroken line of writings from Martin Luther and Heinrich Bullinger to Karl Hall in the twentieth century, it was assumed that early Anabaptism began with the revolutionary Thomas Müntzer and reached its logical conclusion at Münster. In American historiography, not till the twentieth century did scholars such as John Horsch, Harold S. Bender, and Cornelius Krahn successfully challenge that interpretation of Anabaptist origins.

Aftermath

The Melchiorite Anabaptist tradition did not die with the fall of the kingdom of Münster. It was a diverse movement. Various persons sensed kinship with the whole but did not succumb to the efforts of the two Jans to usher in God's rule through a violent revolution in Münster. Gradually the nonrevolutionary and peaceful impulses began to take on a distinct form of their own. Principal spokespersons for an emerging nonrevolutionary Melchiorite tradition were the brothers Obbe and Dirk Philips. They came from the Melchiorite congregation in Leeuwarden begun by Sikke Freerks and were baptized by the emissaries of Jan Matthijs. This diverse Melchiorite pedigree of Dirk and Obbe demonstrates the varied character of the movement.

Fleeing from Leeuwarden when his name appeared on a list of insurrectionists, Obbe Philips made his way to Amsterdam in February 1534. Here he became a leader of the group previously associated with Jan Volkertsz Trijpmaker. He spent most of his time in the provinces between Amsterdam and East Friesland, while Jacob van Campen acted as bishop in Amsterdam. Obbe's brother Dirk did not yet have a leading role in the movement.

While in Amsterdam in March 1534 to confer with Jacob van Campen, Obbe had watched the gruesome executions of Pieter de Houtzager and Bartholomeus Boekbinder, who had ordained him. On May 10, 1535, Jan van Geelen, an emissary from Münster, had tried to overthrow the city government of Amsterdam with the help of a number of Melchiorites in the city. Jacob at first approved use of the sword in self-defense, but then withdrew support from Jan van Geelen's planned attack and warned his cobelievers of the consequences. Nonetheless, Jacob as well as Jan van Geelen and about forty other rebels were executed. Jan van Geelen had previously escaped from a violent uprising in March at Oldeklooster, following which more than a hundred Anabaptists were executed.

Likely these and other such incidents raised questions for Obbe about the direction of the movement. By the end of 1534 Obbe and Dirk, as well as Jacob van Campen, David Joris, and others from the northern Low Countries, were preaching against establishment of the new age by force. But they did not successfully persuade their congregations to accept the idea. Nonetheless, Obbe was still an active Melchiorite leader and likely spent the early part of 1535 in prison because of it.[15]

Following the fall of Münster, the core of those Melchiorites who had not succumbed to the lure of the revolution, as well as disillusioned revolutionaries, gradually became one of the distinct Melchiorite groups. For the years immediately following the fall of Münster, David Joris emerged as the most visible leader of this group. Obbe Philips was also visible, eventually succeeded by his brother Dirk and Menno Simons, who successfully wrested the movement from the spiritualist direction of David. This group of Melchiorites rejected the sword as a means for bringing in the reign of God. They came to see the gathered church as the only literal manifestation of God's reign to expect in this world.

A second group consisted of the old-line Melchiorites in Strasbourg and scattered across the Low Countries. Jan Matthijs van Middelburg was an important leader. This faction also rejected the use of violence but still expected an outpouring of the Spirit and a divine inbreaking in the near future.

A third group followed Jan van Batenburg. He believed that the time of grace, forgiveness, and baptism was past, and that the moment had come for vengeance. Full membership in the group came through acceptance of group marriage. Jan van Batenburg and his followers engaged in a series of raids across

Westphalia and the Low Countries, robbing churches and plundering and burning homesteads.

A fourth group carried on ideas of the Münsterites, with polygamy and the defense or erection of God's reign through force. They rejected as senseless, however, the banditry of Jan van Batenburg. Heinrich Krechting, ex-chancellor of King Jan van Leiden, succeeded for a time in establishing a following in Oldenburg and exerted influence in Westphalia and in the Low Countries.[16]

Oppression in the aftermath of Münster gave the various perspectives a certain cohesion in spite of their differences. A conference at Bocholt in August 1536, attended by some twenty or twenty-five Melchiorite leaders from the various groups, tried to restore some unity to the movement. That representatives from the several factions attended also indicates the intermingling and diverging streams of a movement not yet solidified into clearly demarcated camps.

Most of the important leaders, however, did not attend. Obbe feared an ambush by Batenburgers. Jan van Batenburg also avoided a dangerous journey but likely also anticipated condemnation of his tactics. Representatives from Strasbourg set out for Bocholt but turned back because of a dream experienced by one of the traveling party. Heinrich Krechting did not attend, and Hoffmann, of course, was in prison. The decision of the significant individuals not to attend probably rendered minimal any real chance to establish unity on an enduring basis, but it did open the possibility of increased stature in the movement for David Joris.

David Joris

The major conflict at Bocholt was between the Münsterites and the Melchiorites of Jan Matthijs van Middelburg. The latter condemned the Münsterite perspective as irreconcilable to the teachings of Melchior Hoffmann, while the Münsterites countered by threatening to kill their enemy brothers. In this charged environment, it was David Joris,[17] baptized a year and a half earlier by Obbe Philips, who developed the compromise solution. He asserted their common agreement on the Melchiorite points of celestial-flesh Christology, free will, perfection of the saints, and adult baptism. To the disputed question of vengeance against the godless, David argued a pacifist position. He maintained that vengeance would still be carried out by God and his saints. However, following the parable of the wheat and tares (Matt 13:24-30), he equated the elect with the wheat and identified the reapers as angels. Since the chosen people cannot simultaneously be wheat and reapers, Anabaptists should not wield the sword of vengeance. David then rejected further speculation on the identity of the reapers. He diffused the question of polygamy by postponing a definitive decision, but stated that for himself the number of wives was not important "so long as they obey God and His truth."[18]

David's compromise was thus the continuation of a moderate Melchiorite program, with a tendency to spiritualize points of conflict. The big loser at Bocholt was Jan van Batenburg. When he was arrested the following year, he listed his principal opponent as David Joris, along with Heinrich Krechting, Obbe and Dirk Philips, and Jan Matthijs van Middelburg.

David's role at Bocholt and afterward advanced his career as the most recognized leader of the Melchiorite movement in the late 1530s and early 1540s. Before his career as full-time religious leader and prophet, David had worked as a skilled glass painter. He was impacted by the sacramentarians and had long been one of the many dissenters in the Netherlands. Expelled from his hometown of Delft for iconoclastic preaching in 1528, David spent time in Rotterdam and in East Frisia, and he carried on discussions about Christology with Jan Volkerts Trijpmaker. With his wife, David was in The Hague as a Melchiorite sympathizer in December 1531 when Trijpmaker and the nine others were executed. He continued discussions with Melchiorite apostles through 1532 and 1533 but was hesitant to cast his lot with them. He was nonetheless impacted by Melchiorite ideas and likely adopted Hoffmann's belief that the current age would end in 1533.

David was attracted by the rhetoric from Münster but never joined the trek. After extended conversations he finally accepted baptism sometime in the winter of 1534 to 1535. As a figure of some renown, he was recognized as a potential leader, and soon Obbe Philips ordained him as a bishop. At first David was a reluctant leader, but his attendance at conferences, such as at Waterland and then the Bocholt conference, raised his confidence. In addition, he experienced a vision in December 1536 that appears to have kindled prophetic ambition.

David and his wife, Birkgen, and family were refugees more than once from intolerant magistrates in Delft. While there, he lived in hiding, worked at his glass-painting trade, and operated as leader of the Delft Anabaptists.

In the years 1536 to 1539, David provided the majority of peaceful leadership in the Netherlands outside of Friesland and Groningen. His approach to the Bible sought a middle ground between Melchior Hoffmann and Bernard Rothmann. David never advocated taking the sword of vengeance as did Rothmann and the Münsterites, but David did believe that vengeance would happen as a divinely initiated event. Thus, in Münster's aftermath he could affirm both vengeance and patient suffering, the compromise he articulated at Bocholt.

Spurred on by his late 1536 vision, David asserted himself as a divinely called, Spirit-inspired leader. He based his leadership not on Scripture but on inspiration by the Holy Spirit. It was as the inspired prophet that he undertook to bring all the post-Münster Melchiorites under his control. He developed a quite devoted following and gained some followers from other groups.

Obbe Philips completely surrendered the expectation of a near return of Jesus, calling that earlier hope an unhappy illusion. His disillusionment carried him out of the movement by about 1540. Some of Obbe's people moved under David's leadership, while others stayed with this faction under Obbe's brother Dirk, and Menno Simons, who had just joined at the time of the Bocholt meeting.

The left wing, in the circle of the Batenburgers, had an increasing emphasis on plundering churches and other banditry. Both David and Batenburg made charismatic claims to leadership, and they had a heated rivalry. Batenburg had predicted that the one who outlived the other would be God's anointed. When Jan van Batenburg was arrested in late 1537 and executed early in 1538, some of his followers then migrated to the faction of David Joris.

Striking was David's ability to escape the danger that took many Anabaptists between the conference at Bocholt and the end of 1544. At least one hundred of his supporters were executed. David lived as a fugitive, and his survival frequently depended on the courage and artifice of his followers, who underwent torture and took great risks to protect David.

David's aspirations to charismatic leadership also met challenges. In June 1538 David made an unsuccessful trip to Strasbourg in an effort to convert the original, old-line Melchiorites to his fold. The three days of discussion focused primarily on the basis of leadership. David wanted the Strasbourgers' affirmation. He claimed that he was the one to perfect Hoffmann's original doctrine; following in the line of Hoffmann's charismatic leadership, David stressed his own divine inspiration. The Strasbourgers demanded scriptural and rational proof, which indicates that they were moving away from charismatic leadership and toward a more formal basis of authority.

David did not convince the Strasbourgers, and he left without their acceptance of his leadership. Soon thereafter the surviving Münsterites also rejected his leadership. Although he retained a significant following, David was well short of his goal of controlling all post-Melchiorite Anabaptism in the Netherlands.

In 1539, David moved his family to asylum in Antwerp. Here he quickly became the patron of two wealthy families, and his daughter married one of their sons. The attitude toward nobility and authorities reflected in his writing shifted from suspicion to praise. With more time to reflect in the relative security of Antwerp, the spiritualist direction in which David had been developing reached its culmination. He considered himself the "third David," who was inspired to finish the work of the second David, who was Jesus Christ. As third David, he would rebuild the city of God, which was within each believer. Spiritual identity came from within rather than conformity to mere externals. Therefore, it was possible to conform to externals, such as infant baptism and attendance at worship services of the established church, while remaining inwardly separate.

From his exile in Antwerp, David continued to exert leadership over his followers further north, through his writing and his emissaries, Nicolaas Meyndertsz van Blesdijk and Jorien Ketel, who spread his teaching across the Netherlands and Germany. During this time, he also engaged in an extensive literary struggle with the followers of Menno, who vigorously opposed David and who was rising in stature among Dutch Anabaptists.

The Wonder Book, published in 1543, reflects David's thought during the years in Antwerp. In this large work, David "sought to bring all knowledge into the service of the Holy Spirit." He made the divinely inspired third David "the center for all true wisdom," but toned down the apocalypticism of Melchior Hoffmann.[19]

David Joris left an extensive literary record, and his great productivity contributed significantly to the development of his leadership in the period after Münster. His writings, however, come from all phases of his religious career, with 240 printed works surviving. Of those that can be dated, fourteen fall in the Anabaptist period before 1539, forty-eight from his stay in Antwerp, and 102 from his years in Basel.[20]

Anneken [Anna] Jans exemplifies the impact of David's leadership and his ability to rally ex-Münsterites to his movement.[21] At about twenty-three or twenty-four years of age, in February or March of 1534, Anneken and her husband were baptized in Briel by Münsterite emissaries. Anabaptists had just come to power in Münster, and no doubt Anneken and her husband were attracted by the apocalyptic message about Münster as the city of refuge and about God's vengeance on the wicked. A collection of hymns published by David Joris about 1539 contains "I Can Hear the Trumpet Sounding," a hymn written by Anneken. She was caught up in the apocalyptic rhetoric and expectations of vengeance, but waited for God to enact that vengeance when the children of God will "wash your feet in the blood of the godless."[22] David had not joined the trek to Münster in spring of 1534, and he accepted baptism later that year only after long discussions with Obbe Philips. The fact that Anneken's hymn does not feature the Münsterite sword of vengeance may well reflect the pacifist influence of David Joris.

When her husband was in England to escape authorities in Briel, David and a companion stayed in Anneken's house in Briel when he sought refuge from authorities in Delft. David and Anneken became quite close and likely fell in love, although prayer and the disciplinary intervention of other Anabaptists reportedly kept them from sexual impropriety. In any case, it is evident that David had opportunity to influence Anneken and to publish her hymn. Anneken also exerted significant influence on David. A letter that reached David in 1536 that likely came from Anneken sent him into an eight-day "psychological state of ecstasy."[23] It may have been the letter that kindled his aspirations for the status of prophet as well as moving him in a spiritualist direction.[24]

However, Anneken's outcome differed greatly from David's. In December of 1538, Anneken and another women were recognized as Anabaptists and arrested; Anneken confessed that she was on her way to consult with David Joris. On

January 24, 1539, Anneken and her companion were drowned in Rotterdam. On her way to the water, she offered a significant sum of money to anyone who would promise to raise Isaiah, her fifteen-month-old son. A baker with six children accepted the money and raised him. Isaiah became a brewer and mayor of Rotterdam, but he did not accept his mother's call to follow her as an Anabaptist. Just before her drowning, Anneken wrote a *Testament* to Isaiah. It was soon printed and distributed widely as an Anabaptist tract.[25] In it she stated her willingness to follow the model of Jesus and submit to suffering as a public witness to hope in God's reign. She kept the general apocalyptic framework of Münster but followed the leading of pacifist Anabaptists such as David. Thus, God's vengeance was delayed, and the sword of the Münsterites was put back in its sheath. Patient suffering based on the model of Jesus rather than the sword of vengeance became the way that Anneken and the Anabaptists to whom she appealed could attain victory over their godless tormenters and wait for God to carry out vengeance. In this witness and victory, Anabaptists were identified with the marginalized in society, a rejection of the world in order to identify with Christ. Hence, their martyrdom was "standing with the Christly minority against the worldly majority."[26] In the aftermath of Münster, Anneken's testimony demonstrates that Anabaptists did not withdraw from society; they were clearly engaged in a witness of another kind—a nonviolent witness to the future reign of God.

Anneken's life and martyrdom display the course of Anabaptism in the Netherlands—from "a proto-Münsterite to a follower of Joris to a patient martyr,"[27] who could be claimed for *Martyrs Mirror* by the Anabaptist tradition of Obbe and Menno. The witness of Anneken's death stands in sharp contrast to David, who took a spiritualist direction that ultimately allowed him to save himself.

The years that David Joris functioned as the dominant leader of Dutch Anabaptists, about 1536 to 1540, paralleled the rise of Menno Simons as a leader among Dutch Anabaptists. Many of the twenty-first century heirs to Dutch Melchiorite Anabaptism, as well as those of Swiss and South German Anabaptism, are called Mennonites, after Menno Simons. The narrative now retreats a few years, in order to bring Menno into the story and develop his career to the point where it intersects with and then surpasses David's in leadership of the Melchiorite Anabaptist movement.

Menno Simons

Menno Simons was born about 1496 in Witmarsum. Since as an adult he knew Latin and some Greek, he likely attended monastic schools. In 1524, at age twenty-eight, Menno was ordained a priest and received Pingjum near Witmarsum for his first parish assignment. He served as the second among three priests. Menno later expressed chagrin at his ignorance of the Bible at that time and wrote that for two years he did not touch the Scriptures, for fear of being misled. Meanwhile, he joined his fellow clerics in "playing [cards], drinking, and in diversions."[28]

Two years after his ordination, the sacramentarian questions—specifically the question of whether the bread and wine of the eucharist actually became the body and blood of Jesus as the Roman church taught—sent Menno to the Scriptures. As he put it, "I had not gone very far when I discovered that we were deceived" about transubstantiation. Menno also read some of the writings of Luther, which strengthened him in the idea of resistance to papal and Roman authority. Although Menno rejected the Catholic understanding of the eucharist, he continued as a priest in Pingjum.

The execution of Sikke Freerks Snijder for rebaptism in 1531 in nearby Leeuwarden sent Menno once again to the Bible to check on the traditional teaching of the Roman church. Menno writes that after a diligent study of the Scripture, he "could find no report of infant baptism." He next consulted the writings of Luther, Bucer, and Bullinger, only to discover that they "varied so greatly among themselves." He concluded that "we were deceived in regard to infant baptism."

Abraham Friesen advances an argument that, if accepted, gives Menno's understanding of baptism a common root in Erasmus with Swiss Anabaptists in Zurich. In chapter 2 we observed that only Anabaptists followed Erasmus in saying that the Great Commission of Matthew 28:19 established the proper order of teaching and then baptism, which invalidated baptism of infants, and that the baptismal practices of the apostles described in Acts show their specific practice of the order as established by Jesus in Matthew 28:19. Menno certainly knew the *Annotations* and paraphrases of Erasmus,[29] and Friesen writes that Menno's explication of the proper order of baptism in his *Fundamentboek* of 1539 "replicates the Erasmian argument more clearly than any other work within the corpus of Anabaptist writings," with the possible exception of passages in Balthasar Hubmaier's writings and in Bernard Rothmann's *Confession Concerning the Two Sacraments*. Menno never mentions Hubmaier. If Menno did not develop the idea de novo, which would require significant coincidences of ideas and language, then Menno took this focus on the order of teaching and baptism exemplified by apostolic practice from either Erasmus or Rothmann. When Marpeck republished much of the *Confession* under his own name in his *Admonition*, the Erasmian argument would have confirmed for South German Anabaptism this emphasis already present through the work of Hubmaier and the Swiss Brethren.[30]

Menno did not act upon his conclusion that the Catholic Church erred in two of its most important sacraments. In fact, a few months after determining the baptism of infants to be erroneous, he accepted promotion to his home parish at Witmarsum, "led thither by covetousness and the desire to obtain a great name." He relates that while he fulfilled the external requirements of the office, gained a certain amount of fame, and generally led a life of pleasure, inwardly he was somewhat troubled in conscience.[31]

It was not Menno's doubts but events related to Münster that finally compelled him to renounce the Roman church. When representatives of Münster visited Witmarsum in 1534, he engaged them in both public and private disputations, which led to the report that he could silence them beautifully. His conscience nagged, however. Menno saw that "though they were zealous they erred in doctrine." Meanwhile, he himself continued to teach people the Catholic doctrine, which he no longer believed.

Jan van Geelen's expedition in March of 1535 made an impact on Menno. On March 30 Jan and three hundred followers occupied the monastery Oldeklooster near Bolsward, Friesland. Jan escaped when the imperial forces recaptured the monastery on April 7, but many of the Anabaptists perished in the battle. Thirty-seven were beheaded at one time, and 132 were taken to Leeuwarden, where fifty-five were executed. A Peter Simons, possibly a brother of Menno, was among those who perished in the battle.

Following the events at Oldeklooster, Menno's conscience no longer permitted him to continue safely preaching the Catholic doctrines he believed false, when he saw "that these zealous children [at Oldeklooster], although in error, willingly gave their lives and their estates for their doctrine and faith." Beginning in May and continuing for the next nine months, Menno publicly preached from his pulpit in Witmarsum a gospel emphasizing the Reformation doctrine of repentance, using Scripture to oppose "all sin and wickedness, all idolatry and false worship." He also publicly attacked the kingdom of Münster by both pen and pulpit. His first publication, *The Blasphemy of John van Leiden*, called Jan an antichrist, but it did not appear until after the fall of Münster.

Menno's evangelical message likely placed him in some personal danger. In January 1536 he completely abandoned his pulpit and his settled life in Witmarsum. He explained that he "sought out the pious," the Melchiorite movement of Obbe and

Dirk, with whom he had likely been in previous contact. After his withdrawal from Witmarsum, Menno went underground for a period of study and writing, during which time he produced several devotional tracts. This material then found more complete expression in his 1539 work *The Foundation of the Christian Doctrine*. Supplemented and revised, the *Foundation Book* became one of his chief tools in the gathering of the Melchiorites into a more unified and stable Anabaptist movement.

From Witmarsum, Menno made a first, temporary stop at Groningen. Here he likely received baptism from Obbe Philips. He also married Gertrud, who accompanied him faithfully through the following years of hardship and persecution. He established himself at Oldersum and perhaps used it as his base for excursions throughout the Low Countries in the period 1536-43. At Oldersum, he could have encountered the lingering influence of Karlstadt's work there in 1529 and 1530.

About a year after he abandoned the priesthood, a delegation of six or eight persons, whom Menno described as "beyond reproach as far as man can judge in doctrine and life," requested him to assume formal leadership of their group. Thus, early in 1537 Menno was ordained, also by Obbe Philips.

The identity of Menno with Obbe's faction of the Melchiorites and Menno's own conflict with David Joris is evident in Menno's statement that those who called him "sincerely abhorred not only the sect of Münster, but [also] the cursed abominations of all other worldly sects." His sharp disassociation of himself from the Münsterite movement as a whole, however, represents the perspective of the older Menno, writing in 1554. In the 1539 edition of his *Foundation Book*, he had characterized the Münsterites as "dear brethren" who had "formerly acted against the Lord in a minor way," and he blamed their use of force on bad leadership.[32] Thus, one observes in Menno's career—as for Obbe Philips and others—that while the Melchiorite movement was quite varied, division into distinct groups occurred only gradually in the years after the episode at Münster.

For the rest of his life, Menno worked to rally and unify Anabaptists scattered from the Low Countries to the Vistula Delta. After baptizing and commissioning Menno, Obbe came to doubt the validity of his mission, due to his own baptism by followers of Jan Matthijs.[33] It is assumed that he became a religious seeker without any formal ties, although there is some likelihood that he joined the Lutheran church.[34]

By about 1540 Menno had come to occupy the leadership role abandoned by Obbe in his faction of Melchiorites. And by 1541 Menno's influence had grown to the point that the Regent Maria, in Brussels, authorized the courts of Friesland to pardon a penitent Anabaptist who would betray Menno. The following year a price of a hundred gulden was placed on Menno's head, a public renown accorded to David Joris already in 1539. In these years Menno was David's most substantial opponent and rival for leadership in the Melchiorite movement, and in 1541-43 they engaged in a passionate literary battle. David lived at Antwerp from 1539 to 1544. The struggle for leadership was not finally resolved until David's move from there to Basel with his wife and eleven children in 1544.

Menno considered the followers of David Joris to be one of the "corrupt sects," alongside the Münsterites. Both Menno and David combined the apocalyptic hopes of the early Melchiorites with a rejection of revolutionary violence, which they believed was counter to the character of New Testament Christians. In spite of that agreement, however, David and Menno represented two different directions within Melchiorite Anabaptism. David Joris claimed to be a new messianic David, with a mission vouchsafed by dreams and visions, to assemble Christ's flock in the last days. On the basis of this foundation, David sought to gain recognition from all the Melchiorite groups. With this self-proclaimed mission, David was clearly trying to continue the Melchiorite tradition of charismatic prophetic leadership, which went from Melchior Hoffmann to Jan van Leiden and Jan van Batenburg.

When Menno rejected all the promised Davids as "blasphemers"—since Christ alone is the true David—Menno was critiquing a powerful element of the Melchiorite tradition. Menno countered with his own Melchiorite symbol: baptism. Batenbergers no longer baptized because the time of grace to which baptism belonged had been replaced by the time of vengeance. David Joris had replaced external water baptism with inward fire baptism of the last days. Hence, Menno's followers were the only remaining baptizers in the Melchiorite tradition. The conflict between Menno and David thus concerned two versions of the tradition of Melchior Hoffmann, a conflict not fully resolved until David withdrew from the scene.

Menno was primarily an heir of Hoffmann, with some of his more peculiar ideas filtered out, while also retaining some elements of Karlstadt as mediated by Melchior Hoffmann. Significant surviving elements from Karlstadt included biblicism, the nature of the church, the signs of baptism and Lord's Supper, absence of chiliastic schemes, rejection of oaths, advocacy of nonviolence, and the possibility of a believing magistrate. Menno did retain a version of celestial-flesh Christology, following Hoffmann and against Karlstadt.

David's notion "that to the pure all things are pure" enabled him to counsel his followers to cover up their true religious convictions through participation in the religious and social activities of the larger society. For David, attendance at Catholic or Reformed worship services and even baptism of infants were insignificant outward manifestations. He claimed that these externals mattered much less than the pure, hidden, and inner faith. Ultimately, David's stress on the new Spirit-baptism of the last days undercut Melchior Hoffmann's starting point of baptism with water, which Menno preserved. David's "purity" orientation also permitted some sexual excesses reminiscent of Münster and enabled Menno to charge David with indirectly countenancing polygamy. To Menno and his colleagues, those who hid themselves in the established church compromised basic honesty and religious integrity. David considered Menno's followers as scriptural literalists, who confused external symbols with true inner faith.

Menno and David exchanged sharp writings. These include comments in Menno's *Why I Do Not Cease Teaching and Writing* (1539), *Admonition on Church Discipline* (1541), and a letter of 1542 in which he calls David a "dunghill of a man."[35] Although the first edition of the *Foundation Book* (1539) was aimed principally at those deceived by Bernhard Rothmann and Jan van Leiden, by the time of its major revision in 1558 it had assumed a primarily anti-Davidite front. After David's departure for Basel, the literary battle continued between Menno and his followers and Nikolaas Meyndertsz van Blesdijk, David's most eloquent spokesman and future son-in-law. Menno, Gillis van Aken, Dirk Philips, Leenaert Bouwens, and Adam Pastor also engaged in at least one disputation with Blesdijk, probably at Lübeck in 1546.

In essence, the conflict between David and Menno concerned the nature of faith and the church. David had a spiritualist orientation that allowed a quite radical separation of true faith from an individual's ethics and external religious expression. In contrast, Menno believed that faith in Christ necessarily exhibited itself in a visible church that emphasized discipline and followed the example of Jesus, including believers baptism, nonresistance, nonswearing of oaths, and endurance of suffering to the point of martyrdom. While this view was a continuation of Melchior Hoffmann's emphasis on the gathering of a purified elect for the end times, Menno gave the stress on purification and separation a structural and congregational focus not found in Hoffmann. Following Obbe's earlier lead, Menno replaced the end-time mission with a consciousness of living in a time of grace that had begun with Jesus. The gathered and separated congregation became the locus of the new Jerusalem in the midst of the wicked world.

Menno also sought to locate the separated church in the social order. As had Melchior Hoffmann and Anneken Jans before him, Menno identified with those who suffered from society over against the established church that persecuted them. He was critical of the established churches, pointing out their corruption and calling on the magistrates to protect his suffering but purer church. In this address to the magistrates, Menno did not specifically articulate whether he considered them Christian, but he addressed them as Christians who should protect the pure church. His view was structurally parallel to Schleitheim, which had acknowledged the legitimacy of the civil authorities while pronouncing their sword outside the perfection of Christ. On community of goods, Menno wrote that members of his church shared their money and possessions, but he did not challenge the right of private property as Münsterites had done. And in contrast to Münster, Menno most certainly stressed that Anabaptists refused the sword and were defenseless.[36]

Although they arrived there by differing routes, both the Dutch Anabaptists and the Swiss Brethren had developed quite similar concepts of the church as a separated, suffering, nonresistant minority.[37] However, Menno sought accommodation from the authorities whereas Schleitheim had articulated a more antagonistic relationship with civil authorities.[38] In the post-Münster era, specific options within the Melchiorite tradition had become clear. One was Menno's way of a separatist but engaged minority church. Another was David's withdrawal into an internalized spiritualism.

David's move to Basel in 1544, which left Menno as the most important leader of Dutch Anabaptism, exemplified David's spiritualist orientation. Under the name of Johann van Brugge, he established an identity as a wealthy and respected Reformed refugee. His daughters married into the city's elite. Meanwhile, he continued to correspond with his followers in the Low Countries and to supply them with his mystical and apocalyptic writings. The revised edition of *The Wonder Book*, published in 1551, reveals his spiritualist development, with

Anabaptism receding into the background. In this second edition, he shifted away from his self-conception as third David, identified the third David with the Holy Spirit, "and spiritualized the kingdom of the promised David to mean little more than the community of those who had experienced the rebirth of Christ."[39]

David's true identity became known only after he died of natural causes in 1556. Family members split into factions, one of devoted Davidites and the other consisting of those disillusioned with David. His true identity became public knowledge when the factions quarreled in settling the estate. City and religious leaders then had the body exhumed, burned it along with his books, and made the family vow not to promote his views. Nikolaas van Blesdijk, one of David's traveling emissaries who had followed David to Basel and married his oldest daughter about 1550 or 1551, was one of the disillusioned ones. Following David's death, he cooperated with the state church and developed into an eloquent opponent of David's teaching.

This account of David Joris has focused on his function within Anabaptism and his dispute with Menno Simons, but David's influence lived on, and he was more than merely an opponent of Menno. Through the second half of the sixteenth century, his followers took up the task of defending David and responding to critics. In the 1580s, "several dozen" of his works were reprinted, including the second edition of his *Wonder Book*. As late as the 1620s, the Reformed Synod of the Netherlands worried that followers of David were still reading his works.[40] In the late seventeenth- and early eighteenth-centuries, German Pietists made extensive use of writings by David Joris. For Christian Hoburg (1607–1675), Gottfried Arnold (1666–1714), and Johann Wilhelm Petersen (1649–1726), David's writings provided an important resource. For persons critical of the state church, its external forms, and contentious theological debates, David Joris "modeled an inward religion of the heart that minimized differences of sacrament and confession. Pietists were attracted by the way in which David undermined the learning of orthodox theologians in favor of a church taught directly by God's Spirit."[41]

When Menno exited Witmarsum in 1536, it would be nearly twenty years until he again enjoyed a relatively settled existence. He traveled continually from 1536 to 1543, perhaps with Oldersum as a base, spending most of his time in West Friesland and Groningen, visiting East Friesland once or twice per year, and preaching at night. For the last two years of his work in the Low Countries, he shifted his focus to Amsterdam and the surrounding province of North Holland. From 1544 on, Menno worked primarily in German areas. He spent the years 1544 to 1546 in the area of Cologne and made contact with the Anabaptists in that region. From 1546 until his death in 1561, Menno based his activities in Holstein. The territory he covered, however, extended from northern Germany east of Groningen and all the way to Prussia.

In addition to visits all over the German areas, he was at Goch in 1547 and West Friesland in April 1549. In the summer of 1549 he journeyed at least as far as Prussia and the Vistula Delta to visit Anabaptist refugees from the Low Countries. This extensive travel, along with his writing, spread Menno's name and enabled him to establish a measure of uniformity over the Melchiorite movement, which by midcentury was beginning to be designated by Menno's name.

Finally, in 1554 the nobleman Bartholomew von Ahlefeldt allowed Menno to establish a permanent residence at Wüstenfelde, a village near Oldesloe between Lubeck and Hamburg. Wüstenfelde belonged to Ahlefeldt's estate in Fresenburg, on which he granted exile to Mennonite refugees fleeing persecution. Although controversies within the brotherhood continued to plague the last years of Menno's life, he enjoyed relative physical safety and stability during the seven years at Wüstenfelde until his death on January 31, 1561.

Dirk Philips, who helped to bring Menno Simons into the Melchiorite movement, outlived Menno by some seven years.

Dirk's leadership was both a consolidation and a carrying forward of the direction set by Menno, who since the early 1540s had been the most important leader. As exemplified in his *The Congregation of God*, Dirk developed a view of the church much like that of Menno: a defenseless church modeled on Jesus, which deserved the protection of civil authorities. With this stance Dirk, like Menno, was distancing his version of Melchiorite Anabaptists from the revolutionary radicals of Münster, the spiritualist followers of David Joris, as well as the corrupt churches of Christendom.

In Dirk's view the church, the congregation of God, is joined with Christ in the heavenly Jerusalem, which gives it an identity much larger than the small earthly unity. As the church living in the midst of the world, it is subject to persecution, but it is a witness to the future reign of God lived in the present. This earthly body is a comprehensive society, characterized by baptism of adults, a nonsacramental Lord's Supper, mutual submission, brotherly love, voluntary sharing of property (in contrast to Münster's mandatory community of goods), and obedience to all the teachings of Jesus, including his rejection of the sword. Like Menno, Dirk was seeking to make a place for the separated minority church within the social order, describing a defenseless minority worthy of protection rather than persecution from authorities. Structurally, this church resembles Schleitheim, but with a view to coexistence rather than antagonism with the social order.[42]

Disputes

Additional controversies both inside and outside Anabaptism highlight other aspects of Menno's theology, as well as the increasing role of Dirk Philips. After Anna, widow of the Count Enno, assumed the regency in 1540, relative tolerance came to East Friesland. Under Anna, the Polish-born John à Lasco worked to transform the Reformation in East Friesland into the pattern of the Reformed church. One consequence of the limited toleration of Anna's regency was a series of discussions between the Reformed leaders and the Anabaptist leaders. John debated with followers of David Joris and with Menno Simons, Dirk Philips, and others. The debate with Menno, January 28-31, 1544, in Emden, focused on five points: (1) the incarnation of Christ, (2) infant baptism, (3) original sin, (4) sanctification, and (5) the calling of ministers. Although they reached no agreement on the first, second, and fifth points, Menno reported that he had received friendly treatment and was allowed to leave the city in peace.

Keeping a promise made during the debate, three months later Menno provided John à Lasco with a written statement on the incarnation and the calling of ministers. Menno had not intended the manuscript for public consumption and was quite embarrassed when the ministers of Emden published it without his consent. The same year Menno then published the statement himself, as *Brief Confession on the Incarnation*. This writing clearly shows that Menno held to a version of the celestial flesh of Christ, similar to the belief of Melchior Hoffmann. In this Christology, Jesus brought his flesh with him from heaven, so that the Word became flesh *in* Mary but not *of* Mary. In Menno's analogy, Jesus was nourished in Mary's body without being a product of her flesh in the way that grain is nourished by a field although the grain has to be sown by a sower.[43] As a result of this disputation and the consequent publications, Menno's non-standard view of the incarnation became well known. Ten years later, the celestial-flesh Christology also drew the most attention in another series of discussions and exchange of publications between Menno and Reformed theologian Martin Micron.

Menno had another round of discussions on Christology with Adam Pastor. Menno and Dirk had ordained Pastor, and he stood with them in the disputes with David Joris. However, Pastor objected to Menno's Christology, which in Pastor's view emphasized Jesus's deity at the expense of his humanity. Pastor's own view went to the other extreme. He developed what could be called an anti-trinitarian position, which emphasized the unity and unchangeableness of God with Jesus the human bearer of the Word of God.[44] Menno and Dirk excommunicated Pastor in 1547.

The latter years of Menno's career included a number of conflicts within the churchly community on questions related to church discipline. Important to the leaders was how to establish a church "without spot or wrinkle." Discipline served the purpose of keeping the church pure. A conference at Wismar in 1554 ruled on a number of issues related primarily to church discipline. For example, they decided that one who married outside of the congregation should be excommunicated, but could be reinstated if he or she then continued to lead a godly life. In contrast to the Swiss Brethren, they opted for shunning, and further recommended that shunning be practiced by the spouse of an excommunicated mate.[45]

In the second half of the sixteenth century, the Melchiorite Anabaptists, now Mennonites led by aging Menno Simons and the somewhat younger Dirk Philips and Leenaert Bouwens, experienced a series of schisms. In these conflicts about discipline and the pure church, Menno's younger colleagues generally pushed him toward a more strict position than he desired. The decade of the 1530s had seen upheavals related to the movement's origins; the fifteen-year span to 1555 saw a crystallizing of perspectives and an emerging group consciousness among the scattered congregations.

The Wismar conference in 1554 exemplifies the new era. It made a formal statement on disciplinary matters, to which congregations were expected to conform, thus assuming a sense of identity larger than the congregation. The easing of external threats to Anabaptism after 1555 allowed some weaknesses to surface that were not apparent earlier. The tensions and schisms that resulted often revolved around questions of discipline. Opinions differed, sometimes sharply, about the relationship between the newfound freedom from the Catholic hierarchy and the need to maintain an orderly, distinct congregation.

The first unsolvable crisis relating to discipline had far-reaching effects, including a schism within the Dutch Anabaptist movement and a contribution to breaking off relations between Dutch and South German Anabaptists. When Leenaert Bouwens banned a man in Emden in 1555 for reasons no longer known, Leenaert also insisted that the man's wife should join the congregation in shunning him. When she refused, Leenaert also banned her. Appeals were made and Menno was called upon to mediate. Early in 1557 Menno engaged in some discussions among the primary protagonists in the dispute and agreed to accept the moderate position, that the spouse need not be forced to avoid her husband. However, when the aging Menno proceeded to Harlingen for a meeting that included both Leenaert and Dirk, these two overruled Menno: the ban was pronounced against the woman and those who had supported her.

This series of events signals the passing of leadership to younger men and Menno's increasing isolation in his later years. The dispute also produced the schism that brought the Waterlanders into existence.[46] They adopted the moderate view of discipline and developed into the most liberal of the Dutch Mennonite traditions. Due to their distaste for the apparent rigidity in discipline and intolerance of belief on the part of Menno's faction, they generally refused to be known as Mennonites, preferring the geographic name of Waterlanders, after an area in North Holland.

From this time, the Flemish party considered itself the true Mennonites. Leenaert referred to the Waterlanders as the Drekwagen [dung cart] among the Mennonites, because they accepted those banned by other Mennonite groups and did not require rebaptism of members transferring from other Mennonite groups.

This episode not only brought the Waterlanders into existence; it also helped to precipitate the separation of Dutch and Swiss/South German Anabaptists. In 1555 in Strasbourg, a conference of Dutch and South German Anabaptists tried to deal with the issue of the incarnation, since the Swiss and South Germans could not accept the celestial-flesh Christology held by Menno Simons, Dirk Philips, and other Dutch Anabaptists. The South Germans also expressed concern about the hard position of shunning advocated by the Dutch leaders.

A delegation authorized by this gathering called on Menno at Wüstenfelde in April 1556 to argue for a moderate position on church discipline. In 1557 another conference of representatives from Alsace, Switzerland, and Moravia again urged moderation in the application of shunning.[47] Within two years, however, both Menno and Dirk Philips had published tracts defending the stricter view on marital avoidance, to which the Strasbourg gatherings had objected.[48] In 1560 Menno followed with yet another tract defending marital avoidance, his last tract before his death almost exactly a year later.[49]

The long-term result of these exchanges between the Dutch Mennonites and the South German Anabaptists was that Dirk Philips and Leenaert Bouwens led the way in having the southerners banned and their baptism no longer accepted as valid.[50] Ongoing contact between Dutch and South Germans was lost,[51] to be reestablished in the next century through the efforts of the Dutch to aid the Swiss Brethren refugees in the Low Countries and the Palatinate.

Within a decade of the Waterlander schism occurred the beginning of the long-lasting division between Frisian and Flemish Mennonites. This split had a religious beginning but was fostered by the cultural differences between the two groups. While the northerners had engaged in extensive efforts to aid and resettle the Flemish refugees from the 1540s and 1550s, the two cultural groups had remained distinct. The Frisians had a more reserved personality and preferred simple clothing while enjoying more elaborate household decorations and furnishings. The Flemish, in contrast, had an exuberant and boisterous personality, cared little for household goods, but liked fancy and fashionable clothing.[52]

Two events from 1565 precipitated the division between Frisians and Flemish.[53] About 1560 four Mennonite congregations in Friesland, representing Franeker, Dokkum, Leeuwarden, and Harlingen, had entered a secret pact or covenant among themselves. The covenant called for mutual assistance in settling disputes, administering financial aid, and the calling and assignment of ministers. The pact became public in 1565, when Dirk Philips was called to mediate a dispute that developed when one of the Frisian congregations objected to the calling of Flemish refugee Jeroen Tinnegieter as minister. While Dirk objected to the covenant as an addition to Scripture, he may also have sought to limit the influence of Leenaert Bouwens, to whom Dirk thought he was losing his influence with the group. On his way home, in Emden, Dirk participated in another affair that involved Leenaert. The exact problem is unclear. It may be that Leenaert's congregation thought that he neglected them through his frequent trips to Friesland. In addition, he was accused of being a drunkard and likely did enjoy the hospitality of the Flemish more than the staid Frisian way. In any case, Dirk was one of seven ministers who heard the case in Emden and decided to suspend Leenaert as an elder but not to ban him. Leenaert Bouwens accepted this decision and moved near Harlingen, where he was apparently well received by the Frisians.

Appeals came regarding the decision on Tinnegieter, with Dirk's position augmented by his suspicions concerning Leenaert's involvement in the affair. The division began to harden along personal and cultural lines, and by August 1556 there were mutual bannings by the different groups. An attempt by Dirk to mediate was unsuccessful. Finally, the quarreling groups signed a commitment to accept the decision of a twelve-person arbitration committee. The meeting of reconciliation was to occur on February 1, 1566, in Harlingen. Both parties were required to confess their guilt and to request forgiveness. The Frisians then rose first to their feet. When the Flemish started to stand, they were informed that the Frisians would assist them, since the Flemish bore the greater part of the guilt. The Flemish felt humiliated, and their more volatile tempers flared. They furiously renounced both the arbitration committee and their confession of guilt, and the situation was worse than before.

More attempts at mediation and arbitration by Dirk and others failed. The dispute hardened into two opposing and separate factions, with a rather ironic alignment of groups and leadership. Leenaert Bouwens, accused of a too-free enjoyment of the Flemish way of life, aligned with the Frisians, while the Frisian Dirk Philips was part of the Flemish party and banned by the Frisian party. Dirk spent his last days at Emden, writing a defense of his actions as well as his version of the controversy. He died there shortly after March 7, 1568. Within twenty years each of the two groups would split again, into Old and New Flemish and Old and New Frisians.

Following the death of Dirk Philips, Leenaert Bouwens resumed his function within the community of the church. Leenaert traveled widely during his ministry and kept a careful list of places visited and persons baptized between 1551 and 1582. The record shows 182 places visited, some as many as five times, ranging from Antwerp to Danzig. He baptized a total of 10,386 persons. The period from 1565 to 1568—the years of silence imposed by Dirk Philips—shows no baptisms. After Dirk Philips's death, Leenaert resumed baptizing, adding another 3,509 persons during the last fourteen years of his life.[54]

Consolidation

The fading out of the leadership of Menno Simons finishes this survey of Anabaptist origins in the sixteenth century. We have identified entities that emerged from the period of origins to become long-standing traditions. The Swiss Brethren and the Dutch Anabaptists, who had different origins and developed along somewhat different lines, came to recognize their commonalities and to consider themselves part of the same ongoing movement, and then again moved apart. The Hutterites in Moravia became another ongoing tradition with roots in earliest Anabaptism. South German Anabaptism died out as a distinct movement, although some of its leaders made an impact on other Anabaptist movements, and whatever continued for a time became somewhat an extension of the Swiss Brethren. In each case, we have carried the story far enough to note the passing from the scene of those who originated or placed their enduring imprint on a movement. These include the Swiss Brethren's major figures, most of whom had disappeared by 1529; Jakob Hutter, who entered a troubled movement in Moravia and gave it long-lasting structure and direction in the short years of his leadership, which ended in 1536; Peter Riedemann, who did much to consolidate the Hutterites when relative tolerance allowed communities to reform; Hans Hut and Hans Denck, who died early in the South German movement, and Pilgram Marpeck, who died of natural causes without leaving an institutional legacy; Menno Simons, who left not only a structured brotherhood, but also his name to a majority of those who eventually would claim sixteenth-century Anabaptism as the origin of their religious history; and finally Dirk Philips, who continued and solidified Menno's legacy.

An enabling force in the emergence of all the Anabaptist movements was the long-standing anticlericalism of the sixteenth century. Reading the Bible with lay leaders, baptizing adults, hiring pastors, disciplining members, refusing to approve government service, and rejecting of medieval sacramentalism—all these acts enfranchised laypersons and the common people and rejected the control and authority of the old clergy and hierarchy that the commoners no longer trusted. These efforts at lay control and enfranchisement rejected not only the old Catholic Church but quite soon took aim at the major Reformers as well, when these retained old sacramental forms and placed the Bible in the hands of a new kind of authoritative teacher.

The concerns for lay control of the church joined forces with the protests of the peasants and artisan classes, who felt themselves increasingly oppressed and alienated from their society in the course of the rapid changes taking place in the early-sixteenth century. In the aftermath of the Peasants' Revolt, numbers of these alienated individuals found religious meaning in Anabaptism. In the Low Countries, Anabaptism for a time also became an outlet for the expression of rising Dutch nationalism in its assertion of independence vis-à-vis the imperial court of Charles V. Thus, many Anabaptists came from the ranks of individuals previously involved in various kinds of social and political protests.

Under these common social concerns and practices existed a great deal of theological diversity and differing expressions of the shared convictions. They differed in approaches to the Bible, views of soteriology, and understandings of the basis of adult baptism. Only some of the Dutch of the sixteenth century accepted Menno's view of the incarnation. Swiss and Dutch disagreed on the use of shunning in church discipline. Opinion on the separation of Christians from government varied from belief in the total incompatibility of officeholding with Christian faith (as at Schleitheim), to Menno's acceptance of a Christian magistrate who would refrain from capital punishment. Beyond this, there were as well the early magisterial and mass-church forms of Swiss Anabaptism and the Münsterites' attempt to usher in the kingdom of God with the sword.

In spite of this diversity, however, sixteenth-century Anabaptists did develop—if something well short of a homogeneous theology—at least enough in common that one can follow its legacy through clearly identifiable streams into the twenty-first century. Enough commonality developed that Anabaptists from Switzerland and the Low Countries could meet together and strive for common understandings and support one another in their efforts to obtain toleration.

At the heart of this shared Anabaptist outlook was a new

understanding of the church—a community of adult believers that existed as an alternative, minority society within the dominant society of the world. Since this new church rejected the established church, in both Catholic and the several Protestant versions, Anabaptists frequently suffered for their structure. One entered this new society voluntarily, which made joining an adult act, testified to by adult baptism. The act of an adult thus came to symbolize the identity of the new church and its rejection of the established church. The life and teaching of Jesus and the example of the early church provided the norms for this new society, whose witness to Jesus was a witness to the future reign of God beginning already in the present. Thus, the Bible, particularly the New Testament as the source for the life and teaching of Jesus, became central to the life of the church, which considered itself a restoration of the church of the New Testament. After initial debate, rejection of the sword came to belong virtually by definition to the Anabaptist understanding of the Jesus way. Anabaptism became known as a pacifist movement. Discipline exercised by the brotherhood preserved the integrity of the church's life. This new church rejected the authority of government in ecclesiological affairs and regarded government service by Christians with great suspicion.

The next chapter offers suggestions on the contemporary relevance of this story, with particular attention to implications for Christians and a church committed to Jesus's rejection of the sword.

5

The Meaning of Anabaptism

The previous chapters tell a story. The present chapter undertakes the multifaceted task of finding the Anabaptist story's meaning for the present. Many things flow from this Anabaptist narrative. The following discussion develops the characteristics of Anabaptism as a comprehensive, Christian orientation to the world.

This telling of the Anabaptist story emphasizes distinctions and contrasts rather than commonalities between an Anabaptist perspective and the established churches of Christendom. Readers interested in the profound differences—theological, ethical, and practical—between these two approaches, as well as the rationale for favoring the interpretation based on what is distinct about Anabaptism, should see the essay on historical interpretation in the Appendix (after this chapter).

Living in the Story

For whom is the Anabaptist story relevant? Who may claim the Anabaptist story? Who lives in the Anabaptist story today? The introductory chapter listed several varieties of contemporary Anabaptists to whom I address the story. One obvious category consists of the movements and denominations whose present historical roots can be traced to sixteenth-century Anabaptists. These include all denominations of Mennonites, Amish, and Hutterites, as well as the Brethren in Christ, who originated as a revival movement among Mennonites in the nineteenth century. This category also includes the several Brethren denominations, whose founder, Alexander Mack Jr., combined historic Anabaptism with Pietism. Congregations of these modern Anabaptist denominations include many members who came from other denominations to join the peace church as adults. The Anabaptist story clearly has relevance for these denominations, which trace their historical lineage to the sixteenth century, whether their members are birthright (received by choice) or convinced.

Other individuals and groups retain membership in denominations that belong historically to the established churches of Christendom but identify themselves as Anabaptists. Concerns for peace and nonviolence are frequently an important interest of such individuals and groups. Whether a (loosely) organized group such as the Anabaptist Network in the United Kingdom, or individuals who consider themselves Anabaptists in a variety of denominations or base communities in Latin America—Anabaptists also come in versions that are not lineal or historical descendants of the sixteenth-century movement. This story belongs to them as well; they claim a share in the spiritual heritage.

The themes that characterize Anabaptism are not unique to Anabaptists, and they can exist in a variety of formats and contexts. These themes depict an outlook visible throughout the entire history of Christianity—sometimes as a motif within the dominant church, sometimes gaining expression through a structural alternative to the established church. One can probably locate all Anabaptist principles somewhere within the monastic tradition. The Czech Brethren, the Quakers, the Apostolic Christian Church, the Disciples of Christ, and the Churches of God, as well as Mennonites and Brethren, are particular traditions that tried to structure an alternative church of voluntary believers modeled on Jesus. This motif is visible in the modern Catholic Church and among Anglicans, Methodists,

Baptists, and others. While most of these movements are not causally related, they all reflect a way of being the church identifiable throughout Christian history. In recent times, the way of being Christian that emerges from Anabaptism has been called the "believers church." This term emphasizes the voluntary character of the church: people choose to join as believing adults rather than being born into a church community. Adult versus infant baptism signifies the two differing ecclesiologies—understandings of the church—with their contrasting kinds of entrée.[1]

Neither birthright Anabaptists, such as Mennonites or Brethren, nor those who have embraced the Anabaptist story most recently have a priority of ownership on this story that expresses the idea of the church as a witness to the social order and an outpost of God's reign. In fact, birthright and convinced Anabaptists have something approaching equal standing in this story. If birthright Anabaptists remain in the Anabaptist story, that is a choice made in the context of the possibility of many other choices available in the modern world. That is the same choice made by newcomers to the Anabaptist story, who are quite aware of other choices of faith they could make.

Within that equal footing, birthright and newcomer Anabaptists have differing but complementary tasks, and each faces a temptation. Birthright Anabaptists have a twofold responsibility. They should be keepers of the tradition; they are the ones with the long memory of the stories that comprise the history. And as keepers of the memory, birthright Anabaptists are also the ones best suited to interrogate the tradition, to acknowledge and challenge its failures and weaknesses. The temptation for birthright Anabaptists is to take the history for granted, to allow it to be forgotten and abandoned as unimportant. As a complement to these efforts, the task of newcomers may be to act as publicists for the tradition they have joined. As newcomers who were not part of the earlier story, they can talk enthusiastically, even proudly, about the history they have joined in ways that birthright members cannot. Thus, newcomers can assist birthright Anabaptists to renew appreciation for the tradition. The temptation of newcomers may be to overvalorize the tradition they have chosen to join, to overlook problems, and not to think critically enough about it. Here is where the interrogation of the tradition by birthright Anabaptists serves the newcomers. Birthright and newcomer Anabaptists each have necessary roles in the movement; neither has priority over the other.

Birthright and newcomers to Anabaptism are on an equal footing in another sense as well. The story of the previous chapters depicted a number of social factors that led individuals in the sixteenth century to leave the established churches and join Anabaptism. The Peasants' War, for example, was a result of economic and political injustices of their society. Many of these people subsequently found religious expressions for these concerns in Anabaptism, where understandings of Jesus and of the New Testament gave theological foundation to this choice. Similarly in the present time, a variety of social factors have brought persons to become disillusioned with Christendom and the churches that identify with European or North American society—the exploitative economic system, the proclivity to violence and war, and much more. This disillusionment has led to separations or to development of new loyalties within some version of Anabaptism, loyalties that again are given theological justification through understandings of Jesus and the New Testament. Whether in the sixteenth century or the beginning of the twenty-first century, the result is Christians who understand the church as an alternative society and a witness to the surrounding social order. Anabaptism or the Anabaptist story is not the exclusive possession of a limited historical tradition. It is a Jesus-focused and Jesus-dominated expression of Christianity. Its version of Christian practice makes the Christology of the Gospels into the primary Christian identifier. It is a Christian practice in which every Christian has a birthright and which potentially every Christian can embrace.

The fact that the United States and Canada have no state or established church can lead to confusion about the true significance of Anabaptist or believers church ecclesiology. With no state or established church in North America, nearly every church and denomination is in a sense a voluntary church, a believers church. Even in denominations that baptize infants, a choice is still required in order to remain since it is always possible to choose to switch denominations or to drop out altogether. However, though these denominations are voluntary, it is also possible to say that nearly every church in North America—at least in the United States—has bought deeply into the ethos of civil religion. Such churches have taken on the real but unofficial role of a state church, a voluntary version of support for and identification with the official society and its civil religion. In contrast, the importance of Anabaptist ecclesiology is to pose the church as a countersociety to the ethos of a national society. Whether to baptize infants or adults is still a theological discussion of import, but as following sections will demonstrate, Anabaptist ecclesiology involves more than adult baptism and voluntary faith.

Multiple Visions

Beginning in the early 1970s, scholarship has underscored complexity and pluralism in the story of Anabaptist origins. The first chapters of this book reflect that complexity. Historians and theologians have also offered several suggestions about the meaning of Anabaptism for the contemporary church, whether for birthright or newcomer Anabaptists.

Well known is Harold S. Bender's synthesis "The Anabaptist Vision," which he originally presented as the presidential address to the American Society of Church History in December 1943.[2] Many of its salient points are found in previously published works of his friend and colleague Robert Friedmann.[3] Further differentiation in the description of Anabaptism came from Mennonite scholars such as Friedmann, Cornelius Krahn, or challenges from without like those of Hans Hillerbrand.[4]

The "vision" actually existed in more than one version in the middle third of the twentieth century, with each version intending to describe Anabaptism and apply it to the present. Although there is some overlap between these interpretations, they were identifiably different perspectives and indicate something of the interpretative possibilities that have always existed within Anabaptism.

There was Harold Bender's normative Anabaptism characterized by the three principles: (1) "the essence of Christianity as discipleship" to Jesus; (2) a resulting new concept of the church marked by voluntary adult membership, separation from the world, suffering, and the "practice of true brotherhood and love among members"; and (3) "love and nonresistance" in "all human relationships." This view interpreted Anabaptists as the most consistent Protestants—those who completed the Reformation begun by Martin Luther and Ulrich Zwingli.[5] Writings of John C. Wenger, who popularized the idea of Anabaptists completing the Reformation, and much Mennonite denominational literature have reflected Bender's perspective. His understanding of Anabaptist origins became virtually the standard view among church historians, at least through the decade of the 1960s and into the early 1970s.

C. Henry Smith posed another version of Anabaptism. Smith characterized Anabaptists as individualistic progenitors of such modern ideas as separation of church and state, freedom of conscience, and tolerance and openness in matters of religion.[6] A number of General Conference Mennonite writers have continued this interpretation.

Finally, a third view envisioned Anabaptism as a countercultural community posing itself as a prophetic alternative to the existing social order. This view shows a willingness to generalize from Anabaptist principles to other issues, as in arguing today that opposition to violence demands a reform of the

American penal and judicial system. The Concern Movement,[7] which produced the pamphlet series of the same name, and *The Politics of Jesus* and other writings of John H. Yoder have given visibility to this perspective. In one essay, Yoder identified the center of an Anabaptist commitment, not held in this fashion by any major denominational heritage, as "liberation from the dominion of Mars," or the supposed necessity of war; "liberation from the dominion of Mammon," or slavery to wealth; and "liberation from the dominion of myself," or the freedom to find the true self in "the rule of God and his righteousness."[8]

An important characteristic of Harold Bender's description of Anabaptist origins was the claim that Anabaptism had its origin in the circle of Conrad Grebel in Zurich. Swiss Anabaptism was the source of all subsequent authentic or evangelical Anabaptist movements, linked in an "unbroken course" from "Switzerland, South Germany, Austria, and Holland throughout the sixteenth century . . . [that] has continued until the present day in the Mennonite movement."[9] By establishing a supposed unbroken line from Grebel to the twentieth century of a uniformly pacifist Anabaptism, Bender was challenging the view of Anabaptist origins that had prevailed from Martin Luther well into the twentieth century, that Anabaptism was a violent movement that originated with Thomas Müntzer and reached its logical culmination at the Münster debacle.

Bender's view of a uniform Anabaptism with a single point of origin in Zurich, Switzerland, was challenged and rejected in the 1970s. The image of a single point of origin for a homogeneous movement, which made Swiss Anabaptism the normative form of the movement, was replaced by a scholarly perspective that described multiple, separate points of origin and a diverse, pluralistic movement, specifically including Anabaptists who were not pacifists. The new image was nicknamed "polygenesis," a term in the title of the article that first called widespread attention to the developing perspective of a diverse Anabaptism.[10] Polygenesis provided a number of interpretative possibilities, including the contention that the contemporary peace church should be less concerned about nonviolence since the sixteenth-century origins displayed Anabaptists as less than consistently pacifist. The first edition of *Becoming Anabaptist* fully embraced a polygenesis perspective, but it had the specific purpose of countering any arguments that diversity and pluralism among sixteenth-century Anabaptists validated or rationalized contemporary pluralism,[11] particularly with respect to views of the sword.

In the decade of the 1990s several efforts arose that intended to move beyond polygenesis—to find some unifying elements in Anabaptism but without rejecting or denying the diversity described by polygenesis. These efforts identified some historical links between Anabaptist movements, or described a commonality present amid the diversity of sixteenth-century Anabaptism. The work of James Stayer and Werner Packull described historical links between Swiss Anabaptists and Anabaptism in South Germany and Moravia. These links included the Swiss Congregational Order that subsequently became operative for Anabaptists in Moravia, as well as a number of individuals from the Swiss Anabaptist story who played significant later roles among Anabaptists in Moravia. The narrative in chapters 2 and 3 incorporated these findings. This data leaves intact the diversity of early Anabaptism and yet does provide links that give some historical priority to Swiss Anabaptism.

A second effort to go beyond polygenesis is Abraham Friesen's argument that Erasmus was the intellectual father of both Swiss Anabaptism and significant elements of Dutch Anabaptism. Friesen has pointed out that Erasmus was alone among Catholic and Reformation writers in believing that the specific order in Matthew 28:19 of teaching or making disciples followed by baptism described apostolic practice in Acts. The circle of Conrad Grebel accepted and followed Erasmus's interpretation, Friesen argued, when they found it in his paraphrase and his *Annotations* that accompanied his Greek

New Testament. Friesen also suggested that the interpretation of Erasmus could have influenced Menno Simons. Friesen's argument about Erasmus would establish a point of intellectual origin for some portions of Anabaptism without denying the diversity described by polygenesis scholarship.[12] These arguments that identify links and commonality within the diversity of Anabaptist movements were integrated into the narrative of chapters 2 and 4.

A different kind of suggestion for getting beyond polygenesis comes from Arnold Snyder. He asserted that in spite of the diversity described by polygenesis scholarship, Anabaptism was indeed one movement as characterized by a theology common to all Anabaptist groups. Based on supposedly neutral historical observation, this theology found to be common to all Anabaptist groups has three layers: a foundation consisting of doctrines shared with all Christians, contained in the classic creeds of Christendom; a second layer consisting of doctrines held in common with classic, Reformation Protestantism, such as justification by faith; and a final layer that contains beliefs unique to Anabaptists, such as an ecclesiology that rejects the state church.[13] The appendix on historical interpretation following this chapter provides a number of reasons why I do not accept this theological definition of Anabaptism and its attempt to find one Anabaptist movement after polygenesis.

In light of this description of alternative understandings of Anabaptism, does it matter which of these interpretations one chooses? And how does one live in or find relevance in the Anabaptist story? The following discussion outlines an approach to these questions and suggests some answers and avenues for further discussion about the contemporary relevance of Anabaptism.

Characteristics of Anabaptism

To write history is to tell a story. The story in chapters 2 through 4 describes the origin and development of several distinct but interrelated sixteenth-century Anabaptist movements. What elements did I choose to emphasize from this story? I answer in a single sentence: This narrative tells the story of what for the sixteenth-century was a new way to be the church within a particular sociopolitical context. In turn, that narrative inspires contemporary efforts to embody this way of being the church in particular contemporary contexts. Although descriptions of this way of being the church have varied considerably for both sixteenth-century and contemporary versions, they almost always have included some form of the following characteristics.

Interrelated themes describe this church. The new model emerged when Christians decided to follow Jesus as their authority for ethics—in *discipleship*—and particularly for issues related to baptism, economics, and the sword. Since choosing to follow Jesus as a norm was a decision made by an adult, this church was a *voluntary community*; its members chose to leave the established or state church. The new church positioned itself as an alternative society both to the social order with its government exercising authority in religious affairs, and to the established church, which depended on the government for support and pretended to encompass all of that society. Thus, Anabaptism was a reform movement that rejected the state church—the action that earned it so much grief. However, more than rejection of a state or established church, Anabaptism also rejected the idea of a "Christian society," or a professed belief that the cause of God's reign is identified with a particular nationality or social order. Discipleship—Jesus as ethical authority—received a specific application in the *rejection of violence and the sword*—although quite obviously not all sixteenth-century Anabaptists rejected the sword. The voluntary community founded on discipleship to Jesus is perforce a peace church that rejects the sword of war—as Jesus did. In theological terms, this church lives as an outpost of God's reign in the world, which has not yet come to acknowledge the rule of God.

Additional ideas and practices are derived from or closely

related to these three characteristics. The idea of *separation* from the disobedience of the world, a clear distinction between church and world, constitutes a stance from which to engage the world. The practice of *church discipline* maintains the distinction between church and world. *Mission* or the acquisition of new members happens when the church goes about its task of being the church whose practices and relationships witness to God's reign in history. The church as a voluntary community means *freedom of conscience* and requires recognition that faith cannot be coerced. The various forms of sharing, mutual aid, and *community of goods* all give expression to the church as a community.

Rejection of oaths and *refusal to hold public office* testify that allegiance to the reign of God takes precedence over earthly loyalties. *Baptism of adults* was the religious ritual that marked and constituted the church as a voluntary community independent of control by civil authorities. *Absence of a hierarchy* in the church reflected the emphasis on the enfranchisement of the lay and common people, and it went with the emphasis on community and concern for all members, expressed in the several forms of community of goods. All Anabaptists rejected the Catholic, Lutheran, and Calvinist ideas on the bodily presence of Jesus in the communion bread and wine; they adopted *symbolic views of the Lord's Supper* similar to and derived from leaders like Karlstadt, Zwingli, and the sacramentarians.

All Anabaptists appealed to the Bible as the source of these beliefs and saw themselves as working to restore New Testament Christianity. However, the entire Reformation asserted the authority of the Bible as a counterweight to the Roman church's assertions of the authority of the pope and tradition. Thus, taking the Bible seriously or emphasizing the authority of the Bible cannot in themselves be singled out as characteristics unique to Anabaptists. They did, however, develop a distinctive way to emphasize the Bible that differed in two ways from both the medieval church and the Magisterial

Reformers. The Reformers tended to retain the right of interpretation for the authoritative teachers, and Catholicism retained an authoritative teaching tradition; on the other hand, Anabaptists put the Bible in the hands of laypersons and involved every member in interpretation, making the believing community of voluntary members the locus of interpretation. Further, the assumption of the normative value of the teaching and example of Jesus and also of the early church gave a priority to the New Testament, and particularly to the narratives about Jesus over other parts of Scripture. Anabaptists thus developed a kind of canon within the canon,[14] and they read the Bible not as a flat series of propositions and timeless allegories, but with a sense of direction and development from Old Testament to New Testament. Hence, there developed what later interpreters could call a *hermeneutics of obedience*,[15] the idea that biblical interpretation resulted from the commitment to read the Bible with a view to discovering how to live in its story, and in particular, to live in the life of Jesus.

This approach to the Bible is far from a mere starting over or ignoring of history. In fact, it must take history very seriously in order to discover and correct deviation from the gospel, which begins with the story of Jesus. Appealing to authoritative tradition, as opponents of Anabaptism were wont to do, actually denies the possibility of correction, while correction can happen when Anabaptists read the Scripture again in the community that empowers every member. The Anabaptist approach holds open the possibility for new light from God as the community reads the Bible with a view to expressing the good news of Jesus in their current context.[16]

Anabaptism as described here did not arrive on the sixteenth-century stage as a whole entity after a few folks in Zurich or South Germany or the Netherlands simply read the Bible. Whether through efforts to reform baptism in Zwingli's Zurich or disillusionment with the Peasants' War in South Germany or Menno's contacts with sacramentarians and Münsterites in the

Netherlands—the radicals who became Anabaptists did not set out with separation from the established church as a formative principle. Their initial efforts at reform intended to challenge and revise the prevailing structure. It was by trial and error that the radicals arrived at the idea of a separated church guided by the narratives of Jesus, which stood as an alternative to existing structures. Whether it concerned Karlstadt in Wittenberg and Orlamünde, or the radicals in Zurich or Waldshut or in South Germany and Moravia, or Melchior Hoffmann in Livonia and the Low Countries—the reform efforts of the radicals began with roles in the existing established churches. While biblicism and the intent to follow Jesus may have supplied impulses that differed from the Magisterial Protestants, it was opposition and persecution that forced the radicals outside the established church and helped to instill a sense of separation. Such things as opposition to the tithe demonstrate a clear social component in their earliest goals for reform.

When they failed to remake the established church along the lines of their vision of a more just society, that social component received expression through the structure of an alternative society, outside of or separated from both established ecclesiological and political structures. This process moved at varying rates of speed for the several groups. For example, reaching the idea of a separated church came much more rapidly for the Swiss Brethren at Schleitheim than it did for Menno Simons, who took up the task of reshaping the Melchiorite movement only after years of doubts about the Catholic Church in which he worked.

This picture of Anabaptism is a description of a way of being the church more than it is a list of principles. Removing one item from a list still leaves most of the list. Omitting a characteristic of the movement, on the other hand, markedly changes the character of the movement. Nonetheless, some characteristics are derivative of or dependent upon other themes, and one principle above all gives meaning to this story.

The characteristic that gives meaning to all others is the commitment (or profession of faith) to Jesus's life and teaching as the authoritative source of truth. The will of God is revealed in the particular humanity of Jesus, which forms the baseline against which Christians evaluate their own activity. From following the supposed words of Jesus in Matthew 28:19, which place teaching before baptism, to accepting Jesus's teaching against the sword, Anabaptists from Grebel to Sattler, to Marpeck and Hutter, to Menno and Dirk—all committed themselves to the normativeness of Jesus in some fashion. This commitment and belief was given prime visibility in "The Anabaptist Vision," when Harold Bender wrote that "fundamental" to the vision was the idea of "the essence of Christianity as Discipleship."[17] The idea of the normativeness of Jesus undergirds John Howard Yoder's *Politics of Jesus* and his description of the multiple ways that standard Christian ethics has claimed that Jesus is not the norm for ethics.[18] Elsewhere, Yoder gave "follow[ing] the risen Jesus" as the basis for Anabaptist liberation from "Mars," "Mammon," "myself" and other characteristics of the contemporary world.[19]

Second, if most of the social order does not have this particular commitment to Jesus as authoritative ethical source, it follows almost as a matter of course that the church accepting Jesus as that source will produce a new social reality: a new community visibly different from the society in which it lives. To follow Jesus involves a new way of life, which expresses itself in redeemed attitudes and relationships among people both within and without the church. This communal or social orientation does not deny individuality or the personal nature of one's faith, but it does mean that the individual's faith attains its fullness in terms of the *believing community*. Thus, Harold Bender's second characteristic of the "Anabaptist Vision" was that "newness of life and applied Christianity" had created "a new concept of the church." John Howard Yoder expressed this concept of the church in terms of "liberation from the dominion of the mass." The "Christian community is not Christendom. . . . It is the visible congregation of those who knowingly gather around the name, the teachings, and the memories of Jesus."[20] Baptism is what incorporates an individual into this body of Christ.

Third, if the particular story of Jesus is a norm for behavior, then peace and the *rejection of violence* also as a matter of course follow as a particular manifestation of discipleship or of following the example of Jesus. Jesus' specific rejection of the violent option of the Zealots through his nonviolent confrontation of evil belongs in a central way to the nature of God's reign as revealed in Jesus's life and teaching. Harold Bender's "Anabaptist Vision" expressed this idea as "nonresistance in all things." John Howard Yoder spoke of "liberation from the dominion of Mars."[21]

These central convictions of Jesus as ethical norm, the church as a witness to the social order, and the inherently peaceful nature of the community of Jesus's followers, as well as the convictions or principles derived from them—these are more than a list of propositions or a creed or confession of faith to which Anabaptists give assent. Living in a story shaped by these convictions is different from assenting to the principles as parts of a creed. These convictions function together to structure a way of life, an alternative society, a way of living in the world that begins by accepting Jesus as Lord and the New Testament as the authoritative repository of writings on the life and teaching of Jesus. They describe an outlook that collapses if any of its three elements is removed. These convictions deal with the relationships between people, so that the church truly is a new society and is authenticated by the way it lives as much as by what it believes. To live in the Anabaptist story means to put oneself inside this ongoing narrative and to embody its convictions—to stand where they stood or to put oneself in their social context—so that they shape the way one lives. For an analogy, a baseball player does much more than assent to the rules of the game and agree that they are true. To be a baseball player means to put oneself inside the rules both formal and informal, so that these rules shape the actions and activity of that baseball player. Even when the ballplayer makes errors and transgresses the rules, it is still obvious that he is playing baseball and not ice hockey, although both sports employ wooden sticks.

This description of an Anabaptist outlook does not describe a program to be imitated or transplanted. The Anabaptist tradition has a number of manifestations and expressions, as briefly pointed out in previous sections as well as in the historical chapters. Each has significance as a particular manifestation of the Anabaptist, believers church. Yet, none of these expressions can be canonized as an absolutized or normative form. Making one normative would imply that we already know that past forms and past answers also have the necessary capacity to answer for all new questions. If we only emulate past models, then the past becomes the future.

Telling the story enables one to see that the story is comprised of choices at every juncture. As a matter of fact, the characters involved could have made other choices, and the story could have unrolled differently. How might the face of Anabaptism in Zurich have been different, for example, if leader Conrad Grebel had decided to work within Zwingli's Reformation or had maintained his scholarship and not returned to Zurich? Or how would it have differed if Zwingli had been more willing to accommodate the youthful impatience of his younger, more-radical colleagues? Would the Hutterite form of community of goods have developed if some anonymous Anabaptist had not carried the Swiss Congregational Order to Moravia? How would Dutch Anabaptism have developed if Menno Simons had stayed and preached reform from within the Catholic Church, as he did for the first months after embracing his new theology, or if the authorities had managed to catch Menno when a price was first put on his head and before he had surpassed David Joris as leader? Such "what if" questions and the decisions and historical options they point to provide an additional indication of why mere imitation is not an adequate motif. The idea of imitation reifies past choices and circumstances. In fact, the past was not foreordained. Seeing these past options and choices helps us see the real options and choices that face Christians and the church today.[22] By exposing these choices and historical options, retelling the story actually frees us from historical determinism and enables us to see a future that is other than or more than the past.

But what is it that guides these new choices and decisions? What makes them decisions that are faithful to Anabaptism, and more important, faithful to the reign of God? Here is where I return to the Anabaptist conviction about Jesus's teaching and example as the authoritative source for the Christian life. In the decisions and choices that are made, there is a continual looping back to the narrative of Jesus and asking again, in the new situation in which we find ourselves, how this narrative will shape our understanding and our actions in this new context.[23] This looping back to Jesus is what Anabaptists in Zurich were doing when they asked about baptism in light of Jesus's teaching and the apostles' practice. Their answer resulted in a new form of church in the sixteenth century.

This process of looping back is never finished; it should occur with every new situation. We are always thinking through again how to live out of the story of Jesus as it addresses the new situation in which we find ourselves.

This appeal to the story of Jesus is not a wooden imitation or literal copying of Jesus, any more than we simply imitate sixteenth-century Anabaptists. John Howard Yoder showed that this process of thinking out of the narrative of Jesus in new and different contexts had already begun in the New Testament. Yoder described how New Testament writers took the narrative of Jesus into five new and different cultural settings and cosmologies. In each of those new settings, the writer used images from the new culture in order to show how Jesus, who was identified by the story, transcended the culture into which the story was taken. The result is five different christological expressions of Jesus already in the New Testament, each of which proclaims Jesus's identity with both the heavenly realm and with human flesh as the basis of his saving work.[24] It is this process of thinking again about the meaning of Jesus that occurs within Anabaptism and that expresses in briefest form what it means to live in the Anabaptist story today. It is why one can say that those who identify with Anabaptism are always becoming Anabaptist.

The idea of looping back allows an Anabaptist outlook to adapt to its inevitably changing environment, to make use of new forms and modern technology and newly developed scholarly tools in the process of continuing renewal. Since the recovery or restitution is never completed, one cannot freeze the formulations and practices of one particular epoch as the definitive ones for recovery or preservation, as though all following novel developments were of necessity misguided or to be rejected. In effect, an attempt to freeze formulations and practices creates a postbiblical canon. While new technology or novel ways of looking at theology or the church can and have led the church astray, the new is not inherently wrong just because it is new. Using the criteria of Jesus, the New Testament, and the earlier tradition, the novel is to be evaluated, adopted, adapted, or rejected as a part of the process of restitution.

The continuing nature of looping back to Jesus allows the church to change its mind about innovations without abandoning the criteria from within history and the New Testament. As a college student in the late 1950s in the midst of the Civil Rights Movement, I was firmly committed to Christian nonviolence as it was commonly understood within the Mennonite tradition. The operative concept was "nonresistance," based on the injunction to "resist not evil" in Matthew 5:39 (KJV). It was believed that if properly applied, the verse meant that the nonresistant Christian should offer no resistance of any kind to evil. From that perspective, marches for civil rights, demonstrations, and lunch-counter sit-ins constituted resistance to evil—even when Martin Luther King Jr. professed faith in nonviolence as a Christian, and when I recognized the injustice of the discrimination that African-Americans experienced in the United States. Even when racial discrimination was sinful and wrong, Christian nonresistance would require King and other African-Americans not to resist discrimination, I believed, rather than to resist it with acts like marches and sit-ins. Hence, at that time I did not support the movement, and I was shocked when one of my college professors, who was as committed to the peace tradition of the Mennonite Church as I, supported and participated in the marches and sit-ins of the civil rights struggle. But that professor's challenge also became the first stage in my learning that a commitment to the nonviolence of Jesus could be expressed in more than one way. I learned that I could change my mind—repent of complicity with racism in refusing to support the civil rights struggle—and become an advocate and participant in active work for peace and justice without giving up a commitment to the nonviolence of Jesus.[25]

If change is not inherently wrong, neither is the new—progress and change—inherently good. Clearly a change can result in abandonment or selling out of the foundational ideas or orientation. Change can take unfaithful as well as faithful directions. One of the potentially innumerable examples comes from John Howard Yoder, who used the development of the idea of a justifiable war as an example of unfaithful change. The new stance, Yoder writes, "rejects the norm of the cross and the life of Jesus Christ as the way of dealing with conflict." It "assigns to civil government . . . a role in carrying out God's will that is quite incompatible with the fruit of the progressive relativization of kingship from Samuel to Jeremiah to Jesus and Jochanan ben Zakkai."[26]

Some Contemporary Conversations

The Anabaptist perspective just sketched has the potential to impact every area of life and thought. It is a thoroughgoing orientation to the world, shaped by the narrative of Jesus in a way that makes visible Jesus's rejection of the sword. This section further develops an Anabaptist perspective with reference to contemporary issues and scholarship. The first three sections feature discipleship, ecclesiology, and nonviolence as highlighted above; yet the lines between such concepts are fluid. To discuss the nature of the church is to describe how peace and nonviolence are made visible in the world, expressing what it means to live in and live out of the story of Jesus. This discussion is then also an example of the ongoing discussion about how Christians live in a way that is always a "looping back to Jesus."

Following: Jesus as Authority

The idea of discipleship—following Jesus's life and teaching as authority for Christian behavior—identifies a reference point for ethics that is outside the individual and beyond the immediate context. It is also a reference point potentially accessible to anyone. Few knowledgeable people—scholars or otherwise—doubt that an individual called Jesus of Nazareth actually lived at one time on earth. A general historical consensus exists as to the major events in the outline of Jesus's life, including his rejection of violence. At least there is a consensus on what the New Testament identifies as the major events, even though interpretations of the story's meaning may vary.

In his classic book *The Politics of Jesus* (1972), John Howard Yoder addresses a prevailing assumption in Christian ethics, that Jesus was not relevant for ethics. Most of the efforts of what has passed for Christian ethics have been to rationalize why Christians could not or should not accept Jesus as the norm or model for behavior. In the first edition, Yoder listed six ways of discounting Jesus: (1) Jesus's teaching does not apply now because it was "an ethic for an 'Interim,' which Jesus thought would be very brief." (2) Jesus was a "simple rural figure," whose teaching does not address the complexities of modern society. (3) Jesus and his followers "lived in a world over which they had no control," which means that his teaching does not apply to the modern setting when Christians do have responsibility for the structures of society. (4) Jesus's message was "ahistorical," dealing "with spiritual and not social matters." (5) Jesus was a "radical monotheist," who pointed people away from "local and finite values" and toward the sovereign God, whom they worshipped. (6) Jesus's mission was not to teach ethics but to make atonement for sins and restore fellowship with God as "a gracious gift." In the second edition of this work (1994), Yoder expands the list. In response to the presumed irrelevance of Jesus for ethics, *The Politics of Jesus* poses a counterhypothesis, "that the ministry and claims of Jesus are best understood as presenting to hearers and readers not the avoidance of political options, but one particular social-political-ethical option."[27] My application of the story of Jesus works out of that hypothesis although I do not follow Yoder in every instance.

The career of Jesus as told in the Gospels displays an activist mission whose purpose was to make God's rule visible. Jesus let his disciples pluck grain on the Sabbath (Luke 6:1-5), healed on the Sabbath (Luke 6:6-11; 13:10-17), traveled through Samaria and interacted with a Samaritan woman (John 4:1-30), freed the woman caught in adultery rather than letting her be stoned (John 8:1-11), disputed with the Pharisees, cleansed the temple (Luke 19:45-47), and more. With such actions, Jesus confronted the purity code taught by the religious leadership. Jesus also sent out the twelve (Luke 9:1-7) and then the seventy (Luke 10:1-17) to "proclaim the kingdom of God" (9:2) and to preach that "the kingdom of God has come near to you" (10:9). The reign of God was near because in his person Jesus made that reign present. His teaching, such as the Sermon on the Mount (Matt 5-7), showed what the reign of God looked like for those who would live it.

The opening of Jesus's public ministry had a strong social

component, shown as he quoted Isaiah 61:1-2:

> The Spirit of the Lord is upon me,
>> because he has anointed me
>> to bring good news to the poor.
> He has sent me to proclaim release to the captives
>> and recovery of sight to the blind,
>> to let the oppressed go free,
>> to proclaim the year of the Lord's favor (Luke 4:18-19).

Jesus went out of his way to minister to outcasts like lepers and prostitutes. He paid attention to widows, orphans, and strangers—those without representation in the patriarchal society of first-century Palestine.

These acts and this teaching of Jesus show that God's reign identifies with the powerless, those without advocates in a given society. Some contemporary parallels might include illegal aliens in the United States, victims of AIDS around the world, Palestinian refugees, and any number of other peoples and groups who experience injustice around the world.

But as important as who Jesus identified with is *how* he identified with them. Those who would follow Jesus adopt his way of being on the side of the victims. Equally important as the fact that he confronted injustices is *how* he confronted them. Jesus's way of confronting injustice and uplifting the poor rejected violence as a way to alleviate suffering. Nonviolent resistance to evil characterized Jesus's life and his way of confronting evil. Nonviolence belonged to the heart of his message about God's reign.

The sayings of the Sermon on the Mount about turning the other cheek, giving the coat with the cloak, and going the second mile—all these are resistance tactics that individuals living in economic exploitation or under military occupation by the Romans could use nonviolently to turn the tables on the oppressors. To hit the right cheek, as specified in Matthew 5:39, an aggressor has to use a backhand. In the mores of that time, the left hand was considered unclean and would not be used in public. The right-handed, backhanded slap was an insult directed at a supposed inferior, as husband to wife, or man to woman, or Roman to Jew. Retaliation by the one being struck would give legal justification for punishment. Jesus suggested that instead of retaliating, the one struck should turn the other cheek. Turning the left check was not only a refusal to cower under the insult; it also denied the power to insult. It left the aggressor with a target that could not be reached by another backhand; the turned left cheek can be hit only by the closed right fist. But striking the inferior with a closed fist makes him or her the equal of the aggressor, which denies the point of the insult. "In that world of honor and shaming, [the aggressor] has been rendered impotent to instill shame in a subordinate." Following Jesus's injunction not to retaliate in kind would thus lead to the socially inferior person gaining the upper hand.

The cloak-and-coat scene comes from debtors court, in a situation where wealthy landowners held unjust, usurious liens against poor tenant farmers, who were perpetually in debt. The poor debtor had only the coat on his back to give as security for his loan. He must appear in court each day the debt is not paid and surrender the coat for security, but he may retrieve it again in the evening to ward off the cold during the night. In that culture, the shame of nakedness fell not on the naked man, but on the one who caused the nakedness. Jesus's counsel was that the next time the debtor went to court, he should strip off his undergarment along with the coat that he surrendered for security, and walk around naked all day to give witness to the unjust system that caused his nakedness.

Going the second mile was a response to Roman military rules. A soldier could demand that a member of the local populace carry the soldier's heavy pack. But the Romans were relatively enlightened occupiers. To prevent undue hardship on any one person impressed into service, the rule banned the soldier from coercing more than one mile out of any commoner.

In that context, Jesus suggested that when commandeered to carry a pack, the commoner should carry it a second mile. Once into that second mile, the commoner has put the soldier into the awkward position of breaking his own regulations and eventually may bring him to beg the commoner not to carry the pack. All three of these commands from Jesus are suggestions by which a person in the disadvantaged position could turn the tables and gain the upper hand against a supposed social superior, yet without using violence.[28]

Integral to these resistance strategies of Jesus was the command "Do not resist an evildoer" (Matt 5:39). Walter Wink shows that the meaning of the text is not to resist violently: "Do not mirror evil. . . . Do not react violently to evil, do not counter evil in kind, do not let evil dictate the terms of your opposition."[29] The tactics of turning the other cheek, giving the cloak with the coat, and going the second mile are ways to resist evil without mirroring it. Jesus prescribed resistance tactics, but those tactics that did not employ violence. Wink also observes that the resistance tactics Jesus suggested can be used vindictively. Hence, it is important to maintain their connection to the command "Love your enemies" in Matthew 5:44.

Jesus's life and his teaching are visible, particular manifestations of God's reign in human history. His witness to the reign of God and his calling disciples and teaching them to live according to that reign—both show that the people of God may live and witness without being in charge of the social order through government, and without exercising violence. The following section on ecclesiology locates the roots of a life-without-being-in-charge in Israel before the Babylonian exile, which means that Jesus already stood in a long tradition. This image of the community of God's people disappeared during the third to fifth centuries, when the church ceased being a minority movement and became established. It was this image of the community of God's people that Anabaptists again made visibile in the sixteenth century.

Gerald Biesecker-Mast uses the term "performance" to describe discipleship. Performance emphasizes the "bodily, material character of our witness . . . and the roles we play in the drama of God's redemption story." Thus, being a disciple—living in the story of Jesus—is a living out of the verbal or textual witness of Jesus, a "performance of words as deeds." And as the actions of the disciple witness to Jesus, it becomes a "performance of deeds as words."[30] Discipleship as performance is conveyed in the full title of *Martyrs Mirror*, which begins *The Bloody Theater or Martyrs Mirror of the Defenseless Christians*. Anabaptist martyrs used their deaths as public witness—a theater spectacle—to their faith. A martyrs death gave opportunity for a public witness that "there are commitments worth having that are greater than life itself, and to recognize the triumph of stubborn defenselessness over brute force."[31]

Professing Jesus as the standard for behavior—committing oneself to "perform" as a disciple of Jesus—does not provide immediate answers for all problems. The Anabaptist claim to make Jesus the authority for belief and practice indicates an orientation and a commitment, but it does not provide specific answers to all new questions in a changing world. It does indicate what Jesus's followers ought not do—willingly engage in violence. And it does provide an orientation from which to engage new problems as one "loops back" to Jesus. That looking back to Jesus to discern how to actualize and embody his life and teaching in the contemporary setting produces the church that is a witness to the world of the presence of God's reign.

Gathering: A New Society

The Anabaptist narrative describes the development of the church as new society, independent of civil authorities. It is a church that functions without claiming to be or needing to be in charge of the social order. What gives shape and meaning to this image of the church is the story of Jesus. As developed in this book, Anabaptist ecclesiology embodies that social-political-ethical teaching of Jesus. It describes a churchly movement that is made visible by the behavior of its members. Jesus's teachings that the poor and outcasts have value in the reign of God, his teachings about economics, his challenge to unjust conditions as described in the previous section—these all show that the church involves relationships among people. This Jesus movement is visible in the New Testament. When the church gradually lost the sense of being the minority around Jesus and became established in the third through the fifth centuries, elements within the established church continued the impulses of Jesus. Examples include the monastic movement as well as dissident groups such as the followers of Peter Waldo.

Jesus did not invent this churchly movement that functions independent of established authorities and lives as a witness to God's reign in the social order. This setting already began in the Old Testament when Israel was carried into exile in Babylon. Exile was a defining moment in understanding what it meant to be the people of God. Exile meant that Israelites lived in a setting where they did not hold the reins of control or determine the direction of society through government. They lived without a political establishment and a monarch. This situation was a decided change from rule by the Davidic dynasty, but it was not an unheard-of condition for the Israelites. A clear strand of Israelite history was defined by the claim to have no king but Yahweh. This skepticism about kingship appears in Gideon's refusal to be king (Judg 8:23), Jotham's parable (9:7-15), and Samuel's reluctance to anoint a king (1 Sam 8; cf. 10).

The prophet Jeremiah told the exiles in Babylon that rather than pining after their lost life in Jerusalem, they should settle down, build houses, raise families, learn trades that benefited the society, and "seek the welfare of the city where I have sent you into exile, and pray to the Lord on its behalf, for in its welfare you will find your welfare" (Jer 29:5-7). In other words, God's people Israel could live without having their hands on the means of political control. "Jeremiah's abandoning statehood for the future is thus not so much forsaking an earlier hope as it is returning to the original trust in JHWH."[32] In this life in exile, they were to maintain their religious traditions and worship, which would serve as a witness to the way of Yahweh in the midst of a foreign nation. Nothing about this witness required that it depend on civil or government authorities.[33]

Stories in the book of Daniel reveal and illustrate this witness. The first chapter of Daniel recounts the narrative of Daniel, Hananiah, Mishael, and Azariah, young Hebrews among the captives brought in for education that would enable them to enter the king's service. The young men were willing to learn the local language and a useful skill, but they refused the royal food and wine that was standard fare for trainees and asked instead for vegetables and water. In other words, the young exiles maintained their own cultural and religious identity, which marked them as people who worshipped the God of Israel rather than the gods of Babylon. The outcome of the story is that the Hebrews thrived on their own kind of food and were allowed to continue with it as they worked for the king. The third chapter of Daniel contains the story of three Hebrews, renamed Shadrach, Meshach, and Abednego. Upon intercession by Daniel, they were appointed to be civil servants with responsibilities for the province of Babylon. After the three refused to worship the gods of King Nebuchadnezzar and the golden statue that he had set up, they were bound and thrown into a furnace. But when the fire did not harm the three, the king acknowledged the God of Israel and gave them a promotion. These stories portray how the Hebrews maintained their own religious and cultural identity, as a witness to the God of Israel, even as they worked for the good of Babylon.

The story of Daniel and the den of lions in chapter six has a similar outcome and meaning. Daniel was one of three presidents that King Darius placed over 120 satraps stationed throughout the kingdom to look after the king's affairs. Daniel's job performance earned him the favor of the king but jealousy from the other civil servants, who plotted against him. They persuaded the king to sign a proclamation requiring worship and prayer to the king only for thirty days. The penalty for disobeying the decree was death in a den of lions, by which the other civil servants hoped to eliminate Daniel, who continued to pray three times daily to the God of Israel. However, after being left in the lions' den overnight, Daniel said, "My God sent his angel and shut the lions' mouths so that they would not hurt me, because I was found blameless before him; and also before you, O king, I have done no wrong" (6:22). As a result, the king issued a decree in support of Israel's God, and Daniel continued to prosper under King Darius. These stories illustrate how God's people Israel could and did live as a visible witness to God's reign in a society where they had no control of political authority, but nonetheless they worked for the blessing of the culture in which they were captives. Their witness required courage and it could be confrontational, but the stories are told with a view to encouraging that witness. Stories of Joseph and Esther carry the same meaning.

This tradition of witnessing to the God of Israel within a political context where Israelites did not hold the reins of control is the tradition inherited by Jesus. John Howard Yoder wrote that the model given visibility by Jeremiah "prefigured the Christian attitude to the Gentile World." The Jesus movement did not begin from "scratch." Instead,

> Jesus' impact in the first century added more and deeper authentically Jewish reasons, and reinforced and further validated the already expressed Jewish reasons, for the already well established ethos of not being in charge and not considering any local state structure to be the primary bearer of the movement of history.[34]

It was this long trajectory, reaching all the way back to Jeremiah, that was undone by Constantine and the church leaders who accepted and legitimated the change.

With this discussion of the people of God living as exiles without controlling the political order, it should also be obvious that this tradition pictures a nonviolent people of God. Describing the people of God living independent of established authorities means telling of a pacifist movement, a movement that depended on Yahweh rather than earthly political authorities. The basis of pacifist thought for Christians is not limited to a few Bible verses and some examples of Jesus. It is a long-standing stance of God's people, with kingship as a deviation. Jesus inherited this movement and further validated it. Anabaptist ecclesiology is one of a series of movements throughout history that have given continued or renewed visibility to this stance. The following section continues the discussion of nonviolence in contemporary contexts.

That the church witnesses to the way relationships among people should exist under the rule of God is a vitally important message for the early twenty-first century. John Howard Yoder has listed five practices of the church that model for the world what God's will is for human relationships under the rule of God. (1) The practice of "binding and loosing" involves personal intervention and works toward restoration of broken relationships and healing of offenders rather than punishment. (2) Breaking bread together in the Lord's Supper acts out the sharing of a family in which every member is valued and social stratification is overcome. (3) Baptism initiates individuals from different communities and ethnic groups into a new humanity, a new creation in Christ. (4) The "fullness of Christ" gives this new humanity a mode of group relationships in which each member has a manifestation of the Spirit that serves the common good of the community. (5) The "rule of Paul" states that since every member has a gift, every member—including a woman—has the power to speak in the assembly of the community. Yoder summarizes the witness character of this new society of the church:

The believing body of Christ is the world on the way to its renewal; the church is the part of the world that confesses the renewal to which all the world is called. The believing body is the instrument of that renewal of the world, to the (very modest) extent to which its message is faithful. It may be "instrument" as proclaimer, or as pilot project, or as pedestal.[35]

The meaning of the church as a community is not limited simply to the free association of consenting adults after they recognize their parallel but individual experience of salvation. The reconciled relationship between individuals, made visible by the practices Yoder has depicted, is God-given—a product of grace. Religion is not simply the story of "my personal salvation and my religious history." Reconciliation between individuals belongs as much to the essence of salvation as does reconciliation to God; the two dimensions are inseparable. As Robert Friedmann said in the language of a previous generation, "One cannot come to God except together with one's brother. . . . The binding together of the brethren is as essential for the disciple as is dedication to obedience to God."[36] The sense of community has many dimensions and applications, for American society as well as for the churches.

In contrast to the communal nature of the believers church, modern Western society is characterized by a rampant individualism. In the words of Robert Bellah, "Individualism lies at the very core of American culture."[37] A few, obvious examples illustrate the point. This individualism is exemplified by a comment I hear frequently from students in my ethics class: "What is right for me may not be right for you, but the important thing is that each of us makes up our minds for ourselves." Students seem quite comfortable with the fact that this outlook makes each individual a supreme authority unto oneself. Only when I start asking whether the right of the individual to decide right and wrong applies to serial murderers or to terrorist acts against the United States do they start to realize that individualism is actually a social stance with problematic implications, and that some kind of standard exists apart from the individual.

This rampant individualism—call it selfishness—is obvious in television commercials. A tool commercial pictures a man working with great care to build his own sailboat, for which he obviously will need the best tools. Accompanying the picture, a voice sings, "You're doing it right, 'cause it means more when you're doing it for yourself." In other words, he obviously would not work that hard or carefully for an employer. A nationally known candy bar used to brag that it was big enough to be shared with a friend, and TV commercials showed friends happily sharing the treat in communal goodwill. A more recent commercial for that candy bar had the consumer hiding in a closet so he could eat the whole thing by himself without having to share. Another pictures a man stuffing his face with breakfast cereal before his wife has a chance at the box. In a commercial for a snack cracker, the woman hoards her supply and tells her presumed husband, "Get your own box." Still another commercial pictures a hand inching toward goodies on a plate, when slowly the camera pans up to discover the menacing face of an elderly woman who clutches a fork, tines down, with which she threatens to jab the hand of her husband creeping up to steal the goodies from her plate— and the hand withdraws. Such messages work because of the assumption that the individual takes supremacy over the common good and over sharing or anything one does for others.

This appeal to individualism and to selfishness appears front and center in political campaigns. A winning candidate in a presidential race asked, "Are you better off now than you were four years ago?" In that campaign, civil rights or ecological concerns—issues that envision minority cultural groups or the common good—took a backseat to economic issues touching middle-class American pocketbooks.

Little has changed since then. Campaign rhetoric still

caters to individual wants and to the right of the nation to be the wealthiest country in the world at the expense of others. A candidate could not get elected on a platform that called for the United States to live with less and to stop consuming such a disproportionately large share of the world's resources.[38] The frequently heard slogan "God bless America" claims divine sanction for the sense of entitlement that accompanies this overconsumption by the United States. In effect, this national assertion of entitlement is mass selfishness. Few people would display a bumper sticker saying GOD BLESS ME, but one sees many reading GOD BLESS AMERICA.

Robert Bellah's words underscore this focus on individualism—selfishness—whether at the personal or the national level. He stated that both biblical and classic republican traditions measure the health of a society by "how it deals with the problem of wealth and poverty." In American society, he wrote, "We have put our own good, as individuals, as groups, as a nation, ahead of the common good. . . . We are attracted . . . to the idea that poverty will be alleviated by the crumbs that fall from the rich man's table."[39]

The idea of community of goods that runs through the Anabaptist story of the sixteenth century—whether a shared treasury in Switzerland or the Hutterites of Moravia living in community, without private ownership—is a decided contrast to the rampant individualism of North Americans today. If Christians paid more heed to this Anabaptist idea, they would be doing more than practicing a Christian virtue. Modeling this idea for North American society would contribute to greater justice and peace in the world. Reaction against the United States' selfish exploitation of the world's resources and its claimed right to a go-it-alone foreign policy—a national individualism—contributes to the resentment that the United States encounters in the world. If the United States consumed less and gave greater attention to the needs of other peoples and nations, the United States and the world would be more peaceful.

Jesus's followers are not on their own, guided only by the sincerity of their motives. They take their cues from the Bible and the tradition as mediated and interpreted by the community of God's people, the church. The believing community should help the broader society remember the humanity of all individuals; it should testify that the justice of a society is measured by how it treats the powerless rather than the powerful. As Yoder's *Body Politics* maintains, the communal-oriented church calls attention to the common good and to the solidarity of the human race.

Anabaptism originated in a time of social upheaval. Local control of the church and enfranchisement of laypeople appealed to peasants who felt alienated from the established church and exploited by the nobility and ruling classes. In the twenty-first century, poor people in Latin America, Africa, the Philippines, and other third-world countries also find themselves exploited by a wealthy minority ruling class that frequently receives the support of an established church. The poor are not synonymous with the church, nor does poverty of itself make them harbingers of God's reign or the locus of God's activity in the world. Poor people, however, do belong to the church, and increasingly they are coming to question the unequal status in which they find themselves within it. The church faces the challenge of being the alternative society in a way that liberates the poor and oppressed instead of comforting the oppressors.[40] How to accomplish that goal in a peaceful way, modeled on Jesus, is a difficult and multifaceted endeavor. However, it remains abundantly clear that we must work at that task if we are to be the church.

In spite of the official separation of church and state that is written into the constitution of the United States, the notion of being a "Christian society" that exists in this country exercises a powerful erosive force and exerts a strong temptation that threatens Anabaptist ecclesiology. One way to picture this temptation is through consideration of what lies behind the claims to be a "Christian society" or a "Christian nation." In fact, the "Christian society" of North America, and in particular of the United States, is a continuation in a new form of the established church rejected by Anabaptists in the sixteenth century.

In an evolutionary series of changes in the third through fifth centuries of the Christian era, the church lost or abandoned its identity as an illegal, minority movement. Christianity became the majority religion, and the church became established when the emperor intervened in church affairs and the bishops accepted that intervention. Bishops even appealed to the emperor for support, and emperors assumed the task of protecting the church. In effect, there was a fusion of church and society. It was assumed that everyone in the social order would conform to the Christian religion, and that the church thus served the entire society.

This fusion of church and the social order was never complete. The church maintained its own structures and hierarchy; yet from within the church, the monastic movement can be interpreted as a protest against this fusion of church and civil society. Throughout the Middle Ages the bishops and pope were in continual competition with secular rulers such as emperors and kings, to see who had the most power in the church: Could civil rulers appoint church officials in their territories? Did church authorities hold the authority to invest civil rulers? Nonetheless, these conflicts and the less-than-total fusion of church and society did not call into question the assumption made by officials on both sides that there was one faith encompassing the entire social order. These competitions concerned which authority—church or civil—had ultimate jurisdiction over the one church that encompassed the social order.

The Reformation of the sixteenth century brought two changes to this picture. For one, the fracturing of the Roman Catholic Church meant that there now was a choice of religious preferences for civil authorities to establish. However, none of the new, major Protestant alternatives challenged the idea of an established church. The second change concerned a shift in the balance of power between church and civil authorities. As a result of fostering reformation in their territories, Protestant civil authorities in particular gained ascendancy over church authorities in the struggle to control the one church that was assumed to encompass the social order in their jurisdiction. Only Anabaptists rejected the idea of a state church and developed the idea of a church independent of civil authorities.

The first settlers to North America brought the idea of an established church along with them. The famed Puritan settlers in New England, whose name comes from their belief that the Church of England was not sufficiently purified of all vestiges of Catholicism, sought to establish what they considered the correct church order. Catholics and Anabaptists, for example, were not welcomed.

Official separation of church and state happened for what became the United States in 1791, when the first amendment added to the U.S. constitution said: "Congress shall make no law respecting an establishment of religion, or prohibiting the free exercise thereof." That separation, however, was only at the federal level. The last vestige of official establishment at the state level disappeared in 1831,[41] when Massachusetts removed the favored tax status for Congregational ministers, the denomination that was the lineal descendent of the founding Puritans.

Many churches and churchmen opposed disestablishment. The response was that if the government would not make the United States "Christian," then Christians would have to "Christianize America voluntarily." The host of parachurch organizations that arose in the mid-nineteenth century—Bible societies, tract societies, YMCA, YWCA, Sunday school societies, home mission societies, revival crusades, and more—had as a primary motivation the task of Christianizing America voluntarily.[42] This struggle to Christianize America voluntarily is still going on, and the idea of a "Christian society" or of "Christian America" is a lineal descendant of the medieval state church, but without official governmental support. In the twenty-first century many of those proclaiming "Christian America" are still trying to recover government coercion for their programs of choice.

Several issues currently function as symbols for those who seek to "Christianize America." The desire for prayer in public school classrooms illustrates the drive for a "Christian society." As often said in other contexts, Christians can pray anytime anywhere, eyes open or shut, including in school, because God is everywhere and can hear prayers from anywhere. As the old joke goes, "As long as teachers give tests, there will be prayer in schools." But such spontaneous and voluntary prayer does not satisfy the prayer proponents. They want government-sanctioned, public prayer. The legislative drive targets only public classrooms and ignores other public places, as for example, airport terminals, restaurants, or supermarkets. This selectivity occurs because schools are institutions of the government, which perform the function of socializing the nation's young people into the national mythology of American purity and righteousness. The desire to legislate prayer into the classrooms recognizes the public schools as a national institution and reflects the identity of American nationalism and religion, which the existence of prayer in the classroom would symbolize. One can quickly determine that it is something recognizable as Christian prayer that is desired. Anything remotely recognizable as Muslim or Hindu prayer in schools, for example, would not be tolerated by the proponents for prayer in schools.

The lack of official prayer in public schools and the inability to talk about the supposed Christian foundation of the nation[43] are among several impetuses behind many private schools. Curricula such as the ACE (Accelerated Christian Education), widely used in many private schools and for home school, has "Christian America" as one of its central themes. Its focus on working alone and on individualized achievement also underscores the American individualism discussed earlier.

In addition to prayer in public schools, a number of other issues are also symbols of Christian society or Christian America. Each generates its own set of emotions and conversations, whether the issue is abortion or gay marriage or display of religious objects such as replicas of the Ten Commandments or crèches in courtrooms and other governmental and public space.

Why are such issues that symbolize a "Christian society" a temptation for the Anabaptist peace church? Precisely because they are considered religious views to be imposed on the entire society. Concerns about these issues can lead Anabaptists to follow the "Christian" rhetoric and to forget the basis of the church that embodies the witness of Jesus in the world. That church is founded on faith in Jesus Christ. It is a faith community, and not a community defined by national boundaries or national ethnic identity. The assumption behind views such as prayer in public schools is that "Christian" applies to the entire social order—which was the case when civil rulers in the sixteenth century made the decision about which liturgy—Catholic, Lutheran, or Calvinist—all the people in the ruler's territory would be required to use. Arguing that an issue such as school prayer is a "Christian" issue that should be imposed through governmental legislation is a twenty-first century parallel to the assumption in sixteenth-century Zurich that city council should establish policy on baptism or the Lord's Supper for the entire city.

It is therefore very important that the Anabaptist tradition reflect a theology and an orientation making clear that Christian faith transcends national interests and is not the tribal religion of one nation or of the West European and North American military alliance. This sense that Christian faith is an alternative to, rather than the supporter of, the existing society is a necessary stance if the Christian faith is to judge society rather than be controlled by it.

As a faith community that transcends national boundaries, Anabaptist ecclesiology has a global dimension. A global economy operates through multinational corporations, economic institutions such as the World Bank and the International Monetary Fund, and international agreements such as NAFTA. These structures are controlled by and function for the benefit of the wealthy nations of the world, primary of North America and Europe. By imposing policies such as privatization on poor countries as the prices of international loans or participation in trade, this global economy often foists economic injustice—a form of structural violence—on poor countries.[44] In fact, Wes Howard-Brook and Anthony Gwyther consider the imperialism of this global economic edifice the contemporary equivalent of the Roman Empire as dragon, which is confronted by God's reign in the book of Revelation.[45] An Anabaptist ecclesiology—with its rejection of violence and its concern for those without political and economic clout, as symbolized by the common treasury of sixteenth-century Anabaptists—addresses this global economy and those exploited by it.

Canadian national identity lacks the messianic quality of American national religion. Canada does not have nearly as strong a sense as does the United States of being a "nation under God." Canada is officially a cultural mosaic, which encourages religious and ethnic groups to maintain a particular identity rather than to subsume it under a larger religio-national identity as happens with the melting pot in the United States. Canada's context may, however, pose an equally dangerous though more subtle challenge to Anabaptist efforts to be the alternative society. The easy access which peace people of any stripe have to Canadian politics and business make it easy to lose the distinction between church and world. When the national identity does not pose a direct challenge to the peace church, it is tempting for the church to lose its sense of being a witness to the reign of God.

Standing: Peace and Nonviolence

As previous sections have made clear, the rejection of violence and the sword is intrinsic to the discussion of Jesus as authority for ethics, and it is intrinsic to discussions about the character of the church that strives to continue Jesus's mission of witness to the presence of God's reign in the world. Because of the militarism and proclivity to war of North America, and especially the United States, I follow the lead of those who single out peace and nonviolence with particular significance for a contemporary Anabaptist standing. The discussion below presumes the earlier depiction of Jesus's life and teaching and of Anabaptist ecclesiology.

In the time between the first and second editions of the book in hand, the United States experienced the attack of September 11, 2001, on the World Trade Center, and it has undertaken three major wars—the attack on Iraq in 1991, the invasion of Afghanistan in 2001, and the invasion of Iraq again in 2003—as well as a series of lesser military operations. None of these violent acts fulfilled its intended purpose.

The war against Iraq in 1991 was supposed to teach Saddam Hussein a lesson and, as President Bush said (on Jan. 28, 1991), establish "a New World Order." It accomplished neither goal: Saddam Hussein remained defiant, and the "New World Order" looked suspiciously like the old one and faced the same problems as the old one. The perpetrators of September 11 thought their violent acts would teach the United States a lesson. The specific intent was never quite clear, but the lesson was certainly related to United States and Western inroads in Muslim regions as well as the impact of United States foreign policy on Palestinians. Whatever the specific intent of the perpetrators, the attacks on the World Trade Center only succeeded in provoking the United States to more violence. The result was declaration of a "war on terror," whose first element was the invasion of Afghanistan, followed by the invasion of Iraq. However, as has become increasingly and painfully clear, rather than eliminating terror, the "war on terror" is provoking more hostility to the United States, and even national political commentators have said that the invasion of Iraq spawned terrorists and turned Iraq into a seedbed of terrorists. As these words are written, it is far from clear how the United States will extract itself from Iraq before a great many more people die—from both the United States and Iraq.

But even without knowing the outcome in Iraq and apart from the now well-known lies and fabricated evidence used to justify the invasion, there is still a lesson to be learned from these recent wars and terrorist acts, regardless of the side with which one identifies. *Violence does not solve problems. Violence only provokes more violence.* In these violent exchanges, both sides believed that violence would produce peace and justice, and violence worked for neither side.

If people want peace, they have to take steps to stop the cycle of violence and make choices to turn the course of events in a different direction. Emphasizing the truth of nonviolence, which is ultimately anchored in the story of Jesus, who embodies God's reign, is one of the most important contributions of the Anabaptist story to the world.

Harold S. Bender's third major characteristic of Anabaptism was "the ethic of love and nonresistance as applied to all human relationships." This nonresistance meant "complete abandonment of all warfare, strife, and violence, and of the taking of human life."[46] This description focused primarily on what Anabaptists did not do. It did not provide data on how to live out an ethic of love or how Anabaptists should act positively to overcome violence. It did not say anything about how the nonresistant Anabaptist community interacted with the social order, other than to say that this community did not resist evil.

The narrative of chapters 2, 3, and 4 (above) shows clearly that not all Anabaptists espoused the rejection of the sword described by Bender. Some have argued that acknowledgment of violent Anabaptists undercuts the certainty and clarity of Bender's vision of Anabaptism. Thus, the argument goes, contemporary Anabaptists should be humble about their stance and more open to acknowledge some possible ethical uses of violence.

Gerald Biesecker-Mast's book *Separation and the Sword*

in Anabaptist Persuasion has inaugurated a new stage in Anabaptist studies. Using the tools of rhetorical analysis, Biesecker-Mast brings a cutting-edge argument both to six-teenth-century Anabaptist disputes about the sword and to the way these disputes are relevant for the church of the twenty-first century.

Rhetorical analysis of the Schleitheim Articles, the first systematic statement of Anabaptist ecclesiology, identified two different stances toward the social order within the articles. In articles 3 and 4, the church is perceived as in a separation of *antagonism* to the social order. Church and world belong to two different systems, one of Christ and the other of Belial. These exist in opposition to each other, and a Christian must make a choice to belong to one or the other. In this mutually exclusive and antagonistic relationship, the church opposes the social order. That opposition is what it means to be Christian and to belong to the church of Jesus Christ. But in article 6, on the sword, the rhetorical analysis reveals a separation of *dualism* between church and world.

As the term *dualism* is commonly used in the discipline of rhetoric, a dualistic relationship is one in which two differently oriented and competing entities or groups are shown to be complementary and thus not mutually exclusive. The Anabaptists at Schleitheim were pursuing a dualistic relationship when they wrote that the sword was ordained of God for the preservation of order in society but was outside the perfection of Christ. In other words, Anabaptists were willing to acknowledge the authority of the civil government, including the authority to wield the sword, in exchange for legitimacy and recognition that they posed no threat to civil authority.[47] Hence, in working out the implications of a new ecclesiology, Anabaptists used both antagonistic and dualistic strategies in dealing with the social order. These two strategies are already present in the Schleitheim Articles and subsequently appear among Swiss, South German and Moravian, and Dutch Anabaptists, in documents of the Amish division, and in the later Mennonite confessional tradition into the eighteenth century.

This rhetorical analysis leads to two quite important points about peace and nonviolence for both sixteenth-century and contemporary Anabaptists. For one, this analysis shows how nonviolence is an intrinsic part of the Anabaptist story even when a number of Anabaptists were not pacifists. Rejection of the sword is not simply an item of debate to point out after one has listed the items all Anabaptists agreed on.[48] Biesecker-Mast showed the source of the pacifist perspective in the narrative of Jesus, as well as identifying various ways that Jesus's rejection of the sword was rendered nonfunctional, ways parallel to arguments on the sword expressed by the opponents of Anabaptism.

Second, the rhetorical analysis demonstrates that Anabaptist positions are not a trump card that definitively settles a contemporary debate. Instead, Anabaptist texts challenge us to make choices about how we will express allegiance to God's reign. No position from the sixteenth century should be absolutized for later emulation. Neither the dualistic nor antagonistic stances in any of their variations were developed as static or unchanging answers. Each was a struggle for faithfulness of the church in a particular time and set of circumstances. Understanding this characteristic of the stances in the sixteenth century should lay to rest any effort to determine the "correct" sixteenth-century answer for copying or recovery in the present. Seeking for the relevance of the Anabaptist story is not a matter of finding the correct stance and copying it, but a matter of recognizing that we are always negotiating how the church exists or coexists with the social order. Finding relevance in the Anabaptist story is thus not a matter of identifying the right set of heroes to emulate or principles to adopt. It means rather to continue to live in an ongoing historical stream shaped by the same central posture that emerged from the Anabaptist story in the sixteenth century. This outlook is another expression of ongoing renewal and reform that comes from "looping back" to the narrative of Jesus.

Mennonite peace thinking went through a marked change in the last half of the twentieth century, from passive nonresistance to more activist nonviolent peacemaking. The analysis of antagonistic and dualistic stances among sixteenth-century Anabaptists provides insight into this shift, which is relevant to contemporary Anabaptists far beyond the Mennonite experience.

As previously quoted, Harold Bender's "Anabaptist Vision" identifies the stance of nonresistance, which focuses on avoiding involvement in any situation or activity that involves violence. Guy Hershberger, whose works defined Mennonite peace theology for a generation in mid-twentieth century, wrote that nonresistance describes those Christians "who cannot have any part in warfare . . . and who renounce all coercion, even nonviolent coercion."[49]

Although many Mennonites continue to profess a belief in nonresistance, a decided shift in emphasis from nonresistance to active nonviolent peacemaking is visible in the last half of the twentieth century.[50] Perhaps it is more accurate to say that nonresistance was not abandoned, but that many Mennonites added nonviolent activism to their peace outlook and peace practice. Several things contributed to this shift. One was the Civil Rights movement, which led nonresistant Mennonites to see that passive nonresistance actually accommodated racial injustice. Earlier I described the incident that precipitated the beginning of my personal appropriation of this shift. A second impetus came from the growing national resistance to the Vietnam War. Mennonite young people became active in that war resistance.[51] Ronald J. Sider provided an important stimulus for the shift with an address at the Mennonite World Conference meeting in Strasbourg, France, in 1984. Sider called for the formation of a nonviolent peace force, which would intervene in violent conflicts wherever they occurred.[52] This address led to the formation of Christian Peacemaker Teams, a nonviolent activist organization sponsored by Mennonites, Brethren, and Quakers. CPT has sent violence-reduction teams to a number of trouble spots around the world. In describing this shift from nonresistance to active peacemaking, it is important to emphasize that Mennonites did not invent nonviolent activism. They discovered and came to support a strategy and initiatives that had been in practice for decades.

The phenomena of nonresistance and nonviolent activism fall within the two strategies of dualism and antagonism. Nonresistance fits comfortably within a dualist strategy that does not challenge the social order, in return for being allowed to exist and practice one's religion in peace. Nonviolent activism, on the other hand, has an antagonistic relationship with the social order. It seeks out and confronts injustice and violence and seeks to change the social order, whether it concerns such problems as the structural violence of legal segregation or the direct violence of the war in Vietnam or Iraq. Both stances have existed within Anabaptism, and in each case Anabaptists have assumed that the church poses an alternative to the established church and the social order. Each posture is a strategy related to a particular context rather than an absolutized stance that applies in the same way in all situations everywhere.

The postures of both dualism and antagonism are stances of separation from the social order.[53] The important point is that separation does not mean disengagement or withdrawal. Separation implies engagement with society. Being "separate from the world" was the basis of Anabaptists' witness and their challenge to social structures and the established church. The separations of antagonism and dualism constituted two postures of engagement. Stated from the other side, for Anabaptists to be engaged with the society in which they live did not and does not mean necessarily joining society's structures, such as in participating in officeholding or exercising the sword of war. Engagement also occurs through challenge and maintaining an alternative witness.

I agree with the suggestion in Biesecker-Mast's final chapter that context determines the strategy of choice for particular questions, and that the church in benign and tolerant situations should pursue the more antagonistic strategy. In situations where the church is actively opposed by a hostile government, as was the case in many countries of Eastern Europe prior to the collapse of the Soviet Union, the dualistic strategy may be the better choice. In the 1980s, I had occasions to travel with a pastor in East Germany, then part of the Soviet Empire. The pastor explained that as a response to the suspicious government that officially opposed religion, his church looked for particular ways in which they could cooperate with or support local government initiatives. They worked with the state censors, for example, to show that publications about Old Testament history should not be seen as subversive. As a result, the East German government allowed the publication of significant Old Testament biblical scholarship. In my library I still have a book purchased in East Germany as my copy of a volume also published in the west. Another example from the same context concerned Bible smuggling, or more precisely, opposition to smuggling of Bibles. Some Western TV personalities and missionaries gave high praise to the practice of smuggling Bibles into Communist East Germany. But Christians like the pastor I traveled with discouraged the practice and told their friends who visited from Western countries not to smuggle in quantities of Bibles or Western consumer goods. What such smuggling did, my friend said, was to show the authorities that Christians told lies and could not be trusted.

Christians in the tolerant, officially secular, but largely Christian and democratic countries of North America face a different challenge than did Christians in East Germany. North American society is referred to as "Christian," and churches function without restrictions. Although the United States and Canada have no established church and practice separation of church and state, they are also referred to as "Christian" nations. When candidates for public office profess personal faith and appeal to religious values, it may seem as though the civil and political process is an extension of the church's agenda. In such a context, Christians and the church are not concerned for their existence, and it is easy for them to forget that the church is not identified with the social order. Its roots in God's reign give it a fundamentally different identity. Such a context may call for the church to make an antagonistic response to the social order. In spite of the so-called Christian society, many problems remain—racism and discrimination against people of color, tax policies that favor those with the most wealth, economies dominated by the military while funds for education and social needs are being cut, pre-emptive war,[54] and much more. Rather than finding comfort in a dualistic relationship with the social order, the church should more frequently challenge the injustices of the social order. Such challenges will both remind the church where its primary identity lies in the reign of God, and also move society in a slightly more peaceful and just direction. And, of course, in a context such as Germany under Hitler, antagonism is the only faithful posture.

Glen Stassen and Michael Westmoreland-White developed a twofold definition of violence. It is "(1) destruction to a victim and (2) by overpowering means. *Violence is destruction to a victim by means that overpower the victim's consent.*"[55] This definition includes the overt violence of war and the harm that is done with weapons, but it also recognizes that systemic or structural injustices are also forms of violence. A person denied opportunity because of skin color has experienced violence against one's person. A woman denied opportunity because of her gender has experienced violence against her person. Social policies and conditions that make it impossible for poor people to escape poverty do violence to people. The same applies to persons who experience discrimination because of age or sexual preference. Although such systemic violence is clearly distinguishable from the physical violence of lynching or war, it is important to acknowledge the real harm done to people by unjust structures and policies.

The counterpart to violence is "nonviolence," which Stassen and Westmoreland-White understand as "initiatives and practices of peacemaking. These peacemaking initiatives actively transform violent conflicts or those that could become violent into relationships of relative justice and relative community well-being."[56] It is obvious that Anabaptism, which professes nonviolence and seeks to live nonviolently, can and should confront systemic violence both inside the church as well as in the social order in which it lives. Thus, an Anabaptist outlook embraces peacemaking as activity that opposes not only the violence of war, but also seeks to confront and to change contexts of systemic and structural violence both within the church and in the social order in which the church lives.

The definitions of violence and nonviolence developed by Stassen and Westmoreland-White fit with an Anabaptist outlook that has both dualistic and antagonistic relationships to the social order. Keeping both strategies in mind is necessary and important for the health and witness of Anabaptism as a worldview. It is more than obvious that Anabaptist opposition to the military edifice of the United States will not fundamentally alter or reduce that edifice. Vis-à-vis the military establishment, the church seems well advised to pursue a dualist strategy, for which a central concern would be to maintain provisions enabling conscientious objectors to perform public service that is not connected to the military.

At the same time, the Anabaptist church in North America should pursue an antagonistic social strategy when it considers the many dimensions of systemic violence in North American society. Church policies, statements, and practices should witness against systemic violence. Policies, statements, and practices should put the church clearly on record against the nation's wars. Beyond these actions of the church, some individuals and church organizations will pursue an antagonistic strategy toward the military establishment itself—as when young people refuse to register for the military draft, others become tax resisters and refuse to pay that portion of their taxes that supports the military establishment, and still others engage in public protests against war, such as what happened before the invasion of Iraq in 2003. These activities of an antagonistic strategy express in multiple ways that the church identifies with God's reign and should serve as a witness against the violence and injustices of the social order.

Thinking: New Theological Beginnings

Questions about theology emerge from the observation that Anabaptism was a new way of thinking of the church in the sixteenth century. Does the new ecclesiology have theological implications? Does the new ecclesiology have an impact on the received theology—the classic creeds and formulas—of the state church of Christendom? Does theology exist or develop independent of ecclesiology so that the new ecclesiology simply maintains and repeats the classic theology of the state church? Or does the new ecclesiology also reveal itself in a new theological beginning?

It has been suggested that Anabaptists did not think theologically and did not develop new theological directions but rather "simply" accepted and repeated the standard creeds and formulas of Christendom.[57] That suggestion is incorrect on two accounts. As this section will sketch briefly, Anabaptists did think theologically, and they did not merely repeat the standard formulas and creeds of Christendom. It is true that Anabaptists did not write theology with a stated purpose of producing a new theology for a new ecclesiology. A significant body of evidence exists, however, showing that their theological writing contained new elements and revisions, which reflected the assumption of discipleship that produced a new ecclesiology.

Analysis of atonement theology in the writings of Michael Sattler, Hans Denck, Balthasar Hubmaier, and Hans Hut reveals significant theological differences among these Anabaptists. However, a significant commonality also appears, which marks them as Anabaptists. Although expressed in very different ways, all four of these Anabaptists believed that salvation through Christ would result in a transformed life of the believer. Thus, it is possible to argue that one aspect of their disagreements and disputes is an embryonic beginning of an Anabaptist effort to articulate a new understanding of atonement theology.[58]

The tract "On the Satisfaction of Christ," in *The Legacy of Michael Sattler*, indicates an approach to justification by faith that fits neither medieval nor Reformation imagery. Although the tract uses some imagery of satisfaction atonement, it stresses that what Jesus did for sinners is not a mere substitution. The believer also suffers with Christ. The tract affirms the Lutheran point of justification by faith, but also stresses that faith will result in good works by the believer, which is in line with Catholic thought. These works "are not the work of man, but of God and Christ (through whose power a man does such works) and do not happen because through them man achieves something as his own, but rather because God through them wishes to give to man something of His own." What the sinner then does is done with Christ. Christ has "done enough" for sins, yet continually he will "day by day again do enough in His members and for them, until the end of the world." Thus this tract acknowledges concerns of both Catholics and Reformation Protestants, but goes beyond both Catholic sacramentalism and Lutheran fears of works righteousness.[59] Similarly, Arnold Snyder pointed to the way that schoolteacher Valerius integrated an Anabaptist emphasis on a new life, what has been called discipleship, into an image of satisfaction atonement. In response to forgiveness of sin, "there must be a 'proving' of the already-accomplished redemption by means of concrete response and action."[60] In such revisions of atonement theology, one can observe the beginning of a new theological direction that is missed if the emphasis falls only on Anabaptist agreements with other traditions.

Neal Blough's analysis of the theology of Pilgram Marpeck

has produced comparable results. Marpeck certainly presumed the standard view of the two natures of Christ and trinitarian theology. However, his interpretation and application of those doctrines indicated a specifically Anabaptist rather than Catholic or Lutheran orientation. Marpeck's concern was the spiritualists, whose focus on the inner dimension of salvation undercut the meaning of externals, whether ceremonies such as baptism and the Lord's Supper or ethical conduct such as rejection of the sword. In response, Marpeck argued that since God had become human in the incarnation, God has necessarily linked divine revelation to the outer and material realms of the world. Spiritual reality is then known through the material, and the humanity of Christ is the source of humanity's knowledge of God. Hence, ceremonies, which include such actions as preaching and reading Scripture as well as water baptism and Lord's Supper, are outward manifestations of Christian faith and a continuation of the incarnation, the presence of Christ in the world. Specifically included in these ceremonies is following Jesus or discipleship, as the Holy Spirit gives the believer the power to keep the commandments of Jesus. "Thus," Blough says, "the notions of the humanity of Christ, faith, the Holy Spirit and ethics are all closely related in Marpeck's theology."[61]

In another essay, Blough analyzes Marpeck's atonement theology. Blough argues that Marpeck's theology reflects the stress on Jesus as both Savior and example that is found in medieval, monastic theology and in Anselm's satisfaction atonement. However, Marpeck stressed resurrection as an integral element of Christ's saving work, and the Spirit's transformation of the believer so that the Christian actually and materially lives the teaching of Christ in the world. These elements of actual victory over sin align Marpeck with the atonement motif Christus Victor rather than Anselmian satisfaction atonement

Marpeck agreed with Martin Luther that justification was by faith rather than works. However, Marpeck understood that faith resulted in actual transformation of the believer by the

Holy Spirit, so that salvation manifested itself materially in history as the believer lived the commandments of Christ. This distinguished Marpeck from Luther as well as from medieval theology.[62] Such extensions of the humanity of Christ into an argument for ceremonies and a rejection of the sword, and into revisions of atonement imagery, all show that Marpeck charted a new theological path. That new theological path and the uniqueness of Marpeck's Anabaptist theology are not visible if one chooses to stress his agreement with the received views of trinitarian theology, the humanity and deity of Jesus, and atonement images as these are found in both medieval theology and in Martin Luther.

Menno Simons adopted a Christology that does not conform to standard criteria for correctness, at least as judged by the definition of the council of Chalcedon, whose key phrase asserted the full humanity and deity of Jesus. Menno had a trinitarian outlook, and he took pains to affirm the humanity and deity of Jesus. On the other hand, Menno's Christology was certainly nonstandard. He followed the celestial-flesh Christology of the Melchiorite Anabaptist movement. Briefly stated, Menno believed that Jesus's flesh was human flesh, but it was a human flesh that he had brought with him from heaven. Thus, the heavenly Word became flesh *in* Mary but not *of* Mary; Mary nourished Jesus's flesh, yet his flesh came not from Mary but from heaven. Menno used the analogy of a field that receives seed from a sower; while the field nourishes and grows the crop, the seeds come from outside and are not of the nature of the field.[63] The concern behind celestial-flesh Christology was to explain how the human and therefore sinful Mary could give birth to a human but sinless Jesus.[64] However, if one applies the definition of Chalcedon in strict fashion—that Jesus was fully human and fully divine—Menno's view is unacceptable. Even though it bled when pierced with nails and a sword, flesh that has come from heaven is simply not genuine *human* flesh.

Menno's Christology reflected one kind of medieval misunderstanding about human reproduction, that at conception the male implanted a complete human being into the womb of the female, where it grew until ready for birth. With that model in mind, Menno believed that Jesus must have begun from the Word, which entered Mary and became flesh. Menno's intention was to define Christology in such a way as to ensure the sinlessness of Jesus while also preserving the unity of Jesus's person. For Menno, emphasis on the flesh of Jesus affirmed his humanity, while the heavenly origin of the Word both affirmed Jesus's deity and also preserved the unity of Jesus's person. Menno wanted to defend the sinlessness of Jesus because he believed that the church founded by Jesus was to be a pure church and an extension of Jesus's work on earth. This church would then be separate or distinct from the worldly social order rather than the church of Christendom, which supported that social order.

Menno also described the process of change and conversion in the life of the sinner so that one is transformed in an incomplete way into the flesh of Christ, a transformation that will find its fulfillment at the return of Jesus. Hence, Menno's Christology is oriented by what can be called discipleship—the idea that the earthly life of Jesus constitutes an example and an authority for the life of Christian believers. If one comes to Menno with the idea that new understandings of ecclesiology and of discipleship will provoke other theological changes, then it is quite possible to see Menno's peculiar Christology not just as an idiosyncrasy or an unlearned departure from orthodoxy, but as the beginning of an effort to articulate an Anabaptist theology.

Parallel observations pertain to some of the Philippite hymns from Passau, latter incorporated into the *Ausbund*, which is still used by many Amish believers. The first hymn by Hans Betz, which became number 81 in the *Ausbund*, is an exposition of the Apostles' Creed, but also much more than a mere recitation of the creed. The lyricist felt free to take considerable theological liberties with the text. Instead of referring to the members of the Trinity as "persons," he writes of the three "names" of the Trinity, and the overall emphasis was to stress the unity of the Godhead. In treating the humanity and deity of Jesus, Betz's mystical theology comes close to violating standard christological dogma. He says, for example, that "the Godhead cannot divide itself, . . . Christ's coming into this age happened only according to his humanity which he received." Christ "flowed out from God in the light and clear, bright brilliance which he covered with his pure humanity," and "as a cloud goes over the sun, so that it cannot be seen, thus here in this age was the light covered with humanity." When Jesus finished his suffering on earth, "he went back to the Father into eternity. Understand! Only according to his humanity has he again received glory."[65]

Betz's statements come very close to, if not actually, deviating from standard trinitarian and Chalcedonian theology. In traditional interpretation, reducing the persons of the Trinity to names would appear counter to the standard belief that each person of the Trinity embodies fully all the characteristics of the Godhead. In the fourth or fifth century, it could have been condemned as modalism. And that either humanity or deity would defer to or be subsumed under or covered over by the other—that runs counter to the standard Chalcedonian interpretation that Jesus is fully human and divine, and neither attribute is changed or subsumed under the other at any point from the beginning through earthly mission until ascension and return to unity with God.

However, Betz's hymn also states that Jesus "was visible according to his humanity so that he might teach us." And one who stands in the power of God has faith in God, "who has created him now through Christ, . . . begotten him again to be his son since he fell from God through sin and came into his wrath." In other words, by God through Christ, the sinner is re-created into a child of God, and through the Holy Spirit is "enrolled . . . in the Church."[66] Such comments put a clear Anabaptist-oriented discipleship mold on an outline of the Apostles' Creed. One could argue either that this hymn shows the Anabaptists as theologically deviant, or that they intended to be orthodox because the Apostles' Creed was used. However, I suggest a third interpretation, that the theological liberties taken in this hymn show that the experience of Anabaptism opened the door to new theological reflection.

The second recorded Philippite hymn by Michael Schneider, which became number 2 in the *Ausbund*, deals with the saving work of Christ and lends itself to similar observations. The hymn does feature the suffering of Jesus, in line with a standard theory of satisfaction atonement. However, this hymn accompanies that suffering with a strong discipleship motif. "Christ came to earth for this: to teach the right way, that one should leave one's sins and turn to him. . . . Whoever wants to have fellowship with him and be a partaker of his kingdom must also do like him here on this earth."[67] Like other Anabaptist theologizing we have observed, this suffering actually leads to a victory as the one who suffers with Christ experiences the triumph of God's reign amid the tribulation of imprisonment. This victory through suffering goes beyond the received tradition of suffering with Christ, and it points in the theological direction of Christus Victor. These Philippite hymns in the *Ausbund* reveal a theology committed to a suffering resistance that reveals going beyond the standard, received theology and also the development of a resisting community that begins to express new theology.

In line with these observations about Anabaptist theologizing, Gerald Biesecker-Mast's book *Separation and the Sword in Anabaptist Persuasion* presents a number of illustrations of how Anabaptists were developing a new theological tradition. The sketch here draws on the analysis of a major Hutterite statement, Peter Riedemann's *Account of Our Religion*. Riedemann belonged to the second generation of Hutterites, those who were consolidating an existing movement rather than participating in its creation. If Riedemann's writing shows theological development, that is a clear indication that the new Anabaptist ecclesiology had an impact on other theological issues.

Riedemann's confession is an exposition of the Apostles' Creed. By using this standard document, he no doubt meant the exposition to reassure the authorities of his and the Hutterite's orthodoxy. However, the *Account* is much more than a recitation of the creed. At virtually every turn, Riedemann makes additions and qualifications that take the creed in a Hutterite Anabaptist direction. This is clear in the way he turns a confession of God as Father into a statement of the necessity of living as an obedient child of God, or appeals to the relationship of Father and Son in the Trinity as the basis for community of goods and abandonment of private ownership of property.[68] The significance of such interpretations of the Apostles' Creed are missed if one assumes that Anabaptists are orthodox because they used a classic creed. In fact, Riedemann articulated the beginning of a new theological direction, a direction that becomes clear when one focuses on the revisions and additions, precisely on what is new in Riedemann's treatment of the Apostles' Creed. In fact, Anabaptists did not merely retain standard theological creeds and formulas with their new ecclesiology and a commitment to discipleship. Instead, the new ecclesiology and a commitment to discipleship in fact eventuated in a distinctive theological direction.

Anabaptists did not have a specific *concept* of challenging the standard creeds and formulas and confessions of Christendom, and they did use and quote from the standard, received confessions such as the Apostles' Creed, the Nicene Creed or the Chalcedonian formula. But they did not simply repeat these formulations. They continually added to these formulas and confessions, demonstrating the Anabaptists' sense of the inadequacy of the standard formulas and creeds. They did not perceive the received formulas, creeds, and confessions as a standard "core" to which they were adding. Rather, they considered that what they were adding was actually more important than the received formulations. That they considered the additions of more importance than the received formulations should be obvious—they held to these additions quite stubbornly in spite of great opposition, which included martyrdom. As is said in the introduction to "the Five Articles of Faith" in the Hutterite *Chronicle*, "These five articles of faith are the reason for the great controversy between us and the world. All those of our church who have been executed by fire, water, or the sword were condemned because of these articles."[69] Anabaptists did not become martyrs because they held on to standard theological formulas. They became martyrs because they considered the standard theological formulas inadequate and developed statements that reflected their new understandings of ecclesiology and commitment to discipleship.

If Anabaptist ecclesiology has theological implications, Anabaptist hermeneutics does as well. Earlier the Anabaptist approach to Scripture was described, which located authority for interpretating the Bible in the believing congregation rather than in authoritative teachers (Protestant Reformation) or an authoritative teaching tradition (Catholicism). John Howard Yoder has suggested that this methodology left open, and may even call for, the possibility of challenges and corrections to the received theological tradition. "Is the inherited doctrinal system of a given denomination, which claims to be identical with the teaching of Scripture, really that accurate as a portrayal of what the Bible says? Does this not need to be tested again in every generation? Otherwise, how would we explain the variety of positions each of which claim to be simply identical to the biblical teaching?" After describing the uniqueness of Anabaptist interpretation in terms of the "rule of Paul"—interpretation within the congregation with every member having a voice—Yoder writes: "The other necessary implication of thus placing theological authority in the hands of the congregation was that the congregation must not be bound by tradition or former creedal statements, nor by the supervision of governmental authority. The congregation will recognize the assistance of a teaching tradition, and learn from it as long as it is in accordance with Scripture; . . . There is no denial of history; but there was a refusal to be bound by tradition."[70] The foregoing sketch of revisions and additions to classic formulas and symbols illustrates Yoder's description of Anabaptist hermeneutics.

Anabaptists were not bound by the theological limits of Christendom, but that does not make them theologically irrelevant. On the contrary, not being bound is what makes them theologically interesting and relevant. Examining their theology shows the impact of commitments to discipleship and nonviolence. And when the changes that result from those emphases are recognized, it also points to the absence of those principles as shaping elements in the standard theology of Christendom.

These indications of a new theological direction for Anabaptism are not limited to the sixteenth century. My own work has carried that discussion through the nineteenth century. In *Keeping Salvation Ethical*, I explored what eight different Mennonite and Amish writers of the nineteenth century had to say about issues of violence and atonement theology.[71] Two observations were true about each of the eight figures. Each had an understanding of atonement theology that could be placed within standard satisfaction atonement theology. However, in much the same way that a commitment to discipleship impelled Pilgram Marpeck or Peter Riedemann to make additions and revisions to reflect discipleship and a rejection of the sword, the nineteenth-century Mennonite and Amish authors also made additions and revisions that distinguish their atonement theology from any version of standard satisfaction atonement.

These Anabaptist revisions of inherited theology show that Anabaptists did think theologically and that they did much more than merely repeat the classic creeds and formulas. Their creative theological thinking opens the door to, or begins the process of developing, a new theology that reflects and emerges from the commitment to Jesus as norm of truth, and an ecclesiology that embodies Jesus's teaching in a witness to the world. For me, stepping through that open door resulted in *The Nonviolent Atonement.*[72] It is a continuation of the long-standing Anabaptist efforts to revise standard theology so that it reflects a new ecclesiology and principles such as discipleship and nonviolence—but with an important difference. Rather than adding to or revising the prevailing, dominant atonement motif, this book returns to the Bible to provide a fresh, new articulation of the work of Christ from the biblical material, doing so with a view to making Jesus's rejection of the sword central and visible in the articulation of his work.

The new model makes in-depth use of the book of Revelation. The seven-headed dragon represents the Roman Empire, the representative of the accumulated forces of evil in the world that are defeated by the resurrection of Jesus. A clear example of this victory appears in the dragon's defeat in heaven in Revelation 12:1-12. The Gospels tell this same story of Jesus from an earthly perspective. The life, death, and resurrection of Jesus reveal that his mission was to make visible God's reign in the world. When the forces of evil headed by Rome sought to eliminate his existence by killing him, his resurrection became the triumph of God's reign over the forces of evil, including death. Believers are saved when they place themselves—and are placed by God—in this story and thus share in the victory of God's reign in Christ's resurrection. This model shares the victory motif of classic Christus Victor, but I have called it narrative Christus Victor, both to distinguish it from the classic image and also to stress that its beginning point is the narrative of Jesus. When salvation means to live in this narrative of Jesus, salvation has a material component in history, as Marpeck saw, as well as an eschatological element as the believers share in the future culmination of God's reign, which is promised by his resurrection.

Martyrs appear throughout the Anabaptist story—Felix Manz, Balthasar Hubmaier, George Blaurock, Michael and Margaretha Sattler, Hans Hut, Anneken Jans, and Jacob and Katherine Hutter, to name a few. Anabaptism is the story of people who were willing to die for their faith. Writing in mid-twentieth century, via extensive analysis of *Martyrs Mirror* and the Hutterite *Chronicles*, Ethelbert Stauffer placed Anabaptist martyrs in the context of martyrs throughout the centuries.[73] According to Stauffer's analysis, Anabaptist martyrs saw themselves engaged in a struggle between the kingdom of God and the kingdom of Satan. In this struggle, death was the way that Anabaptists testified to the truth of their confession, and it was also resistance to and ultimately the defeat of Satan. Their deaths were unmerited, their suffering was unmerited, but suffering and death sealed the truth of their confession and witnessed to others of their resistance to Satan. Water baptism included the promise to follow Christ even unto death. Thus, discipleship involved possible martyrdom, since it meant following Christ, who was obedient unto death. Since the struggle of God's reign against Satan's rule continues, followers of Jesus should be prepared to witness through death, confident that the resurrection of Jesus proves death to be the transition to life fully with God.

The emphasis falls at a different point than it did for Stauffer, but narrative Christus Victor does incorporate the commitment to martyrdom he described. Narrative Christus Victor emphasizes the resurrection rather than the death of Jesus. Yet narrative Christus Victor is compatible with and expresses the Anabaptist commitment to martyrdom for the reign of God. Jesus suffered an undeserved death, and with that death and subsequent resurrection, Satan—the dragon of Revelation, the empire of Rome—was defeated. Anabaptists confronted structures in the sixteenth century that carried on the legacy of Rome. In the twenty-first century, the structures and forces that wage war and military occupation and wreak economic violence on the world and foster oppression through racism and gender inequity—these all continue the legacy of the dragon of Revelation. Following Jesus, living in the story of Jesus, means joining in the struggle of God's reign against these forces of violence, oppression, and injustice.

During World War I, two Hutterite conscientious objectors to war died from mistreatment in prison, and a number of Mennonites were harassed and mistreated, with some near lynchings in their home communities.[74] There are similar stories from the Civil War and the Revolutionary War.[75] Aside from these incidents around wars, however, Anabaptists in North America have not faced a widespread threat of death for their faith as was the case in the sixteenth century. However, the theology of narrative Christus Victor should make Christians aware that they may have to pay the ultimate price for allegiance to God's reign made visible in Jesus. The Anabaptist story is another reminder that living in the story of Jesus is an ultimate commitment.

Education for the Peaceable Reign of God

The previous section sketched the possibility of a theology shaped by nonviolence, and a Christian life shaped by such a theology expressing the meaning of Jesus's life and teaching. This section moves beyond theology to consider all academic disciplines or ways of knowing about the world. If being a Christian truly impacts all of life, we should be able to see the evidence in many aspects of life. Stated differently, we should be able to discover ways in which an Anabaptist perspective, with rejection of violence as an intrinsic component, forms a comprehensive outlook, with the potential to impact every aspect of life and thought.

The book *Teaching Peace: Nonviolence and the Liberal Arts*[76] provides one example of such a comprehensive outlook. It has twenty-three chapters that show how nonviolence as a beginning principle has the potential to shape research or teaching in every discipline of the university curriculum. Some contain surprises. A chapter on *actor training* exposes the intrinsic violence of "the method," the dominant theory of actor training. Another chapter states that standard college textbooks in *psychology* discuss aggression and violence almost exclusively as problems of individuals. The failure of textbooks to discuss either the psychological factors that contribute to war or that belong to war's aftermath allows students to assume that war is so normal that there is no need to raise questions about it. A chapter on *global marketization* exposes the structural violence against poorer countries that is inherent in the North American Free Trade Agreement (NAFTA). *Science* chapters on the human immune system and on primate behavior show that presuppositions about the givenness of violence in the paradigms scientists use to interpret data have a significant impact on how much violence scientists presume to find in nature. Chapters on *mathematics* use mathematical models to show that peace and nonviolence are logical, and provide a number of examples to indicate that math is not a "neutral" discipline. How math is taught reflects prior assumptions about violence, nonviolence, and justice.

Beyond these brief examples, *Teaching Peace* has discussions on art, music, criminal justice, biblical interpretation, theology, literature, history, political science, communication, the professions, and more. The book is intended to expand the places in which to look for violence and then visualize nonviolent alternatives. The Anabaptist story reminds us of discipleship, which makes rejection of violence integral to the Christian story. The discussion in this section holds up possibilities for seeing that the nonviolent Anabaptist story does engender a comprehensive Christian orientation, a foretaste of the peaceable kingdom of God. From within the story of Jesus, one can truly see the whole world.

Conclusion

Anabaptism is more than a slight corrective or small-ish addition to one of the presumed standard traditions of Christianity. Neither is Anabaptism a synthesis of other groups. One does not discover the character of Anabaptism by simply identifying roots in some prior medieval or Protestant traditions, or by locating some middle point between two groups. Anabaptism is a comprehensive perspective in its own right. The story told in these pages, and this concluding chapter on the meaning of Anabaptism, have been written to show how Anabaptism is a comprehensive way to look at the world from the perspective of the resurrected Jesus.

Anabaptism of the sixteenth century never achieved a state of homogeneity, and neither have its heirs. In common with all earlier generations, however, all its contemporary inheritors have the task of becoming Anabaptist, the task of understanding what it means to stand in the Anabaptist tradition of discipleship that produces an understanding of the church as a comprehensive movement continuing the incarnation of Jesus. This movement carries on the mission of witnessing to the presence of God's reign in the world. As have all previous generations of persons who have claimed this tradition as their own, we too are striving to form a future on the basis of a serious conversation with our past. Common to all—past and present—is the task of becoming Anabaptist.

Appendix
Essay on Interpretation

The story and statement of implications on the previous pages focus on presenting an integrated historical narrative and a positive and useful statement of its corresponding implications. The account does not burden the presentation with theoretical arguments in support of the particular theological interpretation that have shaped both the narrative and discussion of implications. This appendix supplies that justification and rationale.

The preceding story assumes an interpretative perspective that presents Anabaptism as a distinct movement, different from Roman Catholicism but also different from the other Reformation alternatives in the sixteenth century. I do not present Anabaptism as a combination of Catholic and Protestant elements, or as a middle way between these Catholic and Reformation perspectives. Anabaptism appears as its own kind of movement, with the potential to develop a comprehensive perspective on the world. The story goes beyond a theory of polygenesis to show some connections between diverse Anabaptist movements, following recent scholarship that has identified formative links from Swiss Anabaptism to Moravia involving community of goods and the Swiss Congregational Order, Pilgram Marpeck's influence on Swiss and south German Anabaptists, and perhaps common reading of Erasmus by Swiss Anabaptists and Menno Simons.

In a contrasting effort to move beyond polygenesis with a narrative that is relevant for contemporary Christians, C. Arnold Snyder makes proposals in his important book *Anabaptist History and Theology* and in a later essay "Beyond Polygenesis."[1] This work constitutes the most comprehensive effort since Harold Bender to survey the entirety of sixteenth-century Anabaptism and construct a usable Anabaptist past specifically in service of the contemporary church. Snyder himself clearly assumes a pacifist perspective concerned with the peace witness of the modern church, and his book contains a wealth of accessible data on sixteenth-century Anabaptism.

Snyder's approach goes beyond the diversity and pluralism of polygenesis by discovering a common theological core, characteristic of all Anabaptists in the early years of the movement. According to this argument, the core theology reveals that there was one Anabaptist movement within the flux and diversity of early Anabaptism before the lines hardened along those identified by the differing origins depicted in polygenesis. He says that we can discover this theological core by comparing the theology of all Anabaptists with the inherited theology of Christendom as well as the theology of the major Protestant perspectives. This theological core of Anabaptism has three components, he claims. At the most basic level are the classic creeds and formulas of Christendom, which Anabaptists held in common with both Catholicism and Protestantism. At the next level are the beliefs held in common with the major Protestant Reformers—rejection of Catholic sacramental theology, affirmation of Scripture's authority alone, and acceptance of justification by faith or salvation by grace through faith. Finally, the third category contains the beliefs unique to Anabaptism, described variously in terms of emphasis on the working of the Holy Spirit, discipleship, and an understanding of the church that includes adult baptism, the ban, and practice of the Lord's Supper and mutual aid.[2]

I agree that Anabaptists knew and referred to the classic

creeds of Christendom and that they shared many beliefs with the major Protestant Reformers. However, I do not believe that such an acknowledgment captures the most significant meaning of Anabaptism. Neither does it adequately demonstrate the long-term implications of Anabaptism for Christians today. Finding the meaning of the story is not simply a matter of reading and reporting what the sixteenth-century sources said or with what they agreed. Knowing what Conrad Grebel said about baptism or whether Hans Hut advocated use of the sword or that Menno Simons's Christology deviated from Chalcedon or that Peter Riedemann used the Apostles' Creed—knowing all this does not of itself tell us the significance of those observations, nor does it account for the historical and social meanings of such convictions.

Although Snyder's work has much that is commendable, at the same time I believe that the theological orientation of his project supports rather than rejects Christian identification with the surrounding social order, thereby contradicting a plain theological-ethical commitment of Anabaptist dissent. More specifically in Snyder's case, defining Anabaptism in terms of core theology shared with Christendom makes the move of blending Anabaptism into the dominant churches of Christendom and the social order rather than focusing Anabaptism as a christocentric, discipleship-oriented movement that poses a witness to Christendom and the social order—as Anabaptists themselves described their aims. A number of points support this thesis.

1. The definition of unified Anabaptism in terms of a threefold core was not accessible to sixteenth-century Anabaptists. This definition—or set of observations—is a distinctly modern construct, imposed on the sixteenth-century story. This definition is available only to modern scholars with access to a great deal of data and sources and the privilege of historical distance that Anabaptists in the sixteenth century did not enjoy. Hence, this definition is a modern choice of theology carried to Anabaptism. Consider the implications of this theological choice.

2. The assumption that the essence of Anabaptism is given by agreements, starting with agreements with the theology of Christendom, is inherently biased in favor of Christendom, and contradicts early Anabaptist self-understanding, shaped as it was by the motif of separation from Christendom. In a post-humously published article, John Howard Yoder discussed the difference between ecumenical conversations that begin with points held in common versus a conversation that starts with differences and disagreements.[3] Starting with points of agreement intrinsically favors the side or the group that represents the dominant perspective. The points of difference are the elements that distinguish the small or the minority viewpoint from the dominant group, and these are precisely the points that end up outside the core, relegated to the periphery and outside of the main discussion that focuses on agreements. A dialogue that took both sides equally seriously would begin with points of disagreement, since it is these points that distinguish the minority position. Beginning with these disagreements would bring the particular identifying characteristics of the minority position to the heart of the discussion.

Defining Anabaptism in terms of a theological core shared with Catholicism and with Protestantism is not itself a matter of ecumenical discussion, although it certainly has implications for current ecumenical dialogue. In any event, Yoder's analysis of ecumenical discussion also applies to discussions of historical theology. Defining Anabaptism in terms of agreements with Catholicism and Protestantism produces a result that privileges Christendom's theology and pushes the distinct points of Anabaptism to the periphery. In essence, Anabaptist distinctives become the issues that demonstrate Anabaptist deviation from the norm of Christendom, rather than seeing them as the issues that shape how Anabaptists as a Christian tradition interact with the world, which was the clear perspective of Schleitheim. Since Anabaptists did not agree among themselves on the issue of the sword, that issue—which eventually became one of the most important characteristics of enduring Anabaptism—does not even appear in Snyder's list of Anabaptist characteristics.

3. Defining Anabaptism in terms of the threefold core assumes that the issues distinguishing Anabaptism have no impact on the issues located in the categories of agreement with Protestantism and with Christendom. In fact, as discussion in chapter 5 demonstrated, and in particular the work of Gerald Biesecker-Mast has shown, the distinguishing characteristics of Anabaptism such as discipleship and a new ecclesiology had a marked impact on how Anabaptists thought about such shared beliefs as the Trinity and the incarnation. Defining Anabaptists primarily in terms of agreements with Catholic and Protestant doctrines assumes that doctrinal meanings are somehow impervious to perspectival reconstruction. Such an approach assumes that acknowledging the category of the Trinity is proof of accepting a common meaning.

4. Defining Anabaptist theology in terms of two levels of core beliefs shared with Christendom and a third category of Anabaptist distinctives appears to reflect the separation of ethics from theological doctrine in the classic formulas of Christendom. By contrast, the Anabaptists received the biblical text as a mandate for obedience. When stimulated by practices—lived-out expressions of the gospel—Anabaptists thought it necessary to add to and revise the received symbols and formulas of Christendom. This need to revise theology indicates the absence of ethical, lived dimensions of the classic creedal statements at that point in time.

Specifically, this fourth point is not a statement that Christendom was unethical or lacked ethics. Instead, within a general Christendom outlook, ethics and theology reflect different reference points. This point becomes clear when one recalls that for Anabaptists, the idea of Jesus as authority—expressed via discipleship—led directly to a rejection of the sword and a pacifist outlook. Within the theological traditions in the core shared with Anabaptism, confessing Jesus as Savior does not result in applying Jesus's teaching and example to arrive at rejection of the sword.[4] In this case, ethics begins at some point other than Jesus, which is a separation of theology from ethics. If so, such a view stresses Anabaptism's agreement with classic creeds more than Anabaptism's critique of Christendom's disobedient response to the biblical story addressed by the creeds. Those presenting such an emphasis are in danger of undermining basic convictions by which Anabaptists lived and died.

5. As stated in chapter 5, it is simply not true that Anabaptists "simply" affirmed the classic creeds and formulas of Christendom. While Anabaptists did use these symbols, the data provided in chapter 5 clearly demonstrates that Anabaptists found the classic statements by themselves inadequate and thus they engaged in considerable amplification of and deviation from them.

6. Stated another way, defining Anabaptism in terms of core theological statements shared with Catholicism and Protestantism implies that Anabaptists were theologically unoriginal.[5] In fact, it means that their theological validity depends on agreement with the received formulas, and innovation is problematic. Thus, Anabaptist theology can only be defined in terms of what already is, and any future theologizing perforce looks like the past. We are faced with the conundrum of a new movement whose primary identity can only be old. Anabaptists are thus uninteresting theologically because as newcomers they are presenting only pale versions of what the great theologians of the medieval period or the major Protestant Reformers have already said. The clear implication is that for theology of substance, we need to turn to Catholicism and the Protestant traditions. In fact, as chapter 5 argues, Anabaptists were innovative; their innovation stemmed from the inadequacy of the received symbols of Christendom, and their innovation is theologically significant because it was provoked by their acceptance of Jesus as authority for the Christian life.

7. The foregoing observations all point in the same direction, to show how Snyder's interpretation of Anabaptism lessens the differences between Anabaptism and Catholicism and Protestantism. But Anabaptists were not martyred because they had an outlook that made them look as much like Catholicism or Protestantism as possible. They were martyred because of their differences, and because of the perceived threat such differences posed to Catholic and Protestant regimes. Stated differently, Anabaptists were not martyred on the basis of Anabaptism defined in terms of Snyder's threefold theological definition.

8. If Anabaptists, Catholics, and Protestants shared as much in common as Snyder's approach implies, it would then follow that neither side understood the issues at stake (pun intended!). Those who were killing Anabaptists did not realize how much like themselves the Anabaptists were, and Anabaptists were giving up their lives for a faith that was quite close to that of their persecutors. The implications that neither side understood the situation seems contradicted by the arguments of Peter Blickle, who said that the Peasants' Reformation called for a restructuring of society that posed a clear challenge to the authorities, and that the authorities perceived that challenge. It was this challenge to the authorities that provoked the violent response to the peasants that is called the Peasants' War. Anabaptists also posed a challenge to existing structures of church and society, even if a quite different challenge than that of the peasants. Even when Anabaptists professed to be pacifists, their rejection of the state church and their rejection of the jurisdiction of political authorities in church matters were perceived as threats to the social order. For the most part, Anabaptists were not martyred for a faith with great resemblances to Catholicism and Protestantism, but because Anabaptism posed an implied challenge to the existing structures.

Defining Anabaptism in terms of a theological core of doctrines shared with Catholicism and Protestantism and then a set of Anabaptist distinctives would be establishing Christendom's theology as the norm from which Anabaptism is distinguished. With that approach, the credibility of Anabaptists derives first of all from identity with the received traditions. In the context of the larger picture of Christian traditions and denominations, Anabaptists and Anabaptism then become a smaller and less significant version of the received norm.

My approach, as articulated in this book, is to define Anabaptism as a movement with integrity in its own right. I understand Anabaptism as a Christian tradition that came to accept Jesus's life and teaching as authoritative for life, thereby seeking to live out of that story. A voluntary ecclesiology and rejection of the sword follow from the intent to live out the story of Jesus. This approach does not define Anabaptism in terms of agreement with other traditions, with the Anabaptist distinctives then constituting points of deviation. Rather, my view defines Anabaptism in terms of what it stands for and how it approaches the world and other Christian traditions. In my approach there are still obvious comparisons to make with the traditions of Christendom. But now, differences emerge out of what Anabaptism stands for; Anabaptist distinctives reflect their assumed foundation within the story of Jesus. What distinguishes Anabaptists from other Christian perspectives is then not a deviance from Christendom's norm, but the manner in which it appeals to Jesus' story. The credibility of Anabaptism as a movement thus depends on references to the story of Jesus rather than its agreement with the traditions of Christendom, even though Anabaptism emerged in conversation with these traditions of Christendom.[6]

The question is where authority ultimately lies—in Jesus' story or in later tradition. It bears repeating at this juncture that distinguishing Anabaptism in this way is not an assertion or call for withdrawal. It instead is designating the basis on which Anabaptism engages in and interacts with the traditions of Christendom and with the social order. In this light, Anabaptism is not a deviance from but a corrective for the traditions of Christendom, whose identification of the church with the social order is linked to not accepting Jesus as authoritative, particularly on the issue of the sword. Hence, we return to the original thesis, that defining Anabaptism theologically in terms of core theology shared with Christendom traditions blends Anabaptism into Christendom rather than posing a prophetic witness to those traditions and to the social order.

Notes

In the chapters of historical narrative, at the first significant mention of events (e.g., the Peasants' War) or persons (e.g., Pilgram Marpeck), a note lists the principal sources on which the narrative depends, with author and abbreviated title, supported by the bibliography. Other notes provide references to quoted material, specific points of interpretation, or explanations.

Abbreviation: *MQR* = *Mennonite Quarterly Review*

1. Introduction

1. On the Anabaptist roots of the Brethren, see Donald F. Durnbaugh, "The Genius of the Brethren," *Brethren Life and Thought* 4, no. 1 (Winter 1959): 18–27; idem, "Origins of the Church of the Brethren," *MQR* 36, no. 2 (April 1962): 162–68, 170; and Carl F. Bowman, *Brethren Society: The Cultural Transformation of a "Peculiar People"* (Baltimore, Md.: Johns Hopkins University Press, 1995), 3–6.

2. Sergio Torres and John Eagleson, eds., *The Challenge of Basic Christian Communities: Papers from the International Ecumenical Congress of Theology, February 20–March 2, 1980, São Paulo, Brazil* (trans. John Drury; Maryknoll, N.Y.: Orbis Books, 1981).

3. See §79 of *Gaudium et spes*; ET: Austin Flannery, ed. *Documents of Vatican II* (Grand Rapids: Eerdmans, 1975), 988.

4. National Conference of Catholic Bishops, *The Challenge of Peace: God's Promise and Our Response; A Pastoral Letter on War and Peace* (Washington, D.C.: United States Catholic Conference, 1983), 36–37 (§§118–119).

5. United Presbyterian Church, *Peacemaking: The Believers' Calling* (New York: United Presbyterian Church, 1980).

6. Susan Thistlethwaite, ed., *A Just Peace Church: The Peace Theology Development Team* (New York: United Church Press, 1986), Preface.

7. United Methodist Council of Bishops, *In Defense of Creation: The Nuclear Crisis and a Just Peace*. On support for conscientious objectors and war-tax resisters, see United Methodist Church, *Faithful Witness on Today's*

Issues: Peace with Justice (Washington, D.C.: The General Board of Church and Society of the United Methodist Church), 9; and idem, *Social Principles: The United Methodist Church* (Washington, D.C.: The General Board of Church and Society of the United Methodist Church, 1996), 30.

    8. Evangelical Lutheran Church in America, *For Peace in God's World* (Evangelical Lutheran Church in America, 1995), 1, 11, 12, 23n1.

    9. Douglas Gwyn, et al., *A Declaration on Peace: In God's People the World's Renewal Has Begun* (Scottdale, Pa.: Herald Press, 1991), quote from back cover.

    10. Fernando Enns, Scott Holland, and Ann Riggs, eds., *Seeking Cultures of Peace: A Peace Church Conversation* (Telford, Pa.: Cascadia Publishing House; Geneva: WCC Pubns.; Scottdale, Pa.: Herald Press, 2004). For recent WCC statements on violence, see World Council of Churches, *Overcoming Violence: WCC Statements and Actions 1994–2000* (Geneva: WCC, 2000).

2. Anabaptism in Switzerland

    1. George R. Potter, *Zwingli* (Cambridge: Cambridge University Press, 1977), 70. Much of the data on Zwingli in this narrative is from Potter.

    2. Werner O. Packull describes the two radical groups as representatives of the common people, and he shows the leading role of Andreas Castelberger among the radicals in Zurich. See Packull, "The Origins of Swiss Anabaptism in the Context of the Reformation of the Common Man," *Journal of Mennonite Studies* 3 (1985): 36–59.

    3. A letter from Conrad Grebel shows clear awareness of Erasmus's New Testament and that it was for sale in Castelberger's bookstore. See Leland Harder, ed., *The Sources of Swiss Anabaptism: The Grebel Letters and Related Documents* (Scottdale, Pa.: Herald Press, 1985), 358. For data on the influence of Erasmus in the story of Swiss Anabaptist origins, see A. Friesen, *Erasmus*.

    4. For data on Karlstadt's influence on Zurich Anabaptism, see by Pater, *Karlstadt*.

    5. Also probably present were Georg Binder, Hans Utinger, Hans Hottinger, Wolfgang Ininger, Lorenz Hochrütiner, and Hans Ockenfuss. See Potter, *Zwingli*, 75n2; and James M. Stayer, "Die Anfänge des schweizerischen Täufertums in reformierten Kongregationalismus," in *Umstrittenes Täufertum, 1525–1975: Neue Forschungen* (ed. Hans-Jürgen Goertz; Göttingen: Vandenhoeck & Ruprecht, 1975), 26. The description of these early conflicts follows Stayer, "Anfänge"; and Pater, *Karlstadt*.

    6. The description of the two hermeneutics draws on Werner O. Packull, *Hutterite Beginnings: Communitarian Experiments During the Reformation* (Baltimore: John Hopkins University Press, 1995), 16–32, esp. 31.

    7. Stayer, "Anfänge," 19–49, esp. 21.

    8. Peter Blickle, *Communal Reformation: The Quest for Salvation in Sixteenth-Century Germany* (New Jersey: Humanities Press, 1992).

    9. Harder, *Sources of Swiss Anabaptism*, 242.

    10. Ibid., 276.

11. Ibid., 358; Abraham Friesen, *Erasmus, the Anabaptists, and the Great Commission* (Grand Rapids: Eerdmans, 1998), 38, 44–48.

12. The letter, actually a letter and a long postscript, was written by Grebel, then signed by Andreas Castelberger, Felix Manz, Hans Ockenfuss, Barthlime Pur, Heinrich Aberli, Johannes Brötli, and Hans Huiuff. Several publications of the letter exist, of which the most recent is in Harder, *Sources of Swiss Anabaptism*, 284–94. A complete facsimile of Grebel's original German script, along with German transcription and English translation, are in Konrad Grebel, *Conrad Grebel's Programmatic Letters of 1524, with Facsimiles of the Original German Script of Grebel's Letters* (trans. John C. Wenger; Scottdale. Pa.: Herald Press, 1970).

13. Balthasar Hubmaier, *Balthasar Hubmaier: Theologian of Anabaptism* (trans. and ed. H. Wayne Pipkin and John H. Yoder; Scottdale, Pa.: Herald Press, 1989), 255.

14. The description of the Peasants' War and its backdrop draws on James M. Stayer, *The German Peasants' War and the Anabaptist Community of Goods* (Montreal & Kingston: McGill-Queen's University Press, 1991); and Blickle, *Communal Reformation*. Quotes from Stayer, 50; and Blickle, 142-43.

15. Cited in Stayer, *German Peasants' War*, 50.

16. Quoted in Blickle, *Communal Reformation*, 142–43.

17. For survey of Reublin's many appearances in the Anabaptist story, see biography in Hans-Jürgen Goertz, ed., *Profiles of Radical Reformers: Biographical Sketches from Thomas Müntzer to Paracelsus* (English ed., Walter Klaassen; Scottdale, Pa.: Herald Press, 1982.

18. This comment and the following section counter the statement of Peter Blickle, who wrote that when Swiss Anabaptists were excluded from the Zurich Reformation and the established political and ecclesiastical structures, "the ground had thus been prepared for a withdrawal from the social and political order." Blickle, *Communal Reformation*, 105. This description of a separatism of engagement and the following analysis of Schleitheim is based on Gerald Biesecker-Mast, *Separation and the Sword in Anabaptist Persuasion: Radical Confessional Rhetoric from Schleitheim to Dordrecht* (Telford, Pa.: Cascadia Publishing House, 2006), 101-08.

19. For data on Sattler, see Snyder, *Life and Thought*; idem, "Revolution and the Swiss Brethren"; and idem, "Monastic Origins."

20. The letter, the Schleitheim Articles, and other writings of Michael Sattler and contemporary accounts of his execution are in Michael Sattler, *The Legacy of Michael Sattler* (trans. and ed. John H. Yoder; Scottdale, Pa.: Herald Press, 1973).

21. Snyder, in *Life and Thought*, argued for the origins of Sattler's thought and the Schleitheim Articles in Benedictine monasticism. The word "parallels" used here echoes Dennis Martin's response, which accepted the idea of general parallels between an Anabaptist emphasis on discipleship and the monastic tradition, but not specifically Benedictine origins of Anabaptism. Dennis D. Martin, "Monks, Mendicants and Anabaptists: Michael Sattler and

the Benedictines Reconsidered," *MQR* 60, no. 2 (April 1986): 139–64; and idem, "Catholic Spirituality and Anabaptist and Mennonite Discipleship," *MQR* 62, no. 1 (January 1988): 5–25.

22. G. Biesecker-Mast, *Separation and the Sword*, 103.

23. Ibid., 103. See also Gerald Biesecker-Mast, "Anabaptist Separation and Arguments Against the Sword in the Schleitheim 'Brotherly Union,'" *MQR* 74, no. 3 (July 2000): 381–401.

24. The Swiss Order is translated in Sattler, *Legacy*, 44–45. For Packull's analysis of it, see *Hutterite Beginnings*, 33–46.

3. South German and Moravian Anabaptism

1. Mysticism occurred in many forms. Common to all is the idea of an inner, ecstatic communion with God that for a time transcends ordinary existence. Christian mystics often spoke of a spark of the divine within the individual and sought a mystical union with God at the point when one became *gelassen*, that is, totally emptied of self and submitted to the will of God.

2. For data on Müntzer and the Peasants' War, see biography in Goertz, *Profiles*; idem, "Mystic with a Hammer"; and analysis in G. Biesecker-Mast, *Separation and the Sword*.

3. James M. Stayer, *The German Peasants' War and the Anabaptist Community of Goods* (Montreal & Kingston: McGill-Queen's University Press, 1991), 108–11, esp. 121.

4. For data on Hut, see Packull, *Mysticism* and *Hutterite Beginnings*; Stayer, *German Peasants' War*; and biography in Goertz, *Profiles*.

5. For a detailed analysis of the dispute on atonement and the work of Christ, see J. Denny Weaver, "Hubmaier Versus Hut on the Work of Christ: The Fifth Nicolsburg Article," *Archiv für Reformationsgeschichte* 82 (1991): 171–92.

6. For biographical and theological data on Hans Denck, see Packull, *Mysticism*; Stayer, *German Peasants' War*; and the biography in Goertz, *Profiles*.

7. Manfred Krebs and Hans Georg Rott, eds., *Elsass*, part 1, *Stadt Stassburg 1522–1532*, part 7 of *Quellen zur Geschichte der Täufer* (Quellen und Forschungen zur Reformationsgeschichte 26; Gerd Mohn: Gütersloher, 1959), 110. For an extended analysis of Bucer's comment, see J. Denny Weaver, "The Work of Christ: On the Difficulty of Identifying an Anabaptist Perspective," *MQR* 59, no. 2 (April 1985): 107–29.

8. Werner O. Packull, *Mysticism and the Early South German-Austrian Anabaptist Movement, 1525–1531* (Scottdale, Pa.: Herald Press, 1977), 70.

9. Now Mikulov, Czechoslovakia. This account of Hubmaier and Nikolsburg follows Packull, *Mysticism*; and idem, *Hutterite Beginnings*.

10. Werner Packull gives conflicting statements on whether Hut brought Wiedemann to Anabaptism. See Werner O. Packull, *Hutterite Beginnings: Communitarian Experiments During the Reformation* (Baltimore, Md.: John Hopkins University Press, 1995), 58–59, 64.

11. Ibid., 61.

12. For data on Marpeck, see the biography in Goertz, *Profiles*; Pilgram Marpeck, *Writings of Pilgram Marpeck* (ed. Klassen and Klaassen); idem, *Exposé*; Stayer, *German Peasants' War* (ed. Klaassen, Packull, and Rempel); Packull, *Hutterite Beginnings*; Boyd, *Pilgram Marpeck*; Blough, *Christologie Anabaptiste*; and idem, "Pilgram Marpeck."

13. Walter Klaassen has made the most recent translation of the tract; see Pilgram Marpeck, "Exposé of the Babylonian Whore," in *The Exposé, a Dialogue, and Marpeck's Response to Caspar Schwenckfeld* (trans. Walter Klaassen et al.; vol. 1 of *Later Writings by Pilgram Marpeck and His Circle*; Kitchener, Ont.: Pandora, 1999), 19–48. For a facsimile reproduction, see Hans J. Hillerbrand, "An Early Anabaptist Treatise on the Christian and the State," *MQR* 32, no. 1 (January 1958): 28–47.

14. For a brief discussion of the authorship of *Exposé*, see Stayer, *German Peasants' War*, 120–21. Walter Klaassen first identified Marpeck as the probable author. For this argument, see Walter Klaassen, "Eine Untersuchung der Verfasserschaft und des historischen Hintergrundes der Täuferschrift 'Aufdeckung der Babylonischen Hurn,'" in *Evangelischer Glaube und Geschichte. Grete Mecenseffy zum 85. Geburtstag* (ed. Alfred Raddatz and Kurt Lüthi; Vienna: Evangelische Oberkirchenrat, 1984), 113–29; and Klaassen's introduction to *Exposé* in Marpeck, "Exposé," 22.

15. Arnold Snyder, "The (Not-So) 'Simple Confession' of the Later Swiss Brethren; Part I: Manuscripts and Marpeckites in an Age of Print," *MQR* 73, no. 4 (October 1999): 677–722; idem, "Part II: The Evolution of Separatist Anabaptism," *MQR* 74, no. 1 (January 2000): 87–122.

16. For literature on community of goods and Anabaptism in Moravia, see Packull, *Hutterite Beginnings*; and Stayer, *German Peasants' War*.

17. The modern Czech names of Austerlitz, Rossitz, and Auspitz are, respectively, Slavkov, Rosice, and Hustopeæe.

18. For data on Gaismair, see biography in Goertz, *Profiles*; and Packull, *Hutterite Beginnings*.

19. Packull, *Hutterite Beginnings*, 185–86.

20. For a description of the multifaceted life of Reublin, see biography in Goertz, *Profiles*.

21. Quoted in Packull, *Hutterite Beginnings*, 215.

22. Quoted in ibid., 227.

23. Quoted in ibid., 228.

24. Quoted in ibid., 229.

25. Quoted in ibid., 233.

26. Ibid., 89.

27. For data on Riedemann, see J. Friesen, *Peter Riedemann's Hutterite Confession*; and G. Biesecker-Mast, *Separation and the Sword*.

28. John J. Friesen, trans. and ed., *Peter Riedemann's Hutterite Confession of Faith* (Scottdale, Pa.: Herald Press, 1999), 80.

29. Gerald Biesecker-Mast, *Separation and the Sword in Anabaptist*

Persuasion: Radical Confessional Rhetoric from Schleitheim to Dordrecht (Telford, Pa.: Cascadia Publishing House, 2006), 146.

30. Leonard Gross, *The Golden Years of the Hutterites: The Witness and Thought of the Communal Moravian Anabaptists During the Walpot Era, 1565–1578* (Scottdale, Pa.: Herald Press, 1980).

4. Anabaptism in the Low Countries

1. For a summary of particular individuals associated with sacramentarianism, see Gary K. Waite, *David Joris and Dutch Anabaptism, 1524–1543* (Waterloo, Ont.: Wilfrid Laurier University Press, 1990), 7–12.

2. The Catholic belief that at the words of consecration said by the priest, the bread and wine of the eucharist become the actual body and blood of Christ.

3. In what follows, data on Hoffmann is drawn from Deppermann, *Melchior Hoffmann*; idem, "Melchior Hoffmans Weg"; idem, "Melchior Hoffman and Strasbourg"; the biography in Goertz, *Profiles*; and Packull, "Melchior Hoffman's Experience."

4. Wolmar and Dorpat are, respectively, present-day Valmiera, Latvia, and Tartu, Estonia.

5. For data on Karlstadt in the story of Dutch Anabaptism, see Pater, *Karlstadt.*

6. Klaus Deppermann, *Melchior Hoffman: Social Unrest and Apocalyptic Visions in the Age of Reformation* (ed. Benjamin Drewery; trans. Malcolm Wren; Edinburgh: T & T Clark, 1987), 178, 215. This Christology assumes what we now know to be a false understanding of human reproduction, namely that at conception the male implanted a complete human being in the female, where it grew until ready for birth. A number of medieval personages, including Thomas Aquinas, held to this understanding of human reproduction but did not extrapolate from it to Christology. The intent of the Christology was to ensure that Jesus did not inherit original sin. Most theologians agree, however, that the view denies a genuine humanity of Jesus.

7. Quoted in Calvin Augustine Pater, *Karlstadt as the Father of the Baptist Movements: The Emergence of Lay Protestantism* (Toronto: University of Toronto Press, 1984), 246.

8. An English translation appears as "The Ordinance of God" in George Huntston Williams and Angel M. Mergal, eds., *Spiritual and Anabaptist Writers: Documents Illustrative of the Radical Reformation* (Philadelphia: Westminster, 1957), 182–203.

9. Ibid., 192.

10. In Dutch practice, names like Philips, Simons, and Matthijs were patronymics—abbreviations for son of Philip, son of Simon, or son of Matthew—rather than the "last" or family names in the modern sense. Other designations, such as de Kuyper, which refers to a trade (barrel-maker), and van Leiden, which indicates place of origin, are also not "last" names in a modern sense. This narrative tries to conform to the original Dutch convention rather than using the patronymics and trade names as "last" names.

11. In addition to the writings of Deppermann, this section on Münster also draws on Stayer, *German Peasants' War*; Krahn, *Dutch Anabaptism*; and Williams, *Radical Reformation*.

12. So designated in James M. Stayer, *The German Peasants' War and the Anabaptist Community of Goods* (Montreal & Kingston: McGill-Queen's University Press, 1991), 126.

13. A story from Judith 13:1-10 (in the Apocrypha), in which Judith beheads the invading general Holofernes to save her city Bethulia.

14. Quoted in Stayer, *German Peasants' War*, 134.

15. Albert F. Mellink, "Das niederländisch-westfälische Täufertum im 16. Jahrhundert," in *Umstrittenes Täufertum 1525–1975: Neue Forschungen* (ed. Hans-Jürgen Goertz; Göttingen: Vandenhoeck & Ruprecht, 1975), 213.

16. The four directions are described by Deppermann, *Melchior Hoffman*, 358; and Mellink, "Das niederländische-westfälische Täufertum," 214.

17. For data on David in English, see Waite, *David Joris*; idem, "David Joris' Thought"; David Joris, *Anabaptist Writings of David Joris*; and Stayer, "Davidite vs. Mennonite."

18. Quoted in Deppermann, *Melchior Hoffman*, 360.

19. Gary K. Waite in David Joris, *The Anabaptist Writings of David Joris, 1535–1543* (trans. and ed. Gary K. Waite; Scottdale, Pa.: Herald Press, 1994), 24.

20. These numbers on publications are from Gary K. Waite, *David Joris*, 183.

21. On Anneken Jans, see Packull, "Anna Jansz"; and analysis in G. Biesecker-Mast, *Separation and the Sword*.

22. Cited in Werner O. Packull, "Anna Jansz of Rotterdam: A Historical Investigation of an Early Anabaptist Heroine," *Archiv für Reformationsgeschichte* 78 (1987): 159.

23. Ibid.," 162.

24. Waite, *David Joris*, 68, 70–72.

25. Thieleman J. van Braght, *The Bloody Theater or Martyrs Mirror of the Defenseless Christians* (trans. Joseph F. Sohm; Scottdale, Pa.: Mennonite Publishing House, 1950), 453–54.

26. Gerald Biesecker-Mast, *Separation and the Sword in Anabaptist Persuasion: Radical Confessional Rhetoric from Schleitheim to Dordrecht* (Telford, Pa.: Cascadia Publishing House, 2006), 175.

27. Packull, "Anna Jansz," 167.

28. The autobiographical comments from Menno in this sketch of his life were written some twenty years after the events recounted, in his 1554 "Reply to Gellius Faber," in Menno Simons, *The Complete Writings of Menno Simons, c. 1496–1561* (ed. John C. Wenger; trans. Leonard Verduin; biography by Harold S. Bender; Scottdale, Pa.: Herald Press, 1956), 668–72.

29. Menno Simons, *Complete Writings*, 270, 520–21.

30. Abraham Friesen, *Erasmus, the Anabaptists, and the Great Commission* (Grand Rapids: Eerdmans, 1998), 58–61, esp. 60–61. Menno's comments are in Menno Simons, *Complete Writings*, 120–21.

31. Egil Grislis wrote that Menno's autobiographical statements often reflect the anguish of sin and the joy of salvation, couched in the language of Scripture, rather than the actual details of his life. For example, his stinging description of a typical priest was not likely autobiographical, and he had never broken the vow of celibacy. See Egil Grislis, "Menno Simons' Account of His Conversion and Call in the Light of the Bible," *Journal of Mennonite Studies* 3 (1985): 73–82.

32. Menno Simons, *Dat fundament des Christelycken leers* (ed. H. W. Meihuizen; Den Haag: Martinus Nijhoff, 1967), 202–03, and Pater, *Karlstadt*, 251–52.

33. See Obbe Philips, "A Confession," in Williams and Mergal, *Spiritual and Anabaptist Writers*, 206–25.

34. Cornelius Krahn, *Dutch Anabaptism: Origin, Spread, Life, and Thought* (The Hague: Martinus Nijhoff, 1968; repr., Scottdale, Pa.: Herald Press, 1981), 174.

35. Menno Simons, *Complete Writings*, 1019.

36. G. Biesecker-Mast, *Separation and the Sword*, 180–89.

37. Hans-Jürgen Goertz, *Die Täufer: Geschichte und Deutung* (Munich: C. H. Beck, 1980), 37–38.

38. G. Biesecker-Mast, *Separation and the Sword*, 188-89.

39. Waite in David Joris, *Writings of David Joris*, 24–25.

40. Ibid., 25; Waite, *David Joris*, 186–87.

41. Douglas Schantz, "David Joris, Pietist Saint: The Appeal to Joris in the Writings of Christian Hoburg, Gottfried Arnold and Johann Wilhelm Petersen," *MQR* 78, no. 3 (July 2004): 415–32, esp. 432.

42. G. Biesecker-Mast, *Separation and the Sword*, 189-99.

43. Menno Simons, *Complete Writings*, 436–37.

44. See George Huntston Williams, *The Radical Reformation* (3d ed.; Sixteenth Century Essays and Studies 15; Kirksville, Mo.: Sixteenth Century Journal Publishers, 1992), 739–42.

45. Krahn, *Dutch Anabaptism*, 231; Menno Simons, *Complete Writings*, 1041–42.

46. This account of division follows William Keeney, "Dirk Philips' Life," *MQR* 32, no. 3 (July 1958): 182–83.

47. Krahn, *Dutch Anabaptism*, 235–37.

48. Menno Simons, *Complete Writings*, 959–98; Dietrich Philip, *Enchiridion or Hand Book of the Christian Doctrine and Religion: Compiled (by the Grace of God) from the Holy Scriptures for the Benefit of All Lovers of the Truth* (ed. A. B. Kolb; LaGrange, Ind.: Pathway Pub. Corp., 1966), 223–41.

49. "Reply to Sylis and Lemke," in Menno Simons, *Complete Writings*, 1000–15.

50. Keeney, "Dirk Philips' Life," 183; John S. Oyer, "The Strasbourg Conferences of the Anabaptists, 1554–1607," *MQR* 58, no. 3 (July 1984): 219.

51. Harold S. Bender described the statement of discipline that resulted from the Strasbourg conference of 1568 as the first such statement worked out by the Swiss and South Germans after they and the northerners had gone their separate ways. See Harold S. Bender, "The Discipline Adopted by the Strasburg Conference of 1568," *MQR* 1, no. 1 (January 1927): 58. See also Oyer, "Strasbourg Conferences," 219–20. Van der Zijpp notes that Menno never mentioned the Swiss Brethren, nor did he ever appeal to Zurich origins to parry the claims that his church began with Münster. Further, Sattler was the only non-Dutch martyr in *Het Offer des Herren* of 1562. There are no Dutch translations of Swiss writings except for the Schleitheim Articles in 1560, although Hans de Ries did include some reports on Swiss martyrs in his martyr book of 1615. See Nanne van der Zijpp, "The Dutch Aid the Swiss Mennonites," in *A Legacy of Faith: The Heritage of Menno Simons; A Sixtieth Anniversary Tribute to Cornelius Krahn* (ed. Cornelius J. Dyck; Newton, Mennonite Historical Series 8; Kan.: Faith & Life, 1962), 136–37. Yet note Krahn's statement in *Dutch Anabaptism*, 229–30: "There was constant contact between southern and northern Anabaptists from the earliest days."

52. Keeney, "Dirk Philips' Life," 187n113.

53. This account follows ibid., 186–91.

54. Krahn, *Dutch Anabaptism*, 229–30.

5. The Meaning of Anabaptism

1. For a comprehensive synthesis of these motifs under the rubric of the believers church motif along with historical sketches of a number of believers church traditions, see Donald F. Durnbaugh, *The Believers' Church: The History and Character of Radical Protestantism* (Scottdale, Pa.: Herald Press, 1985); and James Leo Garrett Jr., ed., *The Concept of the Believers' Church: Addresses from the 1968 Louisville Conference* (Scottdale, Pa.: Herald Press, 1960). A brief sketch of contemporary manifestations of the believers church motif appears in John Howard Yoder, *The Priestly Kingdom: Social Ethics as Gospel* (Notre Dame, Ind.: University of Notre Dame Press, 1984), 5–6.

2. It was published in the society's periodical as Harold S. Bender, "The Anabaptist Vision," *Church History* 13, no. 1 (March 1944): 3–24; and in Bender's own periodical as Harold S. Bender, "The Anabaptist Vision," *MQR* 18, no. 2 (April 1944): 67–88. It was reprinted in booklet form as Harold S. Bender, *The Anabaptist Vision* (Scottdale, Pa.: Herald Press, 1944). Following citations are to the booklet format.

3. See Leonard Gross, "Recasting the Anabaptist Vision: The Longer View," *MQR* 60, no. 3 (July 1986): 358–62.

4. Hans J. Hillerbrand, "Anabaptism and the Reformation: Another Look," *Church History* 29 (1960): 404–23; Hans J. Hillerbrand, "The Origin of Sixteenth-Century Anabaptism: Another Look," *Archiv für Reformationsgeschichte* 53 (1962): 152–80.

5. Bender, *Anabaptist Vision*, 18–19, 20, 26–29, 31.

6. C. Henry Smith, *The Mennonites: A Brief History of Their Origin and*

Later Development in Both Europe and America (Berne, Ind.: Mennonite Book Concern, 1920), passim, esp. 320ff. For the challenge that the Bender and Smith versions of Anabaptism posed for each other, see their exchange concerning Smith's *The Story of the Mennonites*, in Harold S. Bender and Ernst Correll, "C. Henry Smith's *The Story of the Mennonites*," review, *MQR* 16, no. 4 (October 1942): 270–75; and C. Henry Smith, "A Communication from C. Henry Smith Concerning the Review of His Book 'The Story of the Mennonites,'" *MQR* 17, no. 4 (October 1943): 246–52.

7. For a history of the Concern Movement, see Paul Toews, "The Concern Movement: Its Origin and Early History," *Conrad Grebel Review* 8, no. 2 (Spring 1990): 109–26. This issue of *CGR* also contains retrospective statements by six of the original seven members of the movement. John Howard Yoder is missing.

8. John H Yoder, "The Anabaptist Shape of Liberation," in *Why I Am a Mennonite: Essays on Mennonite Identity* (ed. Harry Loewen; Scottdale, Pa.: Herald Press, 1988), 339–42.

9. Bender, *Anabaptist Vision*, 11.

10. This article was James M. Stayer, Werner O. Packull, and Klaus Deppermann, "From Monogenesis to Polygenesis: The Historical Discussion of Anabaptist Origins," *MQR* 49, no. 2 (April 1975): 83–122. Its findings were quickly supported and expanded in much subsequent literature.

11. J. Denny Weaver, *Becoming Anabaptist: The Origin and Significance of Sixteenth-Century Anabaptism* (Scottdale, Pa.: Herald Press, 1987), 15.

12. Abraham Friesen, *Erasmus, the Anabaptists, and the Great Commission* (Grand Rapids: Eerdmans, 1998), 20–75.

13. C. Arnold Snyder, "Beyond Polygenesis: Recovering the Unity and Diversity of Anabaptist Theology," in *Essays in Anabaptist Theology* (ed. H. Wayne Pipkin; Text Reader Series; Elkhart, Ind.: Institute of Mennonite Studies, 1994), 11–16; C. Arnold Snyder, *Anabaptist History and Theology: An Introduction* (Kitchener, Ont.: Pandora, 1995), 83–98.

14. The idea of a "canon within the canon" should not pose a problem in itself. For example, carrying a New Testament in place of a whole Bible expresses a judgment about the priority of the New Testament. In contrast to an Anabaptist canon that begins with the Gospels, Martin Luther considered the writings of Paul, particularly Romans, as well as Psalms, to be the leading sources for learning the meaning of "Christ."

15. Ben C. Ollenburger, "The Hermeneutics of Obedience," in *Essays on Biblical Interpretation: Anabaptist-Mennonite Perspectives* (ed. Willard M. Swartley; Text-Reader Series (Elkhart, Ind.: Institute of Mennonite Studies, 1984), 45–61.

16. See John H. Yoder, "The Hermeneutics of the Anabaptists," *MQR* 41, no. 4 (October 1967): 300–4; idem, *Priestly Kingdom*, 63–65, 123–25; idem, *The Jewish-Christian Schism Revisited* (ed. Michael G. Cartwright and Ochs Peter; Grand Rapids: Eerdmans, 2003), 138.

17. Bender, *Anabaptist Vision*, 20.

18. John Howard Yoder, *The Politics of Jesus: Vicit Agnus Noster* (2d ed.; Grand Rapids: Eerdmans, 1994), 5–8, 15–19.

19. John H Yoder, "The Anabaptist Shape of Liberation," 339–43.

20. Ibid., 343–44.

21. Ibid., 339.

22. According to John Howard Yoder, awareness that history was not foreordained and keeping awareness of the choices faced by the protagonists "pushes us to ask far more ambitious and complex questions about all of the forces which were at work, and about how things could have been otherwise, in order to discern options which might have been really available if someone had had the information, or the courage, or the organization to reach them, distinguishing these from other kinds of wishful thinking, and from wasteful or resentful utopias. It drives us to take stock carefully of the powers and resources which were there but were not tapped, or which were at work but did not win out." John Howard Yoder, "'It Did Not Have to Be,'" in *The Jewish-Christian Schism Revisited*, 44. See also idem, "The Burden and the Discipline of Evangelical Revisionism" in *Nonviolent America: History Through the Eyes of Peace* (ed. Louise Hawkley and James C. Juhnke; Cornelius H. Wedel Historical Series 5; North Newton, Kan.: Bethel College, 1993), 23–29.

23. What I have informally called looping back, John Howard Yoder described as an ongoing "restitution," a "continuing series of new beginnings, similar in shape and spirit, as the objective historicity of Jesus and the apostles mediated through the objectivity of Scripture, encounters both the constants and the variables of every age to call forth 'restitutions' at once original and true-to-type, at once unpredictable and recognizable." John Howard Yoder, "Anabaptism and History," in *Priestly Kingdom*, 133.

24. John Howard Yoder, "'But We Do See Jesus': The Particularity of Incarnation and the Universality of Truth," in *Priestly Kingdom*, 46–62.

25. It is important to remember that God's reign is not identified with any particular entity of the social order. Thus, apparent progress on a justice issue does not mean that the reign of God has been brought nearer by political structures. As John Howard Yoder wrote, "The New Testament affirmations claimed no instrumental linkage between their trust in God's future victory and their own present progress." See Yoder, "The Power Equation, the Place of Jesus, and the Politics of King," in *For the Nations: Essays Public and Evangelical* (Grand Rapids: Eerdmans, 1997), 133. As Yoder said in one of many such comments, "Success is not measured by changing the world in a given direction within a given length of time, but by the congruence between our path and the triumph of Christ." See Yoder, "The Racial Revolution in Theological Perspective," in *For the Nations*, 109.

26. John Howard Yoder, "The Authority of Tradition," in *Priestly Kingdom*, 63–79. This essay has an extended discussion on evaluating historical change on the basis of the norm of Jesus Christ.

27. John Howard Yoder, *Politics of Jesus*, 5–8, 11, 15–19.

28. For this interpretation of Matthew 4:38-42, see Walter Wink, *Engaging the Powers: Discernment and Resistance in a World of Domination* (The Powers 3; Minneapolis: Fortress, 1992), 175–84, esp. 176–77.

29. Ibid., 186.

30. Gerald Biesecker-Mast, "Recovering the Anabaptist Body (to Separate It for the World)," in *Anabaptists and Postmodernity* (ed. idem and Susan Biesecker-Mast; The C. Henry Smith Series 1 (Telford, Pa.: Pandora Press U.S.; Scottdale, Pa.: Herald Press, 2000), 207–10.

31. Gerald Biesecker-Mast, "'Bloody Theater' and Christian Discipleship," *Mennonite Historical Bulletin*, October 2001, 4.

32. Yoder, *Jewish-Christian Schism Revisited*, 71.

33. Several discussions of the arc from "no king but Yahweh" to Jeremiah and exile and to Jesus appear in Yoder, *Jewish-Christian Schism Revisited*, including the essays "Jesus the Jewish Pacifist," "On Not Being in Charge," and "See How They Go with Their Face to the Sun."

34. Ibid., 192, 171.

35. John Howard Yoder, *Body Politics: Five Practices of the Christian Community Before the Watching World* (Scottdale, Pa.: Herald Press, 2001), 78.

36. Robert Friedmann, *The Theology of Anabaptism: An Interpretation* (Scottdale, Pa.: Herald Press, 1973), 121, 81.

37. Robert N. Bellah et al., *Habits of the Heart: Individualism and Commitment in American Life* (Berkeley, Calif.: University of California Press, 1985), 142. This important book provides an analysis of the problem of individualism in American society; then it makes some helpful suggestions toward a transformation of American society to bring about a new integration in individual goals and the common good.

38. Numbers frequently quoted are that the United States has about 5 percent of the world's population but consumes 30 to 40 percent of the world's resources.

39. Bellah, *Habits of the Heart*, 285.

40. A denomination-wide example is the discussion of access to health care within Mennonite Church USA. In July 2003, Mennonite Church USA Assembly delegates meeting in Atlanta, Georgia, approved a resolution from the Access Commission to develop a proposal whose outcome would be "Access to appropriate healthcare for all Mennonite Church USA members and more equitable access for our neighbors."

41. George C. Bedell, Leo Sandon Jr., and Charles T. Wellborn, *Religion in America* (2d ed.; New York: Macmillan, 1982), 17–18, esp. 17.

42. For example, see Lyman Beecher, "On Disestablishment in Connecticut," in *Church and State in American History* (ed. John F. Wilson; Boston: D.C. Heath, 1965), 92–93; idem, "A Plea for the West," in *God's New Israel: Religious Interpretations of American Destiny* (ed. Conrad Cherry; Chapel Hill, N.C.: University of North Carolina Press, 1998), 122–30; Henry Ward Beecher, "The Tendencies of American Progress," also in *God's New Israel*, 246–48.

43. The advocates of "Christian America" often refer to the Christian formation of the nation. That claim is much overdrawn if not outright false. It is true that the so-called founding fathers were church members. However, the majority of them were deists, with beliefs far removed from today's advocates of Christian America. Men such as Thomas Jefferson were suspicious of traditional Christianity, and the move to separate church and state was done to keep politics pure and away from the religion they considered spurious. For example, see Jefferson's edition of the New Testament, which removes all miracle stories of Jesus, and Jefferson's posthumously published letters in which he claimed that Christian doctrine was made complicated so that priests could have an easy life explaining it to people duped into the belief that it was necessary for salvation. For these items see Thomas Jefferson, *The Jefferson Bible: The Life and Morals of Jesus of Nazareth* (Boston: Beacon, 1951); and Jefferson's letters to Timothy Pickering and Benjamin Waterhouse in H. Shelton Smith, Handy Robert T., and Lefferts A. Loetscher, *American Christianity: An Historical Interpretations with Representative Documents*, vol. 1, *1607–1820* (New York: Scribner's Sons, 1960), 514–16.

44. For analysis of this economic structural violence and some suggestions for realistic alternatives, see James M. Harder, "The Violence of Global Marketization," in *Teaching Peace: Nonviolence and the Liberal Arts* (ed. J. Denny Weaver and Gerald Biesecker-Mast; Lanham, Md.: Rowman & Littlefield, 2003), 179–93.

45. Wes Howard-Brook and Anthony Gwyther, *Unveiling Empire: Reading Revelation Then and Now* (Maryknoll, N.Y.: Orbis Books, 1999).

46. Bender, *Anabaptist Vision*, 31.

47. Gerald Biesecker-Mast, *Separation and the Sword in Anabaptist Persuasion: Radical Confessional Rhetoric from Schleitheim to Dordrecht* (Telford, Pa.: Cascadia Publishing House, 2006), 101-08.

48. Rejection of the sword does not appear as a defining issue of Anabaptism when Arnold Snyder defines Anabaptist theology in terms of a core of shared beliefs. See Snyder, "Beyond Polygenesis," 12–16; and idem, *Anabaptist History and Theology: An Introduction*, 83–98.

49. Guy F. Hershberger, *War, Peace and Nonresistance* (Scottdale Pa.: Herald Press, 1953), 171. See also John C. Wenger, *Glimpses of Mennonite History and Doctrine* (4th printing, rev., 1947; repr., Scottdale, Pa.: Herald Press, 1959), 152–53.

50. For a history of this transition, see Leo Driedger and Donald B. Kraybill, *Mennonite Peacemaking: From Quietism to Activism* (Scottdale Pa.: Herald Press, 1993).

51. For some of their stories, see Melissa Miller and Phil M. Shenk, *The Path of Most Resistance: Stories of Mennonite Conscientious Objectors Who Did Not Cooperate with the Vietnam War Draft* (Scottdale, Pa.: Herald Press, 1982).

52. The address was reprinted as Ronald J. Sider, "Are We Willing to Die for Peace?" *Gospel Herald* 77, no. 52 (Dec. 25, 1984): 898–901.

53. In fact, G. Biesecker-Mast refers to the separation of antagonism and the separation of dualism. See G. Biesecker-Mast, *Separation and the Sword*, 28.

54. Although defended with language about defense, the doctrine of "preemptive war" proclaimed by U.S. President George W. Bush before the invasion of Iraq in March 2003 has many of the characteristics of a crusade. Crusade characteristics include "transcendent validation," appearing in the omnipresent references to "God bless America"; a "transcendent quality . . . known by revelation," evident in President Bush's claims to speak with God and to be carrying out a divine mission; the lack of "vested rights that have to be respected" for the enemy, evident in the quick dismissal of civilian deaths as "collateral damage"; the U.S. government's arguments that the Geneva Conventions on prisoners of war did not apply to Iraqi prisoners; and "the criterion of last resort does not apply," violated when inspectors were not allowed to complete the search for nuclear weapons, as became overwhelming clear when no weapons were found after the invasion. For crusade characteristics, see John Howard Yoder, *When War Is Unjust: Being Honest in Just-War Thinking* (2nd ed.; Maryknoll, N.Y.: Orbis, 1996), 12–14, esp. 13.

55. Glen H. Stassen and Michael L. Westmoreland-White, "Defining Violence and Nonviolence," in Weaver and G. Biesecker-Mast, ed., *Teaching Peace*, 18, with italics from Stassen and Westmoreland-White.

56. Ibid., 21.

57. "The Anabaptists did not feel called to the task of creative thinking in matters of doctrine. They were pleased simply to repeat the commonly accepted creeds." From C. Arnold Snyder, *From Anabaptist Seed: The Historical Core of Anabaptist-Related Identity* (Kitchener, Ont.: Pandora, 1999), 49, 10; and idem, "Beyond Polygenesis," 11.

58. For analysis of Michael Sattler and Hans Denck in comparison with Martin Bucer, see J. Denny Weaver, "The Work of Christ: On the Difficulty of Identifying an Anabaptist Perspective," *MQR* 59, no. 2 (April 1985): 107–29; for analysis of Balthasar Hubmaier and Hans Hut, see J. Denny Weaver, "Hubmaier Versus Hut on the Work of Christ: The Fifth Nicolsburg Article," *Archiv für Reformationsgeschichte* 82 (1991): 171–92.

59. Michael Sattler, *The Legacy of Michael Sattler* (trans. and ed. John H. Yoder; Scottdale, Pa.: Herald Press, 1973), 108–18, esp. 113, 115.

60. C. Arnold Snyder, *Following in the Footsteps of Christ: The Anabaptist Tradition* (ed. Philip Sheldrake; Maryknoll, N.Y.: Orbis Books, 2004), 53–54, esp. 54.

61. Neal Blough, "Pilgram Marpeck, Martin Luther and the Humanity of Christ," *MQR* 61, no. 2 (April 1987): 203–12, esp. 208.

62. Neal Blough, "Rédemption et histoire: Le salu dans la pensée de Pilgram Marpeck: La lettre 'Concernant l'humilité du Christ' (Février 1547)" (London, UK, 2004); forthcoming in a volume in the series "Perspectives anabaptistes," published by "Editions Excelcis." See also Tom Finger, "Pilgram Marpeck and the Christus Victor Motif," *MQR* 78, no. 1 (January 2004): 53–78.

63. For Menno's writing on Christology, see Menno Simons, *The Complete Writings of Menno Simons, c. 1496–1561* (ed. John C. Wenger; trans. Leonard Verduin; biography by Harold S. Bender; Scottdale, Pa.: Herald Press, 1956), 422–40, 487–98, 763–72, 792–834. For an analysis of Menno's Christology, see William Keeney, "The Incarnation, a Central Theological Concept," in *A Legacy of Faith: The Heritage of Menno Simons; Sixtieth Anniversary Tribute to Cornelius Krahn* (ed. Cornelius J. Dyck; Newton, Kan.: Faith & Life Press, 1962), 55–68. The argument for Menno given here first appeared in my *Anabaptist Theology in Face of Postmodernity: A Proposal for the Third Millennium* (Telford, Pa.: Pandora Press U.S.; Scottdale, Pa.: Herald Press, 2000), 104–5.

64. Traditional Catholic thought solved this problem in a different way. To give Jesus a sinless mother from whom he could then inherit sinless flesh, Catholic thought eventually posited the "immaculate conception" of Mary, in which the Holy Spirit miraculously interceded to prevent the transmission of original sin when Anne and Joachim, Mary's parents according to tradition, conceived her through sexual intercourse. The resultant sinless Mary could then give birth to a sinless son of her flesh. See also comment of n. 6 for ch. 4.

65. Robert A. Riall, trans., and Galen A. Peters, ed., *The Earliest Hymns of the* Ausbund*: Some Beautiful Christian Songs Composed and Sung in the Prison at Passau, Published in 1564* (Kitchener, Ont.: Pandora, 2003), 31, 48, 49, 51, 53.

66. Ibid., 50, 53, 54.

67. Ibid., 62.

68. G. Biesecker-Mast, *Separation and the Sword*, 142–44, 145–46.

69. Hutterian Brethren, *The Chronicle of the Hutterian Brethren Vol. 1*, (ed. and trans. Hutterian Brethern; Rifton, N.Y.: Plough Publishing House, 1987), 251.

70. John H. Yoder, "Hermeneutics of the Anabaptists," 293, 301.

71. J. Denny Weaver, *Keeping Salvation Ethical: Mennonite and Amish Atonement Theology in the Late Nineteenth Century* (Scottdale, Pa.: Herald Press, 1997). For short versions of this discussion, see my "Amish and Mennonite Soteriology: Revivalism and Free Church Theologizing in the Nineteenth-Century," *Fides et Historia* 27, no. 1 (Winter/Spring 1995): 30–52; and my *Anabaptist Theology in Face of Postmodernity*, 71–93.

72. J. Denny Weaver, *The Nonviolent Atonement* (Grand Rapids: Eerdmans, 2001). For summaries of the argument of this book, see idem, "Violence in Christian Theology," *CrossCurrents* 51, no. 2 (Summer 2001): 150–76; and idem, "Violence in Christian Theology," in Weaver and G. Biesecker-Mast, *Teaching Peace*, 39–52.

73. Ethelbert Stauffer, "The Anabaptist Theology of Martyrdom," *MQR* 19, no. 3 (July 1945): 179–214.

74. James C. Juhnke, *Vision, Doctrine, War: Mennonite Identity and Organization in America, 1890–1930* (Scottdale, Pa.: Herald Press, 1989), 218–41.

75. Richard K. MacMaster, *Land, Piety, and Peoplehood: The Establishment of Mennonite Communities in America, 1683–1790* (Scottdale, Pa.: Herald Press, 1984), 249–80; Theron F. Schlabach, *Peace, Faith, Nation: Mennonites and Amish in Nineteenth-Century America* (Scottdale, Pa.: Herald, 1988), 191–92.

76. Weaver and G. Biesecker-Mast, ed., *Teaching Peace.*

Appendix: Essay on Interpretation

1. C. Arnold Snyder, *Anabaptist History and Theology: An Introduction* (Kitchener, Ont.: Pandora, 1995), 83–99; idem, "Beyond Polygenesis: Recovering the Unity and Diversity of Anabaptist Theology," in *Essays in Anabaptist Theology* (ed. H. Wayne Pipkin; Elkhart, Ind.: Institute of Mennonite Studies, 1994), 11–16.

2. The descriptions of this core theology are Snyder, "Beyond Polygenesis," 12–16; and idem, *Anabaptist History and Theology: An Introduction,* 84–93.

3. John H. Yoder, "On Christian Unity: The Way from Below," *Pro Ecclesia* 9, no. 2 (2001): 165–83.

4. This is, of course, based on John Howard Yoder's description of the Constantinian shift, as developed in chapter 5 (above). In a succinct statement of the point made here, Yoder wrote that ultimately what is at stake is the "meaning of the incarnation." The debate in the sixteenth and seventeenth centuries, supposedly about the authority of Scripture, "diverted attention from what was more profoundly at stake, namely, whether the real Jesus of Nazareth is the norm for Christians. Evolutionary visions of the authority of continuing tradition claim grounds, reverently, to leave the earthly Jesus behind. Constantinian triumphalism replaces him with a *Christus Rex* whose preferred instruments are princes and patriarchs. Official Protestantism called for reform, but trusted the princes to do the reforming, and stated the issues at stake primarily on the levels of doctrine." From John Howard Yoder, *The Jewish-Christian Schism Revisited* (ed. Michael G. Cartwright and Ochs Peter; Grand Rapids: Eerdmans, 2003), 139.

5. See comments in C. Arnold Snyder, *From Anabaptist Seed: The Historical Core of Anabaptist-Related Identity* (Kitchener, Ont.: Pandora, 1999), 10, 22, 49.

6. This methodology is parallel to the analysis of John Howard Yoder, who posed questions concerning the "critical study of traditional understandings of the faith" in light of continuing developments in biblical research. "Is the inherited doctrinal system of a given denomination," Yoder asked, "which claims to be identical with the total teaching of Scripture, really that accurate as a portrayal of what the Bible says? Does this not need to be tested again in every generation? Otherwise, how would we explain the variety of positions each of which claim to be simply identical to the biblical teaching?" Later, after describing the uniqueness of Anabaptist interpretation in terms of the "rule of Paul," interpretation within the congregation with every member

participating in interpretation, Yoder wrote: "The other necessary implication of thus placing theological authority in the hands of the congregation was that the congregation must not be bound by tradition or former creedal statements, nor by the supervision of governmental authority. The congregation will recognize the assistance of a teaching tradition, and learn from it as long as it is in accordance with Scripture. . . . There is no denial of history; but there was a refusal to be bound by tradition." A page later, Yoder notes that this approach is to be distinguished from a "primitivism," which would ignore history and expect to repeat the "exact patterns of the primitive church. The concern was for a faithful restoration and moving forward, not for an impossible reversal of the course of history." From John H. Yoder, "The Hermeneutics of the Anabaptists," *MQR* 41, no. 4 (October 1967): 293, 301, 302.

Bibliography

Abbreviation: *MQR* = *Mennonite Quarterly Review*

Bedell, George C., Leo Sandon Jr., and Charles T. Wellborn. *Religion in America.* 2d ed. New York: Macmillan, 1982.

Beecher, Lyman. "On Disestablishment in Connecticut." Pages 92–93 in *Church and State in American History.* Edited by John F. Wilson. Boston: D.C. Heath, 1965.

Bellah, Robert N., Richard Madsen, William M. Sullivan, Ann Swidler, and Steven M. Tipton. *Habits of the Heart: Individualism and Commitment in American Life.* Berkeley: University of California Press, 1985.

Bender, Harold S. "The Anabaptist Vision." *Church History* 13, no. 1 (March 1944): 3–24.

———. "The Anabaptist Vision." *MQR* 18, no. 2 (April 1944): 67–88.

———. *The Anabaptist Vision.* Scottdale, Pa.: Herald Press, 1944.

———. "The Discipline Adopted by the Strasburg Conference of 1568." *MQR* 1, no. 1 (January 1927): 57–66.

Bender, Harold S., and Ernst Correll. "C. Henry Smith's *The Story of the Mennonites.*" Review. *MQR* 16, no. 4 (October 1942): 270–75.

Biesecker-Mast, Gerald. "Anabaptist Separation and Arguments Against the Sword in the Schleitheim 'Brotherly Union.'" *MQR* 74, no. 3 (July 2000): 381–401.

————. "'Bloody Theater' and Christian Discipleship." *Mennonite Historical Bulletin*, October 2001, 1–10.

————. *Separation and the Sword in Anabaptist Persuasion: Radical Confessional Rhetoric from Schleitheim to Dordrecht*. The C. Henry Smith Series. Telford, Pa.: Cascadia Publishing House, 2006.

Biesecker-Mast, Susan, and Gerald Biesecker-Mast, eds. *Anabaptists and Postmodernity*. Foreword by J. Denny Weaver. The C. Henry Smith Series 1. Telford, Pa.: Pandora Press U.S.; Scottdale, Pa.: Herald Press, 2000.

Blickle, Peter. *Communal Reformation: The Quest for Salvation in Sixteenth-Century Germany*. New Jersey: Humanities Press, 1992.

Blough, Neal. *Christologie Anabaptiste: Pilgram Marpeck et l'humanité du Christ*. With a preface by Marc Lienhard. Histoire et Société 4. Geneva: Labor et Fides, 1984.

————. "Pilgram Marpeck, Martin Luther and the Humanity of Christ." *MQR* 61, no. 2 (April 1987): 203–12.

————. "Rédemption et histoire: Le salu dans la pensee de Pilgram Marpeck: La lettre 'Concernant l'humilite du Christ' (Février 1547)." London, UK, 2004. Forthcoming in a volume in the series "Perspectives anabaptistes," published by "Editions Excelcis."

Bowman, Carl F. *Brethren Society: The Cultural Transformation of a "Peculiar People."* Baltimore: Johns Hopkins University Press, 1995.

Boyd, Stephen B. *Pilgram Marpeck: His Life and Social Theology*. Durham: Duke University Press, 1992.

Cherry, Conrad, ed. *God's New Israel: Religious Interpretations of American Destiny*. Chapel Hill, N.C.: University of North Carolina Press, 1998.

Deppermann, Klaus. "Melchior Hoffman and Strabourg Anabaptism." Pages 216–19 in *The Origins and Characteristics of Anabaptism/Les debuts et les caracter-*

istiques de l'Anabaptisme. Edited by Marc Lienhard. The Hague: Martinus Nijhoff, 1977.

————. *Melchior Hoffman: Social Unrest and Apocalyptic Visions in the Age of Reformation*. Edited by Benjamin Drewery. Translated by Malcolm Wren. Edinburgh: T & T Clark, 1987.

Driedger, Leo, and Donald B. Kraybill. *Mennonite Peacemaking: From Quietism to Activism*. Foreword by John A. Lapp. Scottdale, Pa.: Herald Press, 1993.

Durnbaugh, Donald F. *The Believers' Church: The History and Character of Radical Protestantism*. Scottdale, Pa.: Herald Press, 1985.

————. "The Genius of the Brethren." *Brethren Life and Thought* 4, no. 1 (Winter 1959): 4–34.

————. "Origins of the Church of the Brethren." *MQR* 36, no. 2 (April 1962): 162–68, 170.

Dyck, Cornelius J., ed. *A Legacy of Faith: The Heritage of Menno Simons; Sixtieth Anniversary Tribute to Cornelius Krahn*. Mennonite Historical Series 8. Newton, Kan.: Faith & Life Press, 1962.

Enns, Fernando, Scott Holland, and Ann Riggs, eds. *Seeking Cultures of Peace: A Peace Church Conversation*. Telford, Pa.: Cascadia Publishing House; Geneva: WCC Pubns.; Scottdale, Pa.: Herald Press, 2004.

Evangelical Lutheran Church in America. *For Peace in God's World*. Evangelical Lutheran Church in America, 1995.

Finger, Tom. "Pilgram Marpeck and the Christus Victor Motif." *MQR* 78, no. 1 (January 2004): 53–78.

Flannery, Austin, ed. *Documents of Vatican II*. Grand Rapids: Eerdmans, 1975.

Friedmann, Robert. *The Theology of Anabaptism: An Interpretation*. Studies in Anabaptist and Mennonite History 15. Scottdale, Pa.: Herald Press, 1973.

Friesen, Abraham. *Erasmus, the Anabaptists, and the Great Commission*. Grand Rapids: Eerdmans, 1998.

Friesen, John J., trans. and ed. *Peter Riedemann's Hutterite Confession of Faith.* Classics of the Radical Reformation 9. Scottdale, Pa.: Herald Press, 1999.

Garrett, James Leo, Jr., ed. *The Concept of the Believers' Church: Addresses from the 1968 Louisville Conference.* Scottdale, Pa.: Herald Press, 1960.

Goertz, Hans-Jürgen. "The Mystic with the Hammer: Thomas Müntzer's Theological Basis for Revolution." *MQR* 50, no. 2 (April 1976): 83–114.

———, ed. *Profiles of Radical Reformers: Biographical Sketches from Thomas Müntzer to Paracelsus.* English ed., Walter Klaassen. Scottdale, Pa.: Herald Press, 1982.

———. *Die Täufer: Geschichte und Deutung.* Munich: C. H. Beck, 1980.

———, ed. *Umstrittenes Täufertum, 1525–1975: Neue Forschungen.* Göttingen: Vandenhoeck & Ruprecht, 1975.

Grebel, Konrad. *Conrad Grebel's Programmatic Letters of 1524, with Facsimiles of the Original German Script of Grebel's Letters.* Translated by J. C. Wenger. Scottdale, Pa.: Herald Press, 1970.

Grislis, Egil. "Menno Simons' Account of His Conversion and Call in the Light of the Bible." *Journal of Mennonite Studies* 3 (1985): 73–82.

Gross, Leonard. *The Golden Years of the Hutterites: The Witness and Thought of the Communal Moravian Anabaptists During the Walpot Era, 1565–1578.* Studies in Anabaptist and Mennonite History 23. Scottdale, Pa.: Herald Press, 1980.

———. "Recasting the Anabaptist Vision: The Longer View." *MQR* 60, no. 3 (July 1986): 352–63.

Gwyn, Douglas, George Hunsinger, Eugene F. Roop, and John Howard Yoder. *A Declaration on Peace: In God's People the World's Renewal Has Begun.* Scottdale, Pa.; Waterloo, Ontario: Herald Press, 1991.

Harder, Leland, ed. *The Sources of Swiss Anabaptism: The Grebel Letters and Related Documents.* Classics of the Radical Reformation 4. Scottdale, Pa.: Herald Press, 1985.

Hershberger, Guy Franklin. *War, Peace and Nonresistance.* Scottdale, Pa.: Herald Press, 1953.

Hillerbrand, Hans J. "An Early Anabaptist Treatise on the Christian and the State." *MQR* 32, no. 1 (January 1958): 28–47.

Howard-Brook, Wes, and Anthony Gwyther. *Unveiling Empire: Reading Revelation Then and Now.* Maryknoll, N.Y.: Orbis Books, 1999.

Hubmaier, Balthasar. *Balthasar Hubmaier: Theologian of Anabaptism.* Translated and edited by H. Wayne Pipkin and John H. Yoder. Classics of the Reformation 5. Scottdale, Pa.: Herald Press, 1989.

Hutterian Brethren. *The Chronicle of the Hutterian Brethren.* Vol. 1. Edited and translated by Hutterian Brethren. Rifton, N.Y.: Plough Publishing House, 1987.

Jefferson, Thomas. *The Jefferson Bible: The Life and Morals of Jesus of Nazareth.* Boston: Beacon, 1951.

Joris, David. *The Anabaptist Writings of David Joris, 1535–1543.* Translated and edited by Gary K. Waite. Classics of the Radical Reformation 7. Scottdale, Pa.: Herald Press, 1994.

Juhnke, James C. *Vision, Doctrine, War: Mennonite Identity and Organization in America, 1890–1930.* Mennonite Experience in America 3. Scottdale, Pa.: Herald Press, 1989.

Keeney, William. "Dirk Philips' Life." *MQR* 32, no. 3 (July 1958): 171–91.

———. "Eine Untersuchung der Verfasserschaft und des historischen Hintergrundes der Täuferschrift 'Aufdeckung der Babylonischen Hurn.'" Pages 113–29 in *Evangelischer Glaube und Geschichte: Grete Mecenseffy zum 85.*

Geburtstag. Edited by Alfred Raddatz and Kurt Lüthi. Vienna: Evangelische Oberkirchenrat, 1984.

Krahn, Cornelius. *Dutch Anabaptism: Origin, Spread, Life, and Thought.* The Hague: Martinus Nijhoff, 1968. Repr., Scottdale, Pa.: Herald Press, 1981.

Krebs, Manfred, and Hans Georg Rott, eds. *Elass.* Part 1, *Stadt Stassburg, 1522–1532.* Vol. 7 of *Quellen zur Geschichte der Täufer.* Quellen und Forschungen zur Reformationsgeschichte 26. Gerd Mohn: Gütersloher, 1959.

MacMaster, Richard K. *Land, Piety, and Peoplehood: The Establishment of Mennonite Communities in America, 1683–1790.* Mennonite Experience in America 1. Scottdale, Pa.: Herald Press, 1984.

Marpeck, Pilgram. *The Exposé, a Dialogue, and Marpeck's Response to Caspar Schwenckfeld.* Translated by Walter Klaassen, Werner Packull, and John Rempel. Introduced by John Rempel. Vol. 1 of *Later Writings by Pilgram Marpeck and His Circle.* Kitchener, Ont.: Pandora, 1999.

———. *The Writings of Pilgram Marpeck.* Edited and translated by William Klassen and Walter Klaassen. Classics of the Reformation 2. Scottdale, Pa.: Herald Press, 1978.

Martin, Dennis D. "Catholic Spirituality and Anabaptist and Mennonite Discipleship." *MQR* 62, no. 1 (January 1988): 5–25.

———. "Monks, Mendicants and Anabaptists: Michael Sattler and the Benedictines Reconsidered." *MQR* 60, no. 2 (April 1986): 139–64.

Menno Simons. *The Complete Writings of Menno Simons, c. 1496–1561.* Edited by John Christian Wenger. Translated by Leonard Verduin. Biography by Harold S. Bender. Scottdale, Pa.: Herald Press, 1956.

———. *Dat fundament des Christelycken leers.* Edited by H. W. Meihuizen. Den Haag: Martinus Nijhoff, 1967.

Miller, Melissa, and Phil M. Shenk. *The Path of Most Resistance: Stories of Mennonite Conscientious Objectors Who Did Not Cooperate with the Vietnam War Draft.* Introduced by John M. Drescher. Scottdale, Pa.: Herald Press, 1982.

National Conference of Catholic Bishops. *The Challenge of Peace: God's Promise and Our Response. A Pastoral Letter on War and Peace.* Washington, D.C.: United States Catholic Conference, 1983.

Ollenburger, Ben C. "The Hermeneutics of Obedience." Pages 45–61 in *Essays on Biblical Interpretation: Anabaptist-Mennonite Perspectives.* Edited by Willard M. Swartley. Text-Reader Series. Elkhart, Ind.: Institute of Mennonite Studies, 1984.

Oyer, John S. "The Strasbourg Conferences of the Anabaptists, 1554–1607." *MQR* 58, no. 3 (July 1984): 218–29.

Packull, Werner O. "Anna Jansz of Rotterdam: A Historical Investigation of an Early Anabaptist Heroine." *Archiv für Reformationsgeschichte* 78 (1987): 147–73.

———. *Hutterite Beginnings: Communitarian Experiments During the Reformation.* Baltimore: John Hopkins University Press, 1995.

———. "Melchior Hoffman's Experience in the Livonian Reformation: The Dynamics of Sect Formation." *MQR* 59, no. April (1985): 130–46.

———. *Mysticism and the Early South German-Austrian Anabaptist Movement, 1525–1531.* Scottdale, PA: Herald Press, 1977.

———. "The Origins of Swiss Anabaptism in the Context of the Reformation of the Common Man." *Journal of Mennonite Studies* 3 (1985): 36–59.

Pater, Calvin Augustine. *Karlstadt as the Father of the Baptist Movements: The Emergence of Lay Protestantism.* Toronto: University of Toronto Press, 1984.

Philip, Dietrich. *Enchiridion or Hand Book of the Christian Doctrine and Religion: Compiled (by the Grace of God) from the Holy Scriptures for the Benefit of All Lovers of the Truth.* Edited by A. B. Kolb. LaGrange, Ind.: Pathway Pub. Corp., 1966.

Potter, George R. *Zwingli.* Cambridge: Cambridge University Press, 1977.

Riall, Robert A., trans. Galen A. Peters, ed. *The Earliest Hymns of the* Ausbund: *Some Beautiful Christian Songs Composed and Sung in the Prison at Passau, Published in 1564.* Anabaptist Texts in Translation. Kitchener, Ont.: Pandora, 2003.

Sattler, Michael. *The Legacy of Michael Sattler.* Translated and edited by John H. Yoder. Classics of the Radical Reformation 1. Scottdale, Pa.: Herald Press, 1973.

Schantz, Douglas. "David Joris, Pietist Saint: The Appeal to Joris in the Writings of Christian Hoburg, Gottfried Arnold and Johann Wilhelm Petersen." *MQR* 78, no. 3 (July 2004): 415–32.

Schlabach, Theron F. *Peace, Faith, Nation: Mennonites and Amish in Nineteenth-Century America.* The Mennonite Experience in America 2. Scottdale, Pa.: Herald, 1988.

Sider, Ronald J. "Are We Willing to Die for Peace?" *Gospel Herald* 77, no. 52 (25 December 1984): 898–901.

Smith, C. Henry. "A Communication from C. Henry Smith Concerning the Review of His Book 'The Story of the Mennonites.'" *MQR* 17, no. 4 (October 1943): 246–52.

———. *The Mennonites: A Brief History of Their Origin and Later Development in Both Europe and America.* Berne, Ind.: Mennonite Book Concern, 1920.

Smith, H. Shelton, Handy Robert T., and Lefferts A. Loetscher. *American Christianity: An Historical Interpretation with Representative Documents.* Vol. 1, *1607–1820.* New York: Scribner's Sons, 1960.

Snyder, C. Arnold. *Anabaptist History and Theology: An Introduction.* Kitchener, Ont.: Pandora, 1995.

———. "Beyond Polygenesis: Recovering the Unity and Diversity of Anabaptist Theology." Pages 1–34 in *Essays in Anabaptist Theology*. Edited by H. Wayne Pipkin. Text Reader Series. Elkhart, Ind.: Institute of Mennonite Studies, 1994.

———. *Following in the Footsteps of Christ: The Anabaptist Tradition*. Edited by Philip Sheldrake. Traditions of Christian Spirituality. Maryknoll, N.Y.: Orbis Books, 2004.

———. *From Anabaptist Seed: The Historical Core of Anabaptist-Related Identity*. Kitchener, Ont.: Pandora, 1999.

———. *The Life and Thought of Michael Sattler*. Studies in Anabaptist and Mennonite History 27. Scottdale, Pa.: Herald Press, 1984.

———. "The Monastic Origins of Swiss Anabaptist Sectarianism." *MQR* 57, no. 1 (January 1983): 5–26.

———. "The (Not-So) 'Simple Confession' of the Later Swiss Brethren; Part I: Manuscripts and Marpeckites in an Age of Print." *MQR* 73, no. 4 (October 1999): 677–722.

———. "The (Not-So) 'Simple Confession' of the Late Sixteenth-Century Anabaptists; Part II: The Evolution of Separatist Anabaptism." *MQR* 74, no. 1 (January 2000): 87–122.

———. "Revolution and the Swiss Brethren: The Case for Michael Sattler." *Church History* 50, no. 3 (September 1981): 276–87.

Stayer, James M. *Anabaptists and the Sword*. Rev. ed. Lawrence: Coronado, 1975.

———. "Davidite vs. Mennonite." *MQR* 58, no. 4 (October 1984): 459–76.

———. *The German Peasants' War and the Anabaptist Community of Goods*. McGill-Queen's Studies in the History of Religion 6. Montreal & Kingston: McGill-Queen's University Press, 1991.

Stayer, James M., Werner O. Packull, and Klaus Deppermann. "From Monogenesis to Polygenesis: The Historical

Discussion of Anabaptist Origins." *MQR* 49, no. 2 (April 1975). 83–122.

Toews, Paul. "The Concern Movement: Its Origin and Early History." *Conrad Grebel Review* 8, no. 2 (Spring 1990): 109–26.

Torres, Sergio, and John Eagleson, eds. *The Challenge of Basic Christian Communities: Papers from the International Ecumenical Congress of Theology, February 20–March 2, 1980, São Paulo, Brazil*. Translated by John Drury. Maryknoll, N.Y.: Orbis Books, 1981.

United Methodist Church. *Faithful Witness on Today's Issues: Peace with Justice*. Washington, D.C.: The General Board of Church and Society of the United Methodist Church. [1992]

————. *Social Principles: The United Methodist Church*. Washington, D.C.: The General Board of Church and Society of the United Methodist Church, 1996.

United Methodist Council of Bishops. *In Defense of Creation: The Nuclear Crisis and a Just Peace*. Edited by C. Dale White. Nashville, Tenn.: Graded Press, 1986.

United Presbyterian Church. *Peacemaking: The Believers' Calling*. New York: United Presbyterian Church, 1980.

Van Braght, Thieleman J. *The Bloody Theater or Martyrs Mirror of the Defenseless Christians*. Translated by Joseph F. Sohm. Scottdale, Pa.: Mennonite Publishing House, 1950.

Waite, Gary K. *David Joris and Dutch Anabaptism, 1524–1543*. Waterloo, Ont.: Wilfrid Laurier University Press, 1990.

————. "David Joris' Thought in the Context of the Early Melchiorite and Münsterite Movements in the Low Countries, 1534–36." *MQR* 62, no. 3 (July 1988): 296–317.

Weaver, J. Denny. "Amish and Mennonite Soteriology: Revivalism and Free Church Theologizing in the Nineteenth-Century." *Fides et Historia* 27, no. 1 (Winter/Spring 1995): 30–52.

————. *Anabaptist Theology in Face of Postmodernity: A Proposal for the Third Millennium*. The C. Henry Smith Series 2. Telford, Pa.: Pandora Press U.S.; Scottdale, Pa.: Herald Press, 2000.

————. *Becoming Anabaptist: The Origin and Significance of Sixteenth-Century Anabaptism*. 1st ed. Scottdale, Pa.: Herald Press, 1987.

————. "Hubmaier Versus Hut on the Work of Christ: The Fifth Nicolsburg Article." *Archiv für Reformationsgeschichte* 82 (1991): 171–92.

————. *Keeping Salvation Ethical: Mennonite and Amish Atonement Theology in the Late Nineteenth Century*. Studies in Anabaptist and Mennonite History 35. Scottdale, Pa.: Herald Press, 1997.

————. *The Nonviolent Atonement*. Grand Rapids: Eerdmans, 2001.

————. "Violence in Christian Theology." *CrossCurrents* 51, no. 2 (Summer 2001): 150–76.

————. "The Work of Christ: On the Difficulty of Identifying an Anabaptist Perspective." *MQR* 59, no. 2 (April 1985): 107–29.

Weaver, J. Denny, and Gerald Biesecker-Mast, eds. *Teaching Peace: Nonviolence and the Liberal Arts*. Lanham, Md.: Rowman & Littlefield, 2003.

Wenger, John C. *Glimpses of Mennonite History and Doctrine*. 4th printing, rev. 1947. Scottdale, Pa.: Herald Press, 1959.

Williams, George Huntston. *The Radical Reformation*. 3d ed. Sixteenth Century Essays and Studies 15. Kirksville, Mo.: Sixteenth Century Journal Publishers, 1992.

Williams, George Huntston, and Angel M. Mergal, eds. *Spiritual and Anabaptist Writers: Documents Illustrative of the Radical Reformation*. Library of Christian Classics 25. Philadelphia: Westminster, 1957.

Wink, Walter. *Engaging the Powers: Discernment and Resistance in a World of Domination.* The Powers 3. Minneapolis: Fortress, 1992.

World Council of Churches. *Overcoming Violence: WCC Statements and Actions, 1994–2000.* Geneva: WCC, 2000.

Yoder, John H. "The Anabaptist Shape of Liberation." Pages 338–48 in *Why I Am a Mennonite: Essays on Mennonite Identity.* Edited by Harry Loewen. Scottdale, Pa.: Herald Press, 1988.

————. *Body Politics: Five Practices of the Christian Community Before the Watching World.* Scottdale, Pa.: Herald Press, 2001.

————."The Burden and the Discipline of Evangelical Revisionism." In *Nonviolent America: History Through the Eyes of Peace.* Edited by Louise Hawkley and James C. Juhnke. Cornelius H. Wedel Historical Series 5. North Newton, Kan.: Bethel College, 1993.

————. *For the Nations: Essays Public and Evangelical.* Grand Rapids: Eerdmans, 1997.

————. "The Hermeneutics of the Anabaptists." *MQR* 41, no. 4 (October 1967): 291–308.

————. "On Christian Unity: The Way from Below." *Pro Ecclesia* 9, no. 2 (2001): 165–83.

————. *The Jewish-Christian Schism Revisited.* Edited by Michael G. Cartwright and Ochs Peter. Grand Rapids: Eerdmans, 2003.

————. *The Politics of Jesus: Vicit Agnus Noster.* 2d ed. Grand Rapids: Eerdmans, 1994.

————. *The Priestly Kingdom: Social Ethics as Gospel.* Notre Dame, Ind.: University of Notre Dame Press, 1984.

————. *When War Is Unjust: Being Honest in Just-War Thinking.* 2nd ed. Maryknoll, N.Y.: Orbis, 1996.

Index

The Author

Since 1975, J. Denny Weaver has served as professor of religion at Bluffton University. He taught one year at Goshen College (1974-75) and was a visiting professor of theology at Canadian Mennonite Bible College (1990-91). Since the first edition of *Becoming Anabaptist* (1987), he has written *Keeping Salvation Ethical* (1997), *Anabaptist Theology in Face of Postmodernity* (2000), and *The Nonviolent Atonement* (2001). He co-edited *Teaching Peace: Nonviolence and the Liberal Arts* (2003) and has also written numerous articles and book chapters. He is editor of The C. Henry Smith Series, and a frequent speaker in a variety of academic and church settings. In the 1990s Weaver, served with three Christian Peacemaker Teams (CPT) delegations and was also a theological resource person for their training sessions. Weaver is married to Mary Lois (Wenger) Weaver. They have three adult daughters, four grandsons and two granddaughters.

"Few books have a shelf life of a quarter-century, but for nearly that long Denny Weaver's *Becoming Anabaptist* has stood as one of the outstanding historical interpretations of sixteenth-century Anabaptist beginnings. Weaver's keen eye for chronological development and geographic polygenesis takes into full account the diversity of influences that made Anabaptists what they were in the sixteenth century and what they are today. What a treat that Professor Weaver has agreed to provide us with a second edition and that Herald Press keeps the work in print." —*Barry Hankins, Professor of History and Church-State Studies, Baylor University*

"Weaver's study is invaluable." —*Christianity Today*

J. Denny Weaver helps members of the Free Church in our task of becoming Anabaptist. —*Brethren Life and Thought*

"J. Denny Weaver's *Becoming Anabaptist* incorporates the recent scholarship into a brief narrative history of the movement." —*Church History*

"Denny Weaver offers a highly readable history of Anabaptist beginnings which, while providing a synthesis of the recent scholarship, also has in view the practical goal of keeping the legacy alive for adherents of the believers church tradition today." —*The Sixteenth Century Journal*

"The author takes into account recent scholarship and evaluates them with an insightfulness that allows him to keep his church's theology form being blown away 'by every wind of doctrine.'" —Jean Seguy in *Justificatif, Archives de Sciences Sociales des Religions*

Herald Press Titles
by John Howard Yoder